WRITING DALIT HISTORY AND OTHER ESSAYS

Writing Dalit History and Other Essays

Yagati Chinna Rao

KANISHKA PUBLISHERS, DISTRIBUTORS
NEW DELHI-110 002

KANISHKA PUBLISHERS, DISTRIBUTORS
4697/5-21A, Ansari Road, Daryaganj,
New Delhi-110 002
Phones : 2327 0497, 2328 8285
Fax : 011-2328 8285
E-mail : kanishka_publishing@yahoo.co.in

First Published 2007

ISBN 81-7391-880-5

PRINTED IN INDIA

Published by Madan Sachdeva for Kanishka Publishers, Distributors, 4697/5-21A, Ansari Road, Daryaganj, New Delhi-110 002. Typeset by Sunshine Graphics, Delhi, and Printed at Chaudhary Offset Process, Delhi.

To my teachers

Professor K.N. Panikkar
Professor S. Bhattacharya

Preface

"Tell it like it was" runs a common American phrase, echoing, no doubt, consciously or unconsciously, Leopold von Ranke's famous injunction to write history "wie es eigentlich gewesen"—how it really was.[1] As is evident this is neither as simple nor as easy as it sounds; particularly true in terms of India's 'untouchable' past. The actual past, its recovery, its retrieval, what is rendered, are often sadly different, and answers to these questions may be both painful to seek and difficult to find.

A group of radical Puerto Rican historians in the early 1970's stated that "we face the problem that the history presented as ours is only part of our history...what of the history of the 'history less', the anonymous people who, in their collective acts, their work, daily lives, and fellowship, have forged our society through the centuries?"[2] Similarly, Dares Salaam School of history expressed its dissatisfaction saying that "we would end with the singularly useless 'history', celebrating individuals, narrating their biographies and heroic acts or, at the most, erecting monuments for valiant tribes. These would leave the large mass of our people out of history, without history".[3] Fundamentally, post-colonial countries have had to respond to such historiographical concerns acknowledging and accounting for "the relations between an institutionalized national and academic history and the disparate memories of communities and individuals".[4]

History in post-colonial societies assumes a crucial role in not only retrieval of the past but also in constructing identities. Historical enterprise in India encapsulates this crisis in the selective appropriation of the past.[5] The Outcastes constitute a community conscious of its discrimination and exclusion in historical narratives. The current historiographical trends, as regards outcaste history, are ambiguous, elusive in nature. Frequently, the acts of outcastes are categorized as 'parochial' elements. For instance censorious references to them appear in 'nationalist' historiography, a narrative of 'struggle' for freedom. This narrative does not recognize non-elite and non-Brahmin contribution towards national movement. Likewise, Cambridge historiography, while it contests the ideological basis of the nationalist narrative, does not initiate a dialogue with the social periphery and projects the 'lower' castes as mere passive followers of elite leaders. Marxist historians, working within the rigid class perspective, show reluctance to address issues related to caste. Finally, the Subaltern school of thought that emerged in 1980s postulated an alternative framework but their research suffer from the same limitation that they failed to raise fundamental issues related to outcaste historical experience.

The history of these 'untouchables' has yet become a part of Indian historiography, though the study is of immense relevance and significance on account of the inherent radical democratic identity of their movement and their role as productive communities. Available scholarship on these oppressed communities suffers from lack of historical and written documentation. As a result, attempts towards historically locating 'untouchables' are impeded by an acute shortage of direct evidence about the realities of Dalit social life. Recent initiatives to reconstruct Dalit history generally draws from traditional historical sources like archival material, reports of census, commissions, committees and gazetteers. Biographical and autobiographical writings of Dalit organic intellectuals do exist as also literature in the form of poems, novels, dramas, contemporary press reports and caste-association activities, though in the vernacular. The essays in this volume have mainly drawn from these sources.

The essays collected in this volume were presented at various seminars/conferences and workshops. A few of them have also been published in the respective proceedings of the conferences. All these essays are related to various aspects of Dalit history and the region confined to south India in general and Andhra in particular. Since these essays originally were written for a particular conference or workshop, the overlapping and repetition of arguments would be a possible irristant. Retaining such repetition was necessary to maintain the flow of narrative and to cater to the needs of non-specialist readership and each essay was an independent essay and meant for that specialized seminar or a conference.

Notes

1. Leopold von Ranke, 1874, p. vii; Ranier on what Ranke meant and did not mean by this phrase, see G.J. Ranier, 1950, p. 130; also see Bernard Lewis, 1975, p. 71.
2. Angel Quientero Rivera, 1976, pp. 6-7, cited in S. Bhattacharya, 1982, pp. 1-2.
3. Issa G. Shivji, 1976, p. 55.
4. Mamadou Diouf, 1999 and 2000.
5. Priyadarshini Vijaisri, 2004, Introduction.

Acknowledgements

These essays assembled in the volume were presented at various national and international conferences from 1998 to 2006. The essays on caste largely are based on my doctoral research at the Jawaharlal Nehru University, New Delhi and a brief sojourn at the Center for South Asian Studies and Institute for Advanced Studies in the Humanities, University of Edinburgh (2001-2002). I am grateful to Charles Wallace Trust for providing visiting fellowship. I take this opportunity to thank all those people who helped me at various levels in making this work possible; especially Crispin Bates, Duncan Forrester, Daniel O'Connor, Roger Jeffery, Anthony Goods, Deborah Sutton and Andrea Major at the Center for the South Asian Studies, University of Edinburgh; Simon Charsely of University of Glasgow. Also thanks to Adapa Satyanarayana, Muvva Srinivasa Reddy, A. Bobbili, Rajasekhar Basu and Sanjukta Das Gupta, Thomas Blom Hansen, Partha Chatterjee and Fr. Ambrose Pinto for their comments. My wife Vijaisri has been a constant critique and source of encouragement all these years while our son, Vamshi, took it as his duty to keep us on our toes, yet a source of solace on most occasions of disenchantment. Madan Sachdeva and Vivek Chaturvedi were more than eager to see the manuscript in print in record time.

I owe a lot to my teachers, Prof. K.N. Panikkar and Prof. Sabyasachi Bhattacharya. Prof. Panikkar, who was my research supervisor at the JNU guided me through the process of my transition, making it possible to recover a sense of identity both at the academic and the personal level. I am greatly indebted to Prof. Bhattacharya, who has been the Director at the Educational Records Research Unit, with whom it was a memorable experience to work as a Research Officer for a considerably long time. He was not simply an exceptional source of inspiration and encouragement but a guiding spirit who touched lives of many people around him in so many ways. I humbly dedicate this book to both of them as a token of gratitude.

The usual disclaimers are applicable.

14 August 2006.

Yagati Chinna Rao

Contents

Contents

1

Writing Dalit History: A Note on Missionary Sources

It has become one of the truisms of the historical profession that the peasants of traditional societies are silent actors of history. This aphorism is pertinently applicable to the Dalit context in Indian history. Attempt at historically locating the Dalits, thus—far had been impeded by an acute shortage of direct evidence about the realities of the social life of the Dalits even for most of the nineteenth century. Unfortunately, neither the official nor the unofficial sources are detailed and sophisticated enough to be put together a comprehensive picture of the Dalits. Till recently, their origins are obscure, and their presence was neglected. In standard Indian history works, the Dalits are treated either as marginal people without a history of their own or as objects rather than as subjects. Often, these works show reluctance to even mention the name of the Dalits, as if mere mention would tantamount to pollution. Even if a sentence or a paragraph about them figured, it certainly would be on rules, which dwelt on how to avoid them or the type of punishment to be meted out to the Dalits. Fortunately, recent decades have shown that in addition to socially concerned scholars (mostly foreign scholars), an effort is growing among the Dalits to seek directions for the future through a better understanding of their past.

Dalits have not yet become a part of Indian historiography, though such a study is of immense relevance and significance with regard to the inherent radical democratic identity of their movement and their role of being productive community. Available scholarship on Dalits' history suffers from lack of historical and written documentation. Yet, once again, this is not to rule out the immense significance of a few analytical and comprehensive studies on Dalit history.[1]

In an attempt to reconstruct Dalit history, particularly Telugu speaking regions, one generally draws from archival sources like reports of census, commissions and committees and gazetteers. Other sources like in the form of biographical and autobiographical writings[2] of Dalit organic intellectuals do also exist.[3] Of course, such alternative sources like poems, novels, dramas, contemporary press reports and caste-association activities, though in the vernacular are also available aplenty. Another vital source consists of the Christian missionary tracts and archival depositories, awaiting historical recognition in reconstructing the historical experience of the cultures at the periphery. Christian missionary sources are vast though scattered across time and regions. These sources exist as travelogues[4] histories of evangelical groups,[5] some account of caste and Christianity,[6] conversion movements,[7] memoirs of various missionaries.[8] There are also missionary journals, newsletters and pamphlets.

This chapter is an attempt at looking at the missionary sources of the nineteenth and the early twentieth centuries, by the missionaries, who worked in and around Andhra Pradesh. The correspondence between the missionaries within the colony and home their headquarters and in the field so also with government officials, along with rare missionary tracts, provide us immense scope for retrieving the historical experience of the Dalits of Andhra, or for that matter the pan-Indian 'untouchable' communities. This chapter, first tries to discern the earlier imperial policies or attitudes towards missionaries besides gauging the response of the natives. Secondly, it aims at identifying the nature of encounter between missionaries and various communities in the regions with special emphasis on the communities at the periphery. And finally this chapter also provides an extensive note on the missionary sources and their crucial importance in constructing Dalit history and reflecting simultaneously on the problem in utilizing the sources that are looked upon with great suspicion within the discipline.

History Writing and Dalits

History writing in India, was consciously served to a nationalist recovery of India's self, as in post-colonial societies. In the context southern India, history in the pre-colonial period was codified and conserved by the strategic alliances between the powerful kings and the influential priests. The sceptre and pen conjointly functioned as the fundamental instruments in the production, preservation and circulation of the south Indian tradition.[9] This is evident in the two principal sources utilized in the reconstruction of south Indian society. On the one hand, inscriptional sources, most of which were recorded in temples, is a vital source for Indian historiographers.[10] Often, most of these inscriptions are documents recording gifts to Brahmins or temples from wealthy and powerful persons or groups. These inscriptions also provide us with information about the reigning King, his genealogy, conquests and his *dharmic* life, because it is in the Kings' honour that these gifts are bestowed.[11] The alliance between dominant caste groups upholding conventional norms in producing such documents largely resulted in the exclusion of the Dalits. On the other, literary sources in the south are abundant and similarly rich. The relationship between the patron and the court poets and literary figures is also well-recognized fact. They depended reciprocally—the king endowed and honoured poets with gifts, the latter produced literature reinforcing the notions of the king as embodiments of wisdom, compassion, righteousness and generosity.[12]

Even a cursory glance at the history of the Telugu literature, particularly the medieval texts, would reveal how literature was mainly confined to zamindar *darbars* and scholarly gatherings. Until the mid-seventeenth century, writers,. predominantly Brahmins, tried to display their command over language (Sanskrit or sanskritised Telugu) and to score over their rivals.

Available literary sources are often the translations of Hindu epics at least up till the fourteenth century A.D. Starting from Rajaraja Narendra of the eleventh century all rulers, 'generously' donated *agraharas* to the poets, who in turn, devoted all their 'intellect' to praise their patron and depict some of their affairs with women besides trying to preserve the Vedic ritual and consolidated the Varnasrama Dharma. Some literary sources do make scattered references of the *Chandalas* being employed as *Talayaries* or village watchmen.[13] The Edarupalli record mentions them as *Charmakaras*.[14] The Fourteenth and Fifteenth centuries literature like *Kridabhiramam* of Vallabhacharya makes mention of the *Chandala* caste but does not categorize it as separate, outside the pale of Hinduism.[15] Proudhakavi Mallana in his *Rukmangada Charitra* mentions that *Chandalas* were prohibited from attending religious ceremonies performed by the "high caste". These sources evidently show that the *Chandalas* were appendage to the *Chaturvarna* of Hindu society; however, it has to be noted that their main occupation was agrarian labour. Being the productive community they played a major role in the society,[16] worshipped deities such as Ekavira and Mahuramma.[17]

The later medieval period is better known as Rayaluyugam in Telugu literature.[18] Poets of Prabhanda style, included Allasani Peddana (*Manucharistramu*), Nandi Timmana (*Parijatapaharanam*), Ramabhadrakavi, (*Ramabhyudayamu*), Dhurjati (*Kalahasti Mahastyam* or *Kalashastisva Satakam*) and Pingali Surana (*Kalapoornodayam*). But none of them took to reflecting 'society' as a subject. While analyzing the local administration systems under Vijayanagara, T.V. Mahalingam mentions a seventeenth century inscription refers to eighteen professional associations. Even the *Kurantakas* (shoe makers), reportedly formed a part of local assemblies.[19] But the references to "untouchables" do not go beyond this.

In the seventeenth century, Vijayanagar lost its importance and began to come under the increasing political influence of feudatory courts such as Gandikota, Siddhavatam, Nellore, Gingee, Tanjore and Mathura. Literature flourished and some of the popular literary figures were Matli Ananta of

Siddhavatam (Cuddapah district), Pushpagiri Timmana at Nellore, and Raghunadha Nayaka at Tanjore.[20] In northern Andhra literature enjoyed patronage at feudatory courts like Pithapuram and Peddapuram.[21] Surprisingly none of their works deal with social themes. References about "untouchables" occur in the context of taboos, punishment and perpetuation of their servile status. These Prabhanda texts departed from the epic and puranic texts in several respects—a theme might have taken from the Puranas, but restricted to one or two episodes. *Sringararasa* (the erotic emotion) is the predominant element in literature but their usage was confined to the classical standards; narration was subordinate to the description and the two were not integrated.[22] The only qualitative shift was that the target of audience for the Puranas was the common people, but the Prabandhas only catered to the artistic demands of the pleasure-seeking upper class—the kings and the nobility. The prime aim of these texts was to appease the patrons hence were non-relevant for the society at large.[23] However, there was a set of poets outside this circle of literary client-patron nexus, who considerably contributed to Telugu literature in this period. Worth mentioning among them are Tyagayya, Potuluri Vira Brahmam, Paparaju and Vemana among others.

One of the most fascinating aspects with regard to invisibility of such writers is evident in the rediscovery of a subaltern ascetic, Vemana until the first quarter of the twentieth century. But what is more surprising is that no Telugu poet, scholar, critic or even the intellectuals bothered to make any reference to Vemana either in their works or in the debate on reforms and surprisingly thus, no apparent reason is cited for this complete disregard too. Hence, one can only speculate about the reasons for the conscious reluctance to accord due recognition to Vemana and his philosophy. Was it his non-Brahmin status or his rational philosophy ridiculed the caste system or superstitious religious practices? Probably, the first available source of information about Telugu poets and writers in print is the *Biographical Sketches of the Deccan Poets* (1829) by Cavally Venkata Rama Swami gives some answers to this. This work consists of memories of the lives of several eminent bards, both ancient and contemporary, who flourished in different provinces of the Indian peninsula, and it's compiled from 'authentic' documents. In all it deals with 108 poets, of whom 47 are Telugu poets, but even then Vemana does not figure in it. What is more surprising is that even Kandukuri Viresalingam's *Andhra Kavula Charitramu* (1899), which includes many minor poets, even obscure ones, omits Vemana. With some more additions in his revised edition (1917) the total number of poets swells to 220 but still Vemana remained out of bounds with this writer as well.[24] But this 'scholastic' Brahmin negligence in including Vemana was compensated for by western scholars, who recognized his enormous popularity among the masses. French Jesuit Father Le Gac, who in 1730 sent to Louis XV, King of France, a manuscript of 368 of Vemana's poems, is the first recorded contact of the west with Vemana's literature. This manuscript is preserved in Bibliotheque Nationale, Paris.[25] In 1806, French missionary, Abbe J.A. Dubois, writing about Hindu society and culture characterized Vemana as one of the Indian poets who wrote in a 'philosophic vein'.[26] This description caught the attention of Charles Phillip Brown, a British Civil Servant in Madras, who was interested in preparing a Telugu text, a possible aid to Englishmen in learning Telugu. In 1824, with the assistance of Telugu scholars, Brown started reading Vemana in the vernacular and began collecting from different parts of Andhra, palm leaf and paper manuscripts of Vemana's poems from across Andhra.

As a result, in 1829, the first edition of this collection was published by Brown, entitled *The Verses of Vemana: Moral, Religious and Satirical*. Here is an important point that needs to be mentioned. Out of five hundred copies of this edition, fifty copies were presented to him as editor's copies and the remaining four hundred fifty copies disappeared mysteriously. It took Brown ten years to discover that, perhaps to his shock, with the active connivance of the 'high' caste-Hindu *pundits* of the College Board, the missing copies were rolled up as waste paper and tucked away in the lumber room of the college library.[27] However, a host of western rendering of Vemana's work poured in the following the translation by Brown:

Nineteenth century imperialist history had shrouded India's past in darkness, denuded its history of any evidence of change and achievement with permanent marks of inferiority. If the nationalist historians maintained silent on the non-elite and non-Brahmin contribution towards national movement, the Cambridge historians projected 'lower' castes as mere passive followers of elite leaders.[28] And when it comes to Marxist historians, they remained within the classical class perspectives and showed reluctance to address issues related to caste. In Andhra, disillusionment of a Dalit activist with the communist movement led to reassertion of caste centered issues. For instance, when Konada Surya Prakasa Rao,[29] was the President of Krishna District Agricultural Labour Association, Communist Party took a resolution termed 'the Muslim League as political party and the Scheduled Caste Federation of Ambedkar as communal entity'.[30] Innumerable such instances can be found within the political developments in the region.[31] Finally, though the Subaltern school of thought that emerged in 1980s, successfully postulated an alternative framework, it hardly have raised fundamental issues related to the historical experiences of the outcastes.[32]

Colonial Policies

A brief note on the colonial government within which the missionaries emerged and functioned, would help to locate the developments within a specific local context. It needs to be noted that the East India Company never had an official policy on the missionaries. The evangelical and colonial maxim that emerged evolved itself as pragmatic responses to the prevailing circumstances. Initially, the Company had to come to terms with the large number of Roman Catholics present in its territories. In its attempt to foster loyalty of its Catholic 'subjects', the Company adopted a policy of toleration and to a certain extent, even it extended support to Catholicism. But their activities were restricted and any work in British territory demanded prior permission from the Company.[33]

Political rather than religious considerations, were paramount as far as the Company was concerned. Their struggle for supremacy in trade and political arena was also extended to other areas like evangelism. In 1715, the Company suspicious of the priests under the Portuguese Archbishop of Goa as a political suspects, expelled them from Surat and Madras.[34] Similarly, French and Italian priests suspected for political motives were expelled. The Company's position on religious matters in the early days was clearly stated in a 1744 dispatch of the Court of Directors of Madras which maintained that the Church must never be independent of the state.[35] The Company's aim was to limit commercial competition and to keep out 'undesirable' Europeans who could disturb the status quo in its rapidly expanding territory. The Company also was concerned that the disreputable character of many of the interlopers, who managed to find their way to India, would lower Europeans in the eyes of the people and cause problems for internal security.[36]

It was within this background that Protestant missionaries began their activities in India in 1706 with the setting up of a mission at Tranquebar under the patronage of the Danish King Frederick IV. The missionaries soon began to work in British territory, largely because of difficulties they faced in Tranquebar where the Danish authorities were far from sympathetic to them.[37] By 1740 Protestant missionary work in the Company territory was well established, and in 1752 the Court of Directors empowered the Governor of Madras to provide financial assistance 'where it deemed fit'.[38] In 1813, at the periodic renewal of the East India Company's charter, heated discussion occurred over the question of the propagation of Christianity in India. Lord Wellesley observed that 'a Christian governor could not have done less and a British governor ought not do more' found approval on both sides of the debate in 1813.[39]

Missionaries' Intervention

The association of Christian missionaries with Telugu speaking people dates back to the end of 16th century, when two Jesuit priests and a Brother worked their way to Chandragiri in Chittoor district.[40] After a few years of lull, various missions began to increasingly come up in the region. In 1735 Roman Catholic Mission was set up at Cuddapah and the London Missionary Society came up in 1805 at Vishakhapatnam. Later London Missionary Society extended its activities to Ballary, Cuddapah, Anantpur and Vizianagaram areas. In 1832, the Vicar of Apostolic Mission expanded to Nellore, Cuddapah and Anantapur. The American Baptist Mission was established in 1840 and extended to Nellore, Udayagiri, Ongole, Bapatla, Cumbhum and Kurnool.[41] The American Lutheran Mission came in 1842 and spread its wings to Guntur, Repalle, Bapatla, Palnadu, Vinukonda, Bandaru and Rajahmundry.

The Church Missionary Society (CMS) commenced its operation in and around Musalipatnam in 1842.[42] The Free Church of Scotland came to Nellore in 1848 and the Canadian Baptist Mission came in 1890 and spread over to Kakinada, Bheemunipatnam, Srikakulam, Bobbili and Tuni areas. By the end of nineteenth century there were over twenty missionary societies present in the Telugu-speaking region engaged in philanthropic work, especially in the fields of education and health. Consequently, problem of boundaries of each missionary society was resolved through a gentleman's agreement. For instance, the missionaries from the Luthern, Baptist and Church Missionary Society missionaries agreed to not to work in each other's field, though the converts, not infrequently crossed and recrossed mission boundaries.

Initially, one of the objectives of the missionaries was to woo caste-Hindu converts by setting up Anglo-Vernacular high Schools, which were established at Masulipatnam (1843),[43] Ellore (1855) and Bezawada (1857). However, these missionary societies, more particularly the Anglicans, proved as unsuccessful in Andhra, in converting the high caste-Hindus through educational institutions[44] as they had been in Bengal and other areas.[45] Untill 1880 there were only twenty-three caste-Hindu converts: sixteen Brahmins, six non-Brahmins and one Muslim.[46] On the contrary these missionaries received overwhelming response from 'untouchable' communities that eventually led to dramatic en mass conversions—a dominant feature in the evangelical history of southern India. By providing education, medical facilities and other social services, the missionaries won the hearts of untouchables, who resented the rigid customs and ill treatment of caste-Hindus, were increasingly agreeable to conversion to Christianity. The mass movement among 'untouchables' in the CMS territory began with the conversion of a Mala headman named Pogulu Venkayya, notorious for his daring exploits of highway robbery before his baptism in 1859. His testimony regarding the claims of Christianity set in motion a chain conversion movements that eventually brought thousands of Malas and, later Madigas into the Church.[47] Venkayya himself was said to have persuaded over seven hundred people from his community to be baptized. Similarly, the American Baptist Telugu Mission reported that by 1912 there were 61,687 Church members on its rolls in the Telugu region almost all of them from the Madiga community, brought into the Christian fold through the initial leadership of Yerraguntla Periah of Ongole. This mission alone had been baptizing between 1,500 and 3,500 Madigas annually.[48]

The missionaries interceded and protected these converts against money-lenders and the lower echelons of government from the exploitation of higher castes, provided legal assistance and defended them against persecutors.[49] These 'untouchables' were also frequently accused of crimes, whether they were guilty or not.[50] The missionaries greeted the mass conversions with mixed reactions. Although aiding the church quantitatively, the movement brought in hordes of uneducated, poor converts whom many missionaries felt was ill equipped to serve. By 1933, roughly 80 per cent of India's protestant Christians were mass movement converts from Depressed Class backgrounds.[51]

Conversions to Christianity occurred in Andhra at a faster rate than in almost any other part of the South Asian region. During the first four decades of the twentieth century, the Indian Christian population grew at a faster rate than other major communal groups. Between 1921 and 1931, an average of 12,855 converts joined the church each month. The population of Indian Christians increased at a rate of 32.5 per cent during this decade, with Protestant Christians increasing at a much faster rate of 41 per cent during the same period.[52] In 1931, it was estimated that nearly 20 per cent of the depressed classes in West Godavari, 32 per cent in Krishna, and 57 per cent in Guntur districts were converted to Christianity.[53] In some areas, there were converts in almost every 'untouchable' hamlet.[54] The Malas and the Madigas were ordained in increasing numbers and by the early twentieth century, a casual observer might well have been excused for thinking that churches existed solely to serve the needs of the depressed, the deprived and the outcastes.

The Christian missionaries brought about the amelioration to the Dalits in three significant ways: Firstly, those who converted gained a new social consciousness as Christians. Secondly, those who still remained within the fold of Hinduism began to realize that the dogma of untouchability which for so long had justified their miserable condition was false, and that the missionaries do not follow and believe in this dogma.[55] Thirdly, the work of Missionaries stimulated the Hindu socio-religious reformers to reform Hinduism with a view to counter this unprecedented development and increasing influence of Christianity and Islam. Missionary activities also stirred the consciousness of Dalits of Andhra, who became aware of their rights,[56] and realized the inequality of their economic as well as ritual status.[57]

Importance of Missionary Sources

In the light of these developments, let us look at how far missionary sources could be utilized in constructing the Dalit past. Here we would focus on four aspects: the Dalit religion and culture; their education and health; the famine or ecological history and perhaps more importantly the issues of their identity.

The Dalits have always been regarded as part of Hindu society, accommodated in the Chaturvarna scheme of social stratification, as an adjacent or appendage to Shudras, as ati-Shudras. Despite all these the Dalits countered these patronizing ideals through their self-assertive identity struggles. Take for example, the institution of Matangi. Emma Rauschenbusch-Clough has made the first recorded information about the 'Matangis'.[58] The fact is that the custom of 'Matangi' among the cultures could have been lost in the historical wilderness had it not been recorded in the missionary tracts and those associated with evangelical activities. The next mention of this system was by A. Madhaviah,[59] who narrates local myths thereby providing the linkage between the religious identity of the Matangi and the Jogini/Basivi systems.[60] In fact, Edgar Thurston's description of 'Matangi' system draws extensively from these two sources.[61] Similarly, Rev. Henry Whitehead, Bishop of Madras, long association with the Outcastes of the Telugu speaking region resulted in a valuable account of religious practices and beliefs of these communities.[62] Works of this genre emerge as the only sources to construct the historical experience and cultural identity of these cultures, invoking crucial issues which have been neglected and unrecognized within the mainstream historiographical traditions.

With the spread of missionaries and their penetration in rural areas, more particularly in 'untouchable' hamlets, they established churches which worked as school during the day, and as a church during the night. The typical Telugu village chapel-cum-school was usually without walls, or sometimes walls of Palmyra leaves or mud or stone, with thatched roofs.[63] As a part of their philanthropic activities, all these missions added schools and colleges to their churches and worked for the upliftment of the oppressed sections.[64] A cursory look at the state of educational history of Dalits in Andhra would reveal the painstaking efforts the missionaries undertook to sowing seeds of education among Dalits of this region. Often, it is realized that the first generation of educated Dalits later either became activists of future Dalit struggles or worked for the education of their brethren. So, any failure to properly utilize the missionary sources, especially in exploring issues related to Dalit education, would leave the historical picture of the Dalits incomplete and fragmented. Evangelical educational work critically reflects on colonial policies, intra-caste and inter-caste experiences as also the unique model of educational growth in the region. What is to be underlined here is the fact that the missionaries touched upon the souls of the outcastes by way of mainly educating them. This assumes added importance, because their educational activities were inextricably linked with poignant emotions and issues that are yet to gain respectability in mainstream discourses.

Similarly, when one looks at the identity process of Dalits, these missionary sources reveal many interesting and significant facts. What needs to be noted is that a conversion movement is like a kind of group identity, in which the group passes through a negative rejection of its lowly place in Hindu society to a positive affirmation of a new social and religious identity.[65] This new identity does not depend on its acceptance and recognition by the higher castes; but rather it indeed, was chosen and was sustained despite their refusal to accept it. Gradually this process of identity led to significant changes in their occupation and recognized enhancement of status.[66] Emergence of new consciousness entails conflicts at various levels, both ideological and structural. The role of the missionaries in the emergence of a new outcaste personality was interwoven with various shifts during the intense evangelical activity.

Finally, a note on the utility of such sources in ecological or environmental history in relation to the Dalits. What we find often in government records or government managed archival depositories has, always been about policy matters, on how to avoid, what would be future consequences and so on. But a careful reading reveals that there is no reference of the intensity of the disasters or calamities, especially the manner in which it galvanized the precarious conditions in which the outcastes lived. One outstanding example is of Gledstone's *The Story of the Masulipatam Cyclone of 1864.*[67] The event was narrated in the following poignant lines:

> "...It was the morning of All Saints Day, 1864, ... Mr. Maiden, the Port Attendant, noticed as early eight o' clock

> that the barometer was steadily falling...the rain poured through the roofs... about 30,000 [*who*] were drowned that night had a decent burial; and the hospital was drowned with strange sights of dead and dying.... Next to the Noble bungalow was the Sharkey Girls School. There were sixty-six pupils on the rolls on November first and of them only thirty-three lived see the morning."

These narratives of suffering could only find due record in the missionary tracts that were involved at an intimate and humanitarian level than in government controlled documents that could dismiss such details as 'unworthy' or 'irrelevant'.

Merits and Lacunas of Missionary Sources

What strikes the researcher familiar with the missionary literature and archival materials is the wide range and variety of missionaries of knowledge on the Indian society throughout the nineteenth century. Almost everywhere or wherever the missionaries went, they keenly observed, took notes and commented on the nature of social life and conditions. The missionaries were especially interested in the ideological issues of the relationship between Hinduism and the social system. Apart from such theoretical consideration, their comments have related to both issues of material and cultural realities as also those issues that arouse out of their encounter within a specific context. One of the central issues in the missionary literature was the life and condition of the depressed classes in the rural areas, particularly the marginalized and oppressed 'untouchables'. The missionaries became better acquainted with the problems of the cultures at the periphery than most other Europeans did.[68]

This raises fundamental issues; what are the problems associated with the unique nature of missionary sources? And this is in direct relation to the central concern of this chapter: the reconstruction of the Dalit history in a specific local context.

One clear advantage in using the missionary source is that not always present in other records, specifically, in the case of missionaries we already have certain presumptuous about their ultimate objectives and that these biases are likely to be encoded in their critique of the 'native' culture. Whereas in other sources, the writers' motives cannot be so clearly apparent, as in the case of the missionary materials. The missionaries were under considerable pressure to 'produce' 'evidences' and verify everything they claimed. The very success of their reform crusades depended greatly on their collection of reliable information as also on convincing the skeptics and unbelievers. Moreover, in their endeavour especially if they were to enlist the support of others they had to do their research and be prepared to defend the findings. For instance, one of the earliest specimens of evangelical 'social research', vital if they were to sway public opinion, were the surveys they undertook in connection with the custom of *Sati*.[69]

Missionary papers are scattered across libraries and record offices.[70] In most cases the missionary archives that survived are the accumulated records of the sending organizations. These are, of course, most valuable source, containing as they do letters and reports written to their headquarters from the fields, as well as documents recording the formulation and development of mission policy. There are detailed records created in the field: lists of converts and church members, the records of missionary institutions, the minutes of papers of local mission council, particulars of itineration work and so on, were mostly kept in the missionary headquarters. Such records, at least some of them still exist in the missionary fields.[71] Information gleaned from these tracts, documents and accounts, could be of immense value to retrieve the outcaste personality from historical wilderness and complicate the historical space by raising critical issues that have so far been endowed a marginal space in mainstream historical discourses. So also, any just suspicious on the nature of the source could, as in many cases be overcome by cross checking with alternative sources. It needs to be recognized that the historical experience of the Dalits with the missions was interwoven and to dismiss it on grounds of mere 'suspicious' would be a great loss to the discipline.

Some of the aspects in this chapter, have been presented in a Seminar at the Centre for South Asian Studies, University of Edinburgh, Scotland (25 April, 2002) and at a Symposium on 'Contribution of Christianity for the Development of Andhra Pradesh' held at Andhra Loyola College, Vijayawada (3-4 January, 2004). I am grateful to Charles Wallace Trust for enabling me to pursue Post-Doctoral research in UK in 2001-02.

NOTES

1. For details of recent compilation of published sources see Chinna Rao Yagati, 2003a.
2. M.B. Gautam, 1991.
3. Particularly writings of Kusuma Dharmanna, Boyi Bhimanna, Gurram Jashua, Jala Rangaswamy, P.R. Venkataswamy and many others. For details see P.R. Venkataswamy, 1955; Y.B. Abbasayalu, 1979; A. Satyanarayana, 1995 and 1998; Chinna Rao Yagati, 2003a.
4. Perhaps first in its kind was of Abbe Jeane Antoine Dubois, a French missionary's experiences of early decade of nineteenth century of Indian people, society and culture. Chapter five of his work contains one of the earliest documented description of Indian 'untouchables'. This was originally written in 1815, translated by Henry K. Beauchamps. See J. Abbe Dubois, 1953.
5. Here I am giving a list of a few published sources that fairly obvious and easily available, they either deals with one region or the other of what presently known as Andhra Pradesh or an all-India study that contains the Telugu speaking regions. See David Downie, 1892; Paul D. Wiebe, 1988; J.M. Thoburn, 1893; Robert Hunter, 1873; Alexander Duff, 1988; E. Daniel Potts, 1967; Brian Stanley, 1992), Eugene Stock, 1899; Andrew Gordon, 1888; Sushil M. Pathank, 1964; G.A. Oddie, 1979; A.W. Carmichael, 1903; G.G. Findlay and W.W. Holsworth, 1925; R. Lovett, 1899; J. Richter, 1908; C.F. Andrews, 1912; M.A. Sherring, 1884; Stephen Neill, 1954 and 1984; Abbe J.A. Dubois, 1813; John Craig, 1908; Jocob Chamberlain, 1897; P.Y. Luke and John B. Carman, 1968.
6. H.P. Hughes, 1893; Christian Missionary Society, 1927; Duncan B. Forrester, 1974; J.F. Burditt, 1893; E. Asirvadham, 1935; Duncan B. Forrester, 1980.

7. George Smith, 1873; E.A. Annett, 1920; O.C.G. Hayter, 1930; J.Waksom Pickett, 1933 and 1938; Anthony Copley, 1997; D. Kooiman, 1989; Manickam Sundararaj, 1977; G.A. Oddie, 1977.
8. John Noble, 1867; J.N. Oglivie, 1915; Rajaiah Paul, 1961; M.M. Thomas, 1969.
9. Sathinathan Clarke, 1998, p. 59.
10. Thomas, R. Trautman *et.al.*, 1985, p. 7.
11. Burton Stein, 1980, p. 46.
12. For a detailed and complex relationship between the poets and patrons in terms of ritual and ideological interdependency see David Shulman, 1985, pp. 15-46, [emphasis added].
13. *Inscriptions of Andhra Pradesh*, Warangal District, no.87; *Sri Vasavi Kanyakapuranam,* Chapter 46, verse.3, cited in K. Suryanarayana, 1956, p. 265.
14. See *Bharati,* (January, 1968), p. 3., *Ibid.*
15. *Kridabhiramam,* verse 73, *Ibid.*
16. David Washbrook, 1996, pp. 68-86.
17. Praudhakavi Mallana, *Rukmaugada Charitra,* I.V.95, also see M. Somasekhara, 1948, p. 279.
18. Nidadavolu Venkata Rao, 1954, Introduction.
19. *Epigraphia India., XX p.90; Madras Epigraphical Report,1918,* Paras 84-85; K.R.R. Sastry *South India Guilds* pp.6-32, Cited in T.V. Mahalingam, 1969, p. 229.
20. K.A. Nilakanta Sastri, 1976, pp. 405-417.
21. P.V. Chalapati Rao, 1994, pp. 128-138.
22. Bh. Krishnamurthi, 1995, pp. 77-102; also see Velcheru Narayana Rao, 1992.
23. Velcheru Narayana Rao, 1978, pp. 50-60.
24. This conscious neglect was noticed by the Dalit poet of the twentieth century, Gurram Jashuva (1895-1971), who said:

    Vemana's poetry is immortal
    Viresalingam has surely erred
    By ignoring this great poet,
    In his treatise on Andhra poets.

    See his *Gabbilam,* 1991, p. 63; for details of Jashuva's life and works see Yendluri Sudhakar, 1986.

25. J.S.R.L. Narayana Moorty and Elliot Roberts (Tr.), 1995, Introduction.

26. See Abbe, J.A. Dubois, 1953.

27. For details see C.P. Brown, 1840; V.R. Narla, 1971.

28. A. Satyanarayana, 2003, p. 7; and 2005, pp. 117-165.

29. Konada Surya Prakasa Rao born at Pedapalaparru, Krishna District in Dalit labouring family. He passed his SSLC in 1930, later educated at Pithapuram Rajah College at Kakinada. For details see Chinna Rao Yagati, 2003c, pp. 117-153.

30. This has also been mentioned by Boyi Bheemanna, 1988, Foreword.

31. For similar experiences see Vu. Sambasiva Rao, 1994.

32. In the span of twenty years they produced about 80 essays in eleven volumes. There are only three essays that deals with the Dalits and only one by non-Brahmin, non-elite background, that too a non-Dalit.

33. Penelope Carson, 1990, pp. 169-190.

34. Court to Madras, 25 January 1716, para 82, India Office Records, E/3/13.

35. Court to Madras, 7 February 1744, para 42, India Office Records, E/3/109.

36. Cornwallis's Letter to H. Dundas dated 4 April 1790, National Library of Scotland, MSS. 3385, 329.

37. Penelope Carson, 1990, pp. 169-190.

38. J.C. Marshman, 1859, vol. I, p. 39; also see E. Lehmann, 1956.

39. For details of this debate see Penelope Carson, 1988.

40. Uma Ramaswamy, 1974; also see J. Mangamma, 1992, p. 10.

41. For a detailed account of this Mission see, John E. Clough, 1914.

42. Later on this was elevated into Noble College (1893) and named after its founder missionary Robert Noble. For details see Susan Billlington Harper, 2000.

43. For a denomination-wise and region-wise details, Henry Huizinga, 1909. The author also been a Vice Principal and Professor of English at American Baptist Mission College, Ongole.

44. See S. Sathianathan, 1896.

45. F.F. Gledstone, p. 48. But all these caste-Hindu converts, later on occupied highest positions in society, such as Magistrates, Judges, Headmasters and so on.

46. John Bob Williams, 1938, p. 9.

47. John C.B. Webster, 1992, pp. 40-44.

48. A. T. Fishman, 1941, pp. 16-17.

49. J.W. Pickett, 1938, p. 42.

50. J.W. Picket, 1933, pp. 302-303.

51. *Directory of Christian Missions and Churches in India, Burma and Ceylon, 1940-1941*, (Nagpur, 1940), pp. 33-38.

52. "Minutes" of *the Sixth Biennial Meeting of the Andhra Christian Council*, held at Secunderabad (1-4 December), 1933, these estimations were based on Census figures for 1931; also see Dencan B. Forester, 1991, pp. 65-93.

53. See K. Philip, "Annual Letter", October, 1924, Church Missionary Society (C.M.S.) Archives.

54. G.A. Oddie, 1991, pp. 95-124

55. J.N. Farquhar, 1967, pp. 368, 389.

56. M. Suseela, 1913, pp. 127-130.

57. Eugene F. Irschick, 1969, p. 9.

58. Emma R. Clough, wife of a missionary Rev. John E. Clough, member of the Royal Asiatic Society of Great Britain and Ireland. Her remarkable work entitled *While Sewing Sandals or Tales of a Telugu Pariah Tribe*, 1899, more than one hundred years latter, recently been reprinted in India

59. A. Madhaviah, 1905–1906, pp. 301-303.

60. For details see Priyadarshini Vijaisri, K., 2001 and 2003.

61. Edgar Thurston and C. Rangachari, 1909, see vol. IV.

62. Henry Whitehead, 1921.

63. Susan Billington Harper, 2000, p. 190.

64. Chinna Rao Yagati, 2002, pp. 84-120.

65. Duncan B. Forrester, 1991, p. 45.

66. G.A. Oddie,1991, pp. 76-77.

67. For details see F.F. Gledstone.

68. G.A. Oddie, 1996, p. 198.

69. K. Ingham, 1956, p. 45.

70. Many list of guides have been published, notably, Rosemary Keen, 1968; Catholic Archives Society, 1989; C.S. Craig, 1982.

71. For instance, Dornakal Diocesan Archives and Cathedral Compound, Dornakal has a rich collection such as Baptismal records, Marriage Register, *Church Censures: Diocese of Dornakal* and so on.

2

Dalit Education and Identity Formation

The Scheduled Castes of India are a stigmatised people due to which they suffer from a number of disabilities that are buttressed by religion. Some of their disabilities are untouchability, social segregation, lower of economic status, lack of political power, illiteracy and little chance of mobilization. All these mutually reinforcing factors only to worsen their lot. Though legally or constitutionally they are no longer "untouchables" in practice many of them even today bear the stigma that they have been forced to live with for millenia.

Earlier in the past century the Scheduled Castes were also called the Harijans or *children of God*.[1] Many "untouchable" leaders wondered why they were singled out as "children of God"? Were not others also the children of God? If not, whose children are they after all? In this they perceived another attempt to subtle segregation from the rest of the Hindus. The "untouchables" were also called the *avarnas, pariahs* meaning outcastes, because they never were a part of *chaturvarna* scheme of social stratification and were thus below the line of pollution. Not just that they were also considered inferior to the "twice born." They were also known as *panchamas* (the fifth caste) because they supposedly came after the *chaturvarnas*. Their touch and sometimes even their shadow or voice were considered to be polluting the caste Hindus. There are regional variations in the form and content of untouchability. It may range from the notion of pollution by sight, hearing or proximity in the south, to pollution by direct physical contact in the north. But the characterisation has remained with them from times immemorial.

For the purpose of present study the term *dalit*[2] has been used to include all those vast mass of people among the Scheduled Castes who have been traditionally subjected to invidious discriminations on grounds of untouchability and categorized as the "untouchables", the down-trodden, the exterior castes,[3] the ex-untouchables,[4] the Depressed Classes[5] or the Dalits. This study was deciphered with special reference to Andhra.

There are 59 Dalit communities (sub-castes) in Andhra.[6] The Madigas constitute the largest number, their percentage in total Scheduled Caste population 45.8 per cent.[7] They are followed by the Malas constituting 37.9 per cent and the Adi-Andhras[8] 6.8 per cent. These three sub-castes together form the bulk of the total Dalit population in Andhra accounting for as much as 90.6 per cent. The share of the remaining 56 communities is a paltry 9.4 per cent. Due to utter shortage of information and historical evidence, only two major communities—the Malas and the Madigas were taken up for detailed study in this chapter.

The chapter comprises three parts. First, a brief look at the educational development among Dalits with a detailed focus on the role of various agencies and organisations that guided the Dalits and helped to form their ideologies in their effort to challenge an exploitative tradition of the society. It also deals with the attitude and influence of the British officials, the impact of the Missionary activities on the Dalits and the growing realization among the "untouchables" that education holds the key to future development. Secondly, to look at how educational development led to the rise and growth of Dalit movement that helped them form their own identity in the mainstream national socio-political fabric. Between 1920 and1940 they steadily gained importance in the game of numbers in Census reports. Thirdly, this chapter also examined how the process of identity formation culminated in the emergence of "Adi" ideology in the Madras presidency in general and Telugu speaking regions in particular.

The past educational system in the country was not only non-universalistic and parochial but also partisan. Though the content might apparently appeared to be universal at first sight, traditional education was the product of an Indian outlook on knowledge and a corresponding scheme of life and values.[9] In ancient India, the traditional Hindu social structure seemed to have evolved a system of allocation of rewards relating to prestige, power and wealth in such a manner that each of the three "higher" varnas (*dwijas*) could get one of these. Thus, while the Brahmins received the highest social status or prestige in the society, the *Kshatriyas* had the greatest power, and the *Vaishyas* held the largest share of wealth. The remaining sections of the society, broadly called *Shudras*, who were and are the occupational or manufacturing castes, rendered services of a personal nature, and were engaged in growing food and in manufacturing articles of necessity and comfort. Since religion provided the basis for this social stratification, inequality became a structural feature of the traditional Hindu value system. What is more appalling is that while such an inequitious division of social function had a religious legitimacy, the social structure based on caste endogamy ensured its continuity.[10] Maintaining such an order demanded that a value system of thought and logic, which the traditional educational pattern facilitated was in place.

Education was the preserve of only a few privileged sections until the nineteenth century when western education was introduced. Until then, education was directed essentially at preparing a new generation to take the place of the previous generation. And as such that model of education only imposed cultural values,[11] and interests of the "upper" castes or privileged classes. The reproduction of culture through education is known to play a key role in the reproducing of the whole social system.[12] It serves as a potent means of social control.[13] That's why traditional Indian education was limited to a few privileged castes. In the pre-British Indian society education has a religious content and theological causation was supreme. In contrast, the modern educational system introduced by the British was theoretically open to all and also its contents were secular.

Formal education, or for that matter any kind education was for more than one reason was seen as necessary but more or less limited only to the *dwijas* (twice-born castes).[14] The Brahmins, who were engaged with the classical religious texts, interpreted and communicated them to the illiterate masses in their local dialects. The *Kshatriyas* were the ruling class and being the warriors they were also well acquainted with weapons, statecraft and organizational matters thus were educated to some extent. The *Vaishyas* or the business class, also required some studies as the knowledge of arithmetic was necessary to transacting business, keep records and maintain accounts. Even the *Shudras* or the artisan groups, the last clog in the social wheel could acquire the necessary skills for their crafts at home. So it was only the "untouchables" who were left out without access to education of any kind. Manu, the ancient lawgiver, prescribed that the education of *Shudra* children was an offence and this doctrine worked vigorously till about the end of nineteenth century. The denial of education to the Dalits perpetuated their social humiliation, economic exploitation, political marginalization and cultural subordination.

The early modern Europe evolved radically new institutions for "mass", "national", even "popular" education perhaps after got inspired by apocalyptic dreams and millenarian visions.[15] The movement, inspired and advanced by August Hermann Francke (1663-1727) of the Halle University, spread to the royal houses of Denmark and Hanover. The Court of St. James helped found the Society for Promoting Christian Knowledge (SPCK), which in turn promoted educational work in India.[16] By the 1780s, schools run by Christian Friedrich Schwartz and his associates[17] attracted by many non-Christian students, especially those from the Brahmins and other "upper" castes, in the hope that the new learning would better qualify them for positions within the rapidly expanding establishments of the East India Company.[18]

During the first half of the nineteenth century some more new developments took place in the educational sphere of the Madras presidency. Sir Thomas Munro,[19] Governor of Madras (1820-1827), introduced a comprehensive and far sighted scheme, after realising that literacy was confined to the Brahmins, merchants, village lords and "principal ryots" only. Munro, although had no wish to interfere with the existing indigenous educational pattern and held the view that the people should be left to manage their schools in their own way, ordered a general survey of the complete list of schools in each district showing the number of scholars and teachers, the castes to which they belonged, books and the materials they used and the sources of funding.[20] The results of this survey, along with an estimation of census data, provide us a fascinating view on education in the 1820s, more precisely between 1823 and 1825. In Madras Presidency, there were as many as 12,498 schools and 188,000 students in a population of 12,850,941—roughly 1 school per 1000 persons and 1 student per 67 persons during this period.[21] Education was under the control of the Brahmins and religious in its content and the mediums were Sanskrit and Telugu. The Brahmins comprised 60 to 75 per cent of the pupils far out numbering "clean" non-Brahmin, mercantile communities and former-warriors lords of villages.[22] The books used in these institutions were either directly derived from the Vedas and various Shastras, Puranas and other epic literature,[23] and the teachers were all Brahmins.[24]

One striking finding of the survey was the virtual exclusion of untouchables from the sphere of education. The category "pariah" or "unclean" Shudra, invariably found in other Census reports was conspicuously absent here, while a number of Brahminical (Aryan or Sanskrit) social categories found mention, with the Kshatriyas being a notable omission. Moreover, the survey revealed that the Brahmins and Vaishyas made up an average of 34.5 per cent of the pupils in village schools. The untouchable communities, whether it was Pariahs and Pallars in the Tamil speaking areas or the Malas and Madigas in the Telugu speaking areas or any other servile communities, who constituted half of the population, were not counted at all.[25] The main reason for this was that the Brahmins framed the forms and done much of the actual work,[26] so they were unlikely to enter to Dalit *wadas* (hamlets) to find out the actual state of their affairs. Munro's effort to patronize popular education was heroic but short lived.[27] It was heroic because while the Governments of Bengal and Bombay were wavering between oriental and western learning for the upper classes, Munro made a Herculean attempt at popular education of the masses in their vernaculars, with a view to improve their harried lot.[28] It was short lived because although Munro weathered many a storm, his elaborate schemes begun in 1822, were reversed immediately after his death in 1830 in favour of English education.[29] This reversal seems paradoxical because belief in the filtration theory[30] was stronger in Madras presidency than elsewhere.

The Charter Act of 1813, permitted the missionaries to work in the Indian territories of the Company with a view to educate and proselytize the masses. Later in 1823, a General Committee on Public Instruction was formed to give a shape to government policies. In 1837, English was made the language of administration and a Government Resolution of 1844 threw subordinate positions open to Indians. Therefore, English education became attractive to Indians, giving a boost to a subsequent rapid expansion of English education. However, the famous Wood's Despatch of 1854, realised the need to educate the masses not only through English but through the vernacular.

Role of Government Since 1854

After the 1854 Despatch, the Director of Public Instruction took charge of the Department of Education. "Rate Schools" novel to the Presidency and unique to Andhra were started.[31] In this system the villagers were to contribute to the education of their children and the ryots voluntarily subjected themselves to a rate or subscription to maintain schools in their villages. The system of rate schools was directly beneficial to the land-holding classes, who could make the contributions along with their regular revenue payments. The 'Untouchables' formed the bulk of agricultural labourers and did not own any land, due to which they could not benefit from the rate schools. The rate scheme soon lost its voluntary aspect and had to be legalised with the Madras Education Act of 1863.

As discussed above, there were no provisions for education of Untouchables in the indigeneous system of education. Munro's enquiries also provide ample evidence that though there were a few Backward Class pupils, there were none from the "Untouchables". As a result of the dominance of filtration theory and the fear of offending the caste Hindus, the colonial Government made no efforts till the end of nineteenth century to make a provision for the education of the "untouchables".

The policy of protective discrimination developed in stages since the Woods Despatch of 1854. The 'lower' castes had been excluded from higher education in accordance with downward filtration theory that advocated higher education to the "higher" castes alone.[32] The Board of Directors of Education felt that until the public prejudice was overcome in this respect, what was intended to enlighten the largest mass might degenerate into a boon to the lowest classes.[33] The government reply to the letter of the Court Directors of May 5, 1854, stated that nobody should be refused admission to a government school or a college merely on the ground of his or her caste.[34] The Wood's Despatch of 1854 threw open education to all classes, and the despatch of 1857 discouraged the idea of separate schools for the "lower" castes.

However, the opposition of the high castes to the admission of students from the depressed classes in public schools was very strong in the Madras Presidency. The government considered its earlier decision and the Education Commission Report of 1884 recommended establishment of separate schools wherever necessary.[35] In 1891, approving the institution of separate schools, *the Hindu* wrote:[36]

> "...it is impossible to expect caste-Hindu children and these classes to study together in the same schools.

> Nor can much be expected from local boards... Government is perfectly justified in showing special consideration to a class, whose conditions must be a blot on any civilized social system."

In 1893, the Madras Government formulated a series of proposals, which were widely hailed as the Magna Carta of Panchama education.[37] Among the measures recommended by it were: special training schools with a higher stipend for Panchama students and teacher trainees; establishment of special schools by local boards and municipalities for Panchamas in all villages, where they were in large numbers; grant of *poromboke* lands for Panchama schools; Night schools to suite the labouring classes; waiving refunds of building grants if the buildings were used for school purposes for six years.

However, there were difficulties in running even separate schools due to caste prejudices of the concerned officials. Most of the inspecting staff belonging to 'higher' castes, and were reluctant to enter Dalit localities to inspect their schools.[38] An Indian Christian Missionary Society, true to its mission, brought to the notice of the government in 1905, that a caste conscious inspector declined to enter Dalit villages and called the students out well beyond the village, examined their written answers from a distance not less then ten feet and tried to get through the bother as soon as he could.[39] It suggested that even the appointment of Eurasians or native Christians or Panchamas as special assistant inspector would do little justice in this regard. The Government of India had itself confessed that the officials of its educational departments were displaying a hostile attitude towards the lower classes.[40]

Missionary Interventions

Official neglect was compensated by the pioneering efforts of missionaries to educate deprived communities in general and "Untouchables" in particular.

The new branch of modern missionary activity called the "Educational Mission", owes its inception to Alexander Duff of the Free Church of Scotland.[41] He wanted the missionaries to impart western education and values through English medium schools because he considered it to be as an effective instrument of evangelicism. However, the association of Christian missionaries with Telugu speaking people goes back to the fifteenth century, when two Jesuit priests and a Brother began their work at Chandragiri in Chittoor district.[42]

The missionaries took the initiative for the spread of education[43] and to preparing the "untouchables" for higher walks of life.[44] By working for the welfare of the deprived the missionaries succeeded in winning thousands of them to Christianity. During and immediately after the appalling famine of 1876-1879 in the Madras presidency, both to the famine stricken Telugu and Tamil "untouchables", could easily see for themselves the stark contrast between Hinduism that segregated them, and Christianity that helped them in distress, thanks to the humanitarian activities rendered to them by the Missionaries. Many of them embraced Christianity, en mass during this time.[45]

The Christian missionaries strongly believed that caste was the biggest obstacle in their way to spread of their faith.[46] Hence, they adopted a new policy to change the way of life by setting up schools, and introducing social reforms for the deprived communities.[47] Though, proselytization continued to remain the ultimate aim of the missionary, their yeoman service in the other fields gained recognition and popularity among the "untouchables" of Andhra.

By the end of nineteenth century nearly twenty Mission Societies were working towards started their emancipation of the untouchables in the Telugu speaking areas.[48] The Karnatic Mission was established in 1700 at Nellore and it later extended its branches to Cuddapah and Krishna districts.[49] A Roman Catholic Mission established at Cuddapah in 1735, and the London Missionary Society at Visakhapatnam was extended to Bellary, Anantapuram and Vizianagaram. These were followed by the French Society de Missions Strangers in Krishna district and the Vikar of Apostolic Mission in 1832, which later expanded to Nellore, Cuddapah, Anantapuram and Krishna. The American Baptist Mission was established in 1840 and worked in the Udayagiri, Ongole, Bapatla, Khambam and Kurnool areas. The American Lutheran Mission came in 1842 and were active in Guntur, Repalle, Bapatla, Palnadu, Vinukonda, Bandaru and Rajahmundry.

The Protestant Mission commenced its operations from 1843 in and around Nellore, Guntur and Bandaru. They established many educational institutions with the famous Nobel College in Machilipatnam being one of them. The Free Church of Scotland came to Nellore in 1848. The English Church Missionary Society followed suit in 1865. Initially they worked in the vicinities of Krishna, Godavari, Kurnool and Cuddapah districts it extended its branches to a number of towns including Nandyala, Mutyala Padu, Bandaru, Eluru, Bezawada. In 1890, the Canadian Baptist Mission established branches at Kakinada, Bheeminipatnam, Srikakulam, while the Baptist Mission made its presence at Kakinada, Bheemunipatnam, Srikakulam, Bobbili and Tuni. These were followed by the Basel Evangelical Missions, the Schelswing Holstein Luthern Mission and the St. Francis of Sales Mission.

As part of their philanthropic work, all these Missions aggressively promoted Schools and Colleges and worked for the uplift of the oppressed sections. Through this process, the missions introduced the humanistic element of the western civilization to the natives.[50]

The Reformists

By providing education, medical benefits and other social services, the missionaries opened the eyes of the caste-Hindus to the neglect of these unfortunate masses. Starting from second half of the nineteenth century, the "Untouchables" who are resenting the rigid customs and ill treatment by the caste Hindus, were increasingly becoming agreeable to conversion to Christianity.[51] And conversion had two tangible effects on these down-trodden: it not only changed their lifestyle but also influenced the attitude of many caste Hindus towards them.[52]

In Andhra mass conversion to Christianity, particularly among the Dalits, continued well in to the early decades of twentieth century. According to 1931 Census nearly 20 per cent of Depressed Classes in West Godavari, 32 per cent in Krishna and 57 per cent in Guntur districts had been converted to Christianity.[53] In some areas every "untouchable" of each hamlet was converted.[54] Malas and Madigas were converted in increasing numbers and by the early twentieth century, a casual observer might well have been excused for thinking that the Churches existed solely to serve the deprived and the Outcastes.

Different communities received and looked upon the work of missionaries in different ways. The "untouchables" took this in two ways. Firstly, the converts began to experience a new social standing, and they felt that it is certainly better than suffering under Hinduism. Secondly, and more importantly those who still remained within the fold of Hinduism began to realise that the dogma of untouchability that for centuries justified their miserable condition was false.[55] Some caste-Hindus, who saw the amelioration work of the missionaries and who were exposed to western education and knowledge began losing faith in Hinduism and caste.[56] Subsequently, some of them converted to 'half way houses' like Brahma Samaj.[57]

The impact of western humanitarian, liberal and rationalist ideas stirred several Hindu reform movements, from around mid-nineteenth century. The social reformers of this period perceived the caste system as morally and ethically abhorrent, socially debilitating and politically devisive.[58] Two outstanding Telugu Brahmin reformers were: Kandukuri Viresalingam (1848-1919)[59] and Raghupati Venkata Ratnam Naidu (1862-1939).[60] Viresalingam centred his activities in and around Rajahmundry and northern circars, while Venkataratnam Naidu concent-rated in the vicinity of Kakinada and Machilipatnam. They appealed for the eradication of caste discrimination and advocated sympathy towards "untouchables". These two pioneers were followed by others like Unnava Laxminarayana, (a Brahmin writer), Tripuraneni Ramaswamy Choudhary (a

Khamma poet) etc. All these reformers considered education as a crucial instrument to root out untouchability.

A few enlightened individuals began to provided education for the Dalits. The Andhra Deena Sangham was founded at Machilipatnam in 1907 to attend to the social, economic and spiritual aspects of the ameliorative work. It concentrated on education, and by 1924, they could open twelve night schools, nine day schools, and one part-time school for girls in an around Machilipatnam.[61] Handicrafts such as tailoring, drawing, tape-weaving were taught in these schools to help the untouchables lead an independent lives.[62]

Philanthropic caste-Hindus did play a role in uplifting the "untouchables". Viresalingam with support from the Maharaja of Pithapuram started a school to give free education to the children of the Outcastes.[63] The Maharaja of Pithapuram inspired by reformist ideas, began a number of welfare activities for the untouchables. He facilitated admission of the Dalit students into the high school at Kakinada, established two separate hostels for Dalit boys and girls, supported the Ram Mohan Roy hostel of Kakinada for Dalits, who were pursuing college education.[64] In fact, most of the first generation of Dalit intellectuals of Andhra were products of these educational institutions sponsored by the Maharaja.[65]

Though R. Venkataratnam Naidu began his reform activities in the late 1880s, he could do constructive work for Dalit education, only after becoming Principal of Pithapuram Rajah College (1905-1919). He also presided over many anti-untouchability Conferences in the Madras presidency.[66] Another reformist, Chilakamarti Laxmi Narasimham started the Ram Mohan Roy School for Dalits at Rajahmundry in 1909, with English as well as Telugu as medium of instruction. This school also offered free tuitions to Dalit children.[67]

Though religious and revivalist organizations like the Prarthana Samaj, Brahmo Samaj and Arya Samaj were vehemently criticizing the evils of caste system and pleading for the eradication of untouchability did nothing tangible in this field.[68] The members of the Manya Sangam[69] and the Adi-

Andhra Society showed an inclination towards Brahmoism, as it rejected the authority of the Vedas and discarded the Yagnopaneeta or *Jandyam* (the sacred thread). But soon they realized that the untouchable converts to Arya Samaj did not receive the same respect as caste Hindu converts.

In fact, caste Hindus within the Arya Samaj, retained their deep rooted prejudices, as exemplified by an incident in 1914 at the Arya Samaj anniversary at Begampet Vaidik Ashram. A competition was organised for the pupils of various schools to recite *vedamanthras* with their meanings. Also participating were Adi-Hindu Primary Schools. When a Dalit student scored first and received the applause of the audience, the Secretary of the Vaidik Ashram was upset as the Brahmin could not win and made a rude and vulgar remark to the Dalit student. He said "a *Chandal* (an untouchable) did not deserve such an honour". Finally, the prize was not given to the Dalit student.[70] Consequently, the Dalits severed their connection with the Arya Samaj and gradually they withdrew from the cobweb of these reformers.

By the second decade of the twentieth century the social reform movements, initiated by Kandukuri Viresalingam and other individuals had come to an end.[71] The death of Viresalingam in 1919, the mass political agitations spearheaded by the Indian National Congress and the emergence of numerous caste associations were said to have been the reasons for the decline of social reform in Andhra.[72] The Gandhian consensus model "internal reform and self-purification" did nothing constructively but only tried to integrate the Dalits into Hinduism. At another level, the nationalist press began to increasingly focus on the evil practice of untouchability, and sympathetic literature like songs, pamphlets, novels and short-stories.[73]

The Labour Schools

In 1921, the Board of Revenue recommend the appointment of a special agency for promoting the interests of the Depressed Classes.[74] This suggestion was made as it firmly believed that unless a separate agency was created to carry out the government policy, neither the liberal policies and approach nor the facilities created would be able to bring about the desired effect on them. Along with an agency, with "a special officer with a suitable staff under him should be appointed as protector of the Depressed Classes" remarked the Board in its recommendations. The job of this officer was to study the economic conditions of these people and submit proposals to the government for improving them, to ensure that the philanthropic bodies working in the field received the required help from the government to promote education and other better living conditions for them. Fallowing this, the agency also ensured that the students from these castes got admission into publicly–managed schools, stopped government grants to private schools which excluded these children and extended financial assistance through scholarships and reduced the fees among others.

The new special agency was termed 'the Labour Department', not as the name may suggest for the benefit of industrial workers, but for the uplift of Depressed Classes.[75] C.F. Paddison, a senior ICS officer was designated as the Commissioner of Labour; a Deputy Commissioner was appointed in 1920.[76] Also a Labour Advisory Board, comprising one each European, Brahmin and *Adi-Dravaida* was also constituted in the same year.[77] A District Labour Office was also constituted in 1922 for each district where special work was in progress.

The Labour Department started its work in the Godavari District in 1920 and grew fast in size and scope. Between 1921 and 1924, extensive activities on a gradual increasing scale, were undertaken in the Krishna and Guntur districts. Since promoting elementary education was one of its primary concerns, the Department started separate primary schools for the Depressed Classes called "labour schools", and the number of these schools increased as the department widened its activities.

Slowly, more and more Dalit children began to get admission into schools. In 1918-1919, subsidies were made available to the local bodies to open 82 additional elementary schools for the benefit of the Depressed Classes.[78] The Board's elementary schools at Veeravasaram in Peddapuram Taluk, and Kapileswarapuram and Sankatayapalem in Ramachandrapuram Taluk admitted untouchable children; and the Veeravasaram school even had an 'untouchable' teacher.[79]

In spite of the welfare measures and special efforts of the government, their progress on the educational front was slow. In the municipal areas of Anakapalli, Tenali, Narasaraopet, Hindupur and Tirupati the numbers of Depressed Classes admitted into schools was zero. While in the Ganjam, Nellore, and Ballery regions, the number was not appreciable. In the Krishna district, out of 671 caste-Hindu schools under Taluk Boards, only in 28 schools admitted the children of Depressed Classes. The only exception being Godavari district, which by 1922 had 62 schools with 2414 boys and 34 girls along with 43 night schools.[80]

Also, despite the Government orders to District Boards to admit "Untouchables" without any caste restrictions,[81] caste-prejudices against them continued. The Assistant Labour Commissioner asked all schools to admit "untouchable" children and even warned that if they did not do so they would lose the government subsidy.[82] The Director of Public Instruction, too, asked the local Boards and Municipalities to work towards breaking down prejudices by admitting all castes.[83] But caste-Hindu fundamentalists hardly bothered about any such orders and warnings.

Exemplifying this, the Amalapuram Taluk Board passed a Resolution in 1920, following collective petition from the villagers of Sakurru, Indupalli and others to the effect that the admission of Panchamas into public schools was undesirable.[84] In northern circar districts, there was wide resentment among the caste-Hindus, as their children were made to share their seats with the "Untouchable" children. In Dharmavaram, Chandragiri, Narsapur, Gobichettiyapalayam, and Palvancha taluks, the caste-Hindus withdrew their children from the schools following admission of Panchama children.[85]

Table-1 shows the rise and growth of education among the Dalits and other castes from 1891 to 1931. The initial work of missionaries was followed by private philanthropic efforts and encouragement from the colonial government, but the education of the "untouchables" did not make the desired progress. As the table shows, "upper" castes like Brahmin, Komati (Chittiyar), Kapu and Reddy were the highest educated. Even middle level occupational communities like the Kamsali, Balija and Mangali were fairly well placed. The least educated communities were none other than the Untouchables—the Malas and Madigas.

Table–1

Growth of Education (Caste-wise Break up) in Andhra: 1891-1931

Caste	1891		1901		1911		1921		1931	
	Male	*Female*	*Male*	*Female*	*Male*	*Female*	*Male*	*Female*	*Male*	*Female*
Brahmin	72.21	3.73	67.30	4.55	68.19	9.91	59.66	14.98	68.2	9.9
Balija	20.12	1.44	11.70	0.73	20.90	2.03	22.46	3.25	20.9	2.0
Komati	60.46	0.88	49.47	0.86	52.11	2.50	52.13	5.37	52.1	2.5
Kapu/ Reddy	9.45	0.22	3.82	0.06	8.98	0.29	13.56	0.48	12.2	0.7
Kamma	3.41	0.24	4.79	0.15	12.21	0.69	13.56	0.48	12.2	0.7
Mangali	6.61	0.11	3.53	0.12	6.86	0.27	8.61	0.54	6.9	0.3
Mala	1.13	0.05	0.56	0.03	1.3	0.07	1.63	0.14	1.4	0.1
Madiga	0.46	0.02	0.23	Nil	0.82	0.06	0.89	0.11	0.8	0.1
Kamsali	28.53	0.56	16.45	0.47	25.05	1.35	27.61	2.55	25.1	1.4
Golla	2.66	0.06	1.02	0.07	2.76	0.14	2.90	0.25	2.7	1.1

Source: Compiled from the Census Reports of the Madras Presidency for the years shown.

In 1931, the Government decided to admit "exterior" castes (as Dalits were called then) in all aided schools. But as a result, many schools were closed down and from a many other, the caste-Hindus withdrew their children.[86] However, it has to be noted that in spite of the facilities offered, the literacy rate among the Dalits was only one per cent beyond primary stage. Before 1901, this figure was less than one per cent and by 1931, the figure rose marginally to shade over one per cent.[87]

Table–2
Growth of Dalit Education Under 'Labour Department' in Madras Presidency

Year	*No. of Schools*	*Total pupils*
1919-20	6438	1.75 lakhs
1920-21	7007	1.93 lakhs
1921-22	8045	2.22 lakhs
1922-23	8575	2.38 lakhs
1924-25	9086	2.54 lakhs
1931-32	9413	2.63 lakhs
1936-37	10215	2.92 lakhs
1948-49	NA	4.90 lakhs

Source: Compiled from the Annual Reports of Public Instruction in the Madras Presidency for the years shown.

During the later part of 1930s, after the formation of popular governments, further impetus was given to Dalit education including scholarships and hostel facilities. Government ordinances of this period show the steps taken for the development of education. The number of Dalit students admitted to primary (labour) schools increased throughout the period, as shown in Table-2. However, while the Government established new schools, they were at the same time closing down an even greater number of schools except in 1937-38. Ironically, most of the time, the Government's ameliorative programmes existed only on paper with no serious follow-up measures to implement them.

Despite these special programmes, the growth of Dalit literacy was very low compared to that of general population. In addition to caste-Hindu prejudices and non-cooperation with colonial policies, the socio-economic conditions of the Dalits were also responsible for this. The fear of oppression by the caste-Hindus also played a crucial role in this.[88] The maximum dropout rate reveals the fact that poverty was a constant companion, making them withdraw their children from schools during the agricultural season and when there were fewer economic incentives. Besides overt discrimination, most of the Dalits lacked money for tuition, and an encouraging environment for study. Thus, the economic backwardness, in addition to social disabilities and the consequent fear of oppression by caste-Hindus, were impediments in the progress Dalit education in Andhra.

While they're very little development of Dalit education by early decades of the twentieth century, even this was notable since there was no scope for it earlier. The first generation could learn because of the mercy of missionaries, the efforts of philanthropists and those of British Government agencies. In this way, the first few drops of learning that fell among the parched "Untouchables" by the turn of twentieth century as a trickle of educational opportunities began to widen into a small stream slowly. Out of this first generation of educated untouchables cameout, the first teachers and the first to take the few places opened to them in government services, such as the military and the railways. In the 1920s and the 1930s more Untouchables children followed their paths into schools. Their elders, still only a hand full, took their part in the political struggle that the Congress Party and Gandhi was spearheading against the British rule.[89]

On the economic front, a number of major irrigation schemes was launched along the Krishna and Godavari rivers during nineteenth century, laying the basis for intensive cultivation of rice and cash crops for a growing market. As a result, large-scale commercialization of agriculture had taken place by the early years of the twentieth century.[90] This process eroded the traditional caste and *jajamani* ties, which bound the Dalit labourers and aided development of a mobile labour force providing opportunities for many Dalits to move ahead.[91] Thousands of Dalit labourers from the East coast used to go every year for work on the docks of Rangoon in Burma.[92] This Burmese connection played an important role in development of their economic life and some of them even invested in education of their brethren back home.

The Emergence of Dalit Consciousness

During the 1930s, two divergent and strong currents appropriated the development of Dalits, and the end result was to division of the radical Dalit movements. One of the forces was the Gandhian influence, which the second current was the influence from the Communists. The Congress Party's front for the Outcastes called the Harijan Sevak Sangh at Vijayawada in November 1932, entered the province with the formation of the Andhra branch. While two caste-Hindu reformers, K. Negeswara Rao and M. Bapineedu were its President and General Secretary respectively. Two Dalits—Vemula Kurmayya from Krishna district and Naralasetti Devendrudu from West Godavari district were its Joint Secretaries. These two played a major role in organizing the Adi-Andhra conferences. They educated and influenced many Dalit rural people. Gradually, the majority of Dalit intellectuals got absorbed into the Congress, with its "Harijan" terminology and its reiteration of Hindu identity. The end result was that it followed a cautious and a limited philosophy.[93]

The second current to sweep the Dalits during the 1930s was the nascent but fast emerging Communist movement. As a working class movement, it could enter more forcefully into Dalit localities than any other movement in the 1930s and the 40s.[94] Soon the Communists began to organize the rural poor, workers and agricultural labourers.[95] On the whole, the Communist movement certainly played a significant role in increasing the wages of Dalit labourers, by organizing these scattered labourers into a strong force of labour unions, and by teachings of Socialism and Marxism. Active participation of the Dalits in the Communist movement created a consciousness of unity and an awareness of the need to fight for their rights. At a political level, although the Congress claimed credit for bringing in the Minimum Wages Act, that benefited the Dalits more than any other section, the communist mobilization was responsible for steadily upgrading of the minimum wages, as the movement was "economic determinist."[96]

However, the Communists articulated only economic questions, and took the care to see that the Dalits did not develop an independent identity by incorporating Ambedkarism in to Marxism.[97] The Communists did not even develop a paradigm of their own to tackle the disfigured identity of the Dalits. A careful examination of communist literature of the period (and even that upto the 1970s) shows the Communists addressing the Dalits as 'Harijans' while claiming to be Anti-Gandhians. By the mechanical application of dialectical materialism, they thought that only better wages and landholdings, would undo the Brahminical past. Nowhere can one find a semblance of a critique of Brahminical tradition in the theoretical discourses of the Communists.

In the meanwhile, a conscious effort was being made by the Dalit intelligentsia to develop a theory of exploitation that could build a strong unity. For them, education was a double-edged weapon—to instil reform ideas in them to change their habits and superstitious practices; and secondly to arouse in them a consciousness of the oppression and exploitation being meted out to them by caste-Hindus and to organize them for gaining a respectful place in society. They also realized the limitations of both the philanthropic and the governmental initiatives for their uplift. Thus, it was the first generation of educated Dalits, inspired by ideas of reform and the notion of equality, who effectively began to organize educational activities for their communities.

The Dalit intelligentsia criticized the existing educational methods.[98] Gurram Jashua,[99] a powerful and popular Dalit poet lamented that:[100]

> Our books are as meaningless as the corps of our fore fathers,
> If we confine reading to these books.
> The posterity will be as learned as the trained bull
> That shakes or nods its head to the prompting of its master

Thrust such decadent books on the heads of people
And the tree of knowledge will never flower.

Bhagya Reddi Varma (1888-1939), a Dalit intellectual and social reformer from Hyderabad,[101] felt that education was essential for the all around progress and upliftment of the untouchables.[102] His educational activities began with a lower primary school at the *Jagan Mitra Mandali* office at Easamiah Bazar in 1910. It was followed by one at Lingampalli and the third at Bogul Kunta. Later, four more schools were opened at Chanchalguda, Sultan Shahi, Dhulpet and Gunfoundry. All seven schools were started and run with public funds.[103]

By the early 1930s, these Adi-Hindu primary schools grew to 26, and about 2,500 Dalit children became the beneficiaries. But finance became a problem, and in 1933, the Government of Nizam proposed taking over these schools. The proposal was agreed to, on the condition that the medium of instruction should remain the mother tongue of the pupil and not Urdu as was compulsory in government schools in those days, and secondly that the curriculum should include some handi-crafts.[104]

Against a background of widespread illiteracy and ignorance and with the influence from the neighbouring states, the Dalit leaders of Hyderabad started educational activities in coastal Andhra, establishing Schools and Hostels for Dalit Children. Here, the Burma factor is more visible again. Vundru Tatayya (1850-1930) was one of the Burma-returned Dalit reformers with deep pockets. He held 300 acres of landholding in Burma and 150 acres of land in his native village Ponnamanda, in Rajolu taluk of East Goadvari district. He used to visit Burma annually to collect money for Dalit education back in Andhra. During the 1920s he set up a school at Ponnamanda and funded construction of school buildings at three other villages—Anatavaram, Allavaram and Modalukuduru.[105] Apart from this yeomen service for Dalit education Tatayya also persuaded other Dalit leaders, including Golla Chandrayya, Kusuma Tatayya, Tadi Swamy, Pamula Reddi, Kona Venkanna to initiate welfare efforts for their community.[106]

Many of the hostels for Dalit pupils, established by Dalit activists, functioned without government grants. In 1928, two separate hostels for Dalit boys and girls were established at Rajahmundry by Jala Ranga Swamy.[107] In the1930s, Eeli Vadapalli (1911-1972) established a school and hostel at Mandapet.[108] He established the Laxmi Industrial Training School at Ramachandra Puram. Jala Ranga Swamy even went out to streets to collect food and money for feeding the students, since there was no funding available.[109] Another hostel was established in 1936 by Golla Chandrayya (1818-1972) at Rajolu. In 1937, the Bapuji Harijan Hostel was set up by Pandu Laxmana Swamy (1892-1960).

In addition to schools and hostels, Dalit intellectuals also established many journals and newspapers to spreading awareness among the Outcastes. In these awareness programmes, *Bhajan Mandalis* and other cultural activities played a major role in identity formation. The educated Dalits were very few, but they were more than enough to make their presence felt and in creating socio-political and cultural consciousness among their masses.

By the 1920s, particularly beginning with 1917, an emerging non-Brahmin movement began to challenged the Brahmin dominance in the Madras Presidency thus laying the basis for many of the themes influencing Dalit movements, including a non-Aryan or Dravidian identity.[110] During the same time a new generation of literate and militant Dalits were thoroughly rejecting both the Panchama and the Harijan identities and were organizing themselves as Adi-Andhras, the original sons of the soil. Similar situations can be found all over India. In Punjab, it is called Adi-Dharm movement, in Madras it is called Adi-Dravida movement,[111] and in U.P. it is called Adi-Hindu movement.[112] For Andhra the decisive year was 1917. Madari Bhagya Reddi Varma organized Andhra Desa First Panchama Conference at Bezawada from 4-6 November, 1917. Brahmins and caste-Hindus too attended this conference, including Gudur Ramachandra Rao, Ayyadevara Kaleswara Rao and Vemuri Ramji Rao. In his Presidential address, Bhagya Reddi

Varma narrated the atrocities of caste-Hindus unleashed on the "untouchables" and talked about their miserable plight. He argued that the term Panchama was found no mention in the Puranas or other Hindu scriptures and the so-called Panchamas were the original sons of the soil and that they were once the rulers of the country.[113] The delegates then rejected the term Panchama and declared themselves as the Andhra Desa First Adi-Andhra Conference. They passed eighteen relatively non-controversial resolutions, such as appealing to the government to nominate Adi-Andhras to local bodies, and Legislative Councils, and also establish separate schools and wells for them. They decided against making an open call for entry into the temples as they considered it as a futile agitation and an unwanted thing, besides being no way beneficial to the untouchables.[114] But caste tension showed up during the three days of the Conference, with the known Kanaka Durga temple remaining closed fearing of an attempt to enter it.

After this, conferences were held in Andhra every year at the village, taluk, district and regional levels. These conferences constantly passed resolutions urging the government to label them as Adi-Andhras or Adi-Dravidas, according to linguistic areas, forcing the Madras Legislative Council to adopt the following resolutions.[115]

1. That this council recommends to the Government that the term 'Panchama' or 'Paraya' used to designate the Ancient Dravidian community in southern India should be deleted from Government records etc., and the term 'Adi-Dravida' in the Tamil and 'Adi-Andhra' in Telugu districts be substituted instead".

2. An undertaking was given that the Government would have no objection to call the members of this community 'Adi-Dravida' in Tamil, 'Adi-Andhra' in Telugu districts and particular members of the community 'Dravidas', if they prefer to be so-called, but it would not be possible to re-edit old records. The Government accordingly directs that the following

terms shall in future be adopted in place of 'Panchama' or 'Paraya' or similar terms in all official documents:

However, the Adi-ideology and the Adi-Andhra consciousness only intensified, which is clear from the rising number of such conferences in the 1920s and the 1930s throughout Andhra districts. So does the fact that by 1931, the census indicated 838,000 people listing as Malas, 612,000 as Madigas and 665,000 as Adi-Andhras in Madras presidency alone.[116]

Concluding Remarks

The nineteenth century social reform movements regarded education, as a means of enlightenment but progress was limited to the "twice born". Feeble efforts were made to extend education to women and untouchables. Social reforms admitted the Dalits only as marginalised Hindus. This was in reaction to Christian missionaries success in proselytising them. Schools became an institutional form of reiterating the Dalits' under-privileged and unequal status.

The Missionaries' attitude towards the Untouchables was marked by humanism and zeal to solve their problems by satisfying their immediate needs. But such an attitude was badly lacking in the fragile efforts made by many caste-Hindu reformers. The first generation Untouchables became either ideologies of or activists of the Dalit cause. They made efforts to educate the Dalit masses, seeing education as the most effective way to break the strongly embedded caste hegemony. Through their writings in journals, pamphlets, political addresses, novels and poetry, they ridiculed the efforts made by the caste-Hindu reformers and exhorted the Dalits to realise the importance and effectiveness of education. No concrete and collective social movement for Dalit education was taken up by the enlightened caste-Hindus. This is true even of the Communists. Thus, the Dalits did not receive much support from any non-Dalits.

Education became meaningful to the untouchables only in those institutions, which were founded by the missionaries and Dalit reform organizations. The non-Dalit women were recognised as an entity to be reformed and educated in the late nineteenth and early twentieth centuries. As a result, many caste Hindu women achieved high status in the political, educational and professional fields, while the Dalit Women remained uneducated and excluded from schooling system in the throughout the period under review, except a few extraordinary exceptions.

Available sources reveal that education did not do much better the economic status of the Dalits. Even the census reports do not indicate any professional mobility in any field. However, education produced an intelligentsia, a number of social reformers, politicians and writers, who in turn fought for Dalit rights. Such rights became the subject of legislation only in the post-colonial society.

An earlier version of this paper has been presented at National Conference on 'Education and Disprivileged Groups' held at ERRU, School of Social Sciences, JNU (6-7 August, 1998) and at 'South Asian Conference on Education' held at Department of Education (Central Institute of Education), University of Delhi, (14-18 November, 1999).

NOTES AND REFERENCES

1. The term "Harijan" was coined by Narsi Mehta, a Gujarati saint poet. In fact, the term initially used only to refer to the children of *devadasis*, the female temple dancers. Symbolically speaking they were "children of God" in that devadasis (*deva* means God and *dasi* means servant) were dedicated to the services of God/Goddess and sexual union between the agents and servants of God was mystified and even invested with an aura of divinity. See T.K. Oomen, 1994; Tapi Dharma Rao, 1992. But Gandhi widely used the term *Harijan* and popularised it as a Synonym to "Untouchables". See Kamalini Sengupta, 1995, p. 16.

2. The term 'Dalit' means trampled, squeezed, crushed, down-trodden, or Broken to pieces generally. 'Dalit', therefore, originally denoting class rather than caste but it is now being increasingly used for the untouchables. It was Dr. Ambedkar who began using the word Dalit, applying it first only to his caste, the Mahars. Later it spread to all the Scheduled Castes, but the later became

common and settle as legal term. The term got resurfaced in the 1970s, thanks to the Dalit Panthers. For them, Dalit is a symbol of change and revolution. A Dalit believes in humanism, rejects the existence of God, rebirth, soul, 'sacred' books that teach discrimination, fate and heaven, because these have made him a slave an exploited man in his country. See Gangadhar Pantawane, 1986, pp. 79-87. In 1972, Namadeo Dhosal, a Mahar himself a powerful poet and one of the founders of Dalit Panthers, widened the scope of the term to include Scheduled Castes, Scheduled Tribes, and landless labourers and the economically exploited. Now the term applies again to Scheduled Castes, as distinct from tribals and OBCs. See Eleanor Zelliot, 1996, pp. 267-292. For a different analysis, which was not well received although thought provoking, see James Massey, 1994.

3. The term "Exterior Castes" has been used by J.H. Hutton. It was originally suggested by the Census Superintendent of Assam latter added as Appendix I in the *Census of India*, 1931, vol. I, part I Report, (Delhi: Manager of Publications, 1933), pp. 471-501.

4. Now that "Untouchability" is banned, at least legally or Constitutionally, the "untouchables" now called as 'Ex-untouchables.' See Harold R. Issacs, 1965.

5. As late as 1930, the Indian Statutory Commissioned defined Depressed classes as they were, "In origin, these castes seem to be partly "functional" comprising those who followed occupations held to be unclean or degrading, such as scavenging, leather working and partly "tribal" i.e., aboriginal tribes absorbed into the Hindu fold and transformed into an impure Caste. See *Indian Statutory Commission* Report, vol. I, (Calcutta, 1930), p.37.

6. For a list of all the total sub-castes among the Scheduled Castes in Andhra Pradesh, See the *Scheduled Castes and Scheduled Tribes Orders Amendments Act, 1976* (No. 108 of 1976, dated the 18th September, 1976).

7. See *Census of India, 1991*, Series I, India, Paper-I of 1993, *Union Primary Census Abstract for Scheduled Castes and Scheduled Tribes* (India/State Level) (Delhi, Controller of Publication, 1992).

8. The 'Adi-Andhra' sub-caste was a latter addition. Until the 1921 Census there was no one under this nomenclature, but by the 1931 census there were about 6,65,000 counted under this caste. These were offshoots of the Malas and Madigas. Educated untouchables, influenced by the "non-Aryan" themes of the Dravidian movement had started to identify themselves as "Adi-

Andhras", with a claim that they were the original sons of the soil. Though the term 'Adi-Andhra' can be heard from 1917, it was only in 1922 that the Madras Government agreed to delete reference to "Panchama" "Paraya" from its records and the term with a "Adi" prefex to a regional identifier such as "Adi-Andhra", "Adi" Dravida etc. See Government of Madras, Law (General) Department, G.O. No. 817, 25th March 1922, alongwith Legislative Council Resolution—January 1922: *Census of India, 1931*, vol. XIV, Madras, Part I, p. 349. Also see Indu Raja Gopal, 1985, pp. 118-141; Gali Omvedt, 1994, pp. 117-119.

9. R.N. Saxena, 1967, pp. 78-79.
10. Brij Raj Chauhan, 1967, p. 229.
11. Neil, J. Smelsor, 1993, p. 265.
12. Pierre Bourdieu and Jean Cloude Passeron, 1990, Preface.
13. Neil, J. Smelser, 1993, p. 267.
14. Dharma Pal, 1983, p. 20.
15. Robert Eric Frykenberg, 1986, p. 40.
16. K.S. Latourette, 1953, pp. 894-897.
17. His associates including John Z. Kiernander, Daniel Joseph Jaenicke, Christian Wilhelm Gericke, John Kohloff, Philipp Fabricius etc. For Details see Hugh Pearson, 1839.
18. Hugh Pearson, 1839, vol. I, pp. 379-85.
19. For the details of contribution and activities of Thomos Munro, alongwith a critical biographical information see Burton Stein, 1989.
20. "Minute on the Education of the Natives of India" June 25, 1822, Tamil Nadu State Archives, Madras Revenue Consultations, July 2, 1822, also see Aleander J. Arbuthnot, 1981, vol. 2, pp. 326-329, A.N. Basu, 1952, pp. 176-177.
21. "Minute of Sir Thomas Munro, March 10, 1826, (For St. George, Revenue Consultations)", Dharmpal, 1983, pp. 248-251.
22. Richard B. Devitt, 1977, cited in Robert Eric Frykenberg, 1986, p. 44.
23. For instance, at Rajahmundry the books used in schools and colleges were, in addition to the *Vedas and Sastras*, the Bala Ramayananam, Rukmini Kalyanam, Kristna Satakam, Sumati

Satakam, Vasu Charitra, Manucharitra, Bhagavatam, Gajendra Moksham etc. For details see report from the collector, Rajamundry to Board of Revenue, dated September 19, 1823, Tamil Nadu State Archives, Board of Revenue Proceedings, vol. 963, pro. 2.10.1823, pp. 8520-8525, Nos. 29-30.

24. See Abbe J.A. Dubois, 1953, p. 292.

25. Alexender J. Arbuthnot, 1855, p. 45; A.D. Compbell to Board of Revenue, August 17, 1825, para 18, Tamil Nadu State Archives, Madras Revenue Consultations, August 25, 1823.

26. Robert Eric Frgykenberg, 1986, p. 45.

27. A. Mathew, 1988. pp. 14-38.

28. S. Sathinadhan, 1894, p. 6; also see H. Sharp, 1965, pp. 73-81.

29. S. Sathianathan, 1894, pp. 10-11.

30. For "Filtration theory' see Macaulay's Minute, dated 2.2. 1835, C.E. Travelyan, 1838; also see A. Mathew, 1988.

31. For details see J. Mangmma, 1971.

32. Uma Ramaswamy, 1974b, p. 1963.

33. Public Consultations, dated December 30, 1834, Despatch No.16, Madras Revenue Office, Volume 629, item 25; also see M. Sargurudoss, 1961.

34. Y. Vaikuntham, 1982, p. 180, quoting from *Indian Statutory Commission*, 1930, vol. I.

35. Proceedings of Education Department, Government of Madras, G.O. No.68, (Education), Dated February 1, 1893.

36. *The Hindu*, June 3, 1891.

37. Government of India, "Progress of Education in India 1892- 1893", *Third Quinguennial Review*, (London, 1898), pp. 352-353.

38. S. Saraswathi, 1974, p.148.

39. Proceedings of the Education Department, Government of Madras, G.O. No. 763, (Education) dated, November 22, 1905.

40. *The Madras Mail*, August 13, 1908.

41. Julius A. Richater, 1908, pp. 192-193.

42. Uma Ramaswamy, 1974b, pp. 1958-1964.

43. See the "Statement Concerning the State of Education of the Depressed Classes in Bombay Presidency" submitted by Dr. B.R. Ambedkar to the Indian Statutory Commission, on May 29, 1928, cited in A.C. Pradhan, 1986, p. 11.

44. K. Ramanujachari, 1901, p. 328.

45. J.N. Farquhar, 1967, pp. 366-67.

46. A.I. Mayhew, 1941, p. 310.

47. *Ibid.*, p. 308.

48. For details of Missionary activities and mass conversion movements in Andhra, see J.W. Pickett, 1933; J.G. Manor, 1971, pp. 27-41; A.V. Fishman, 1941; Frederic Lamb, 1913; F.F. Gledstone.

49. Akudi Venkatesware Rao, 1939, pp. 699-705.

50. S. Natarajan, 1959, pp. 7-8.

51. J.E. Padfield, 1908, pp. 42-62; Edgar Thurston and K. Rangachari, 1909, vol. iv, pp. 329-330.

52. J.W. Pickett, 1938, p. 60.

53. Duncan B. Forrester, 1991, pp.65-93. Also see the "Minutes" of the Sixth Biennail Meeting of the Andhra Christian Council held at Secunderabad, (1-4 December, 1933).

54. G.A. Oddie, 1991, pp. 95-124; also see M. Suseela, 1913, pp. 127-130.

55. J.N. Farquhar, 1967, p. 368.

56. Julius A. Richter, 1908, pp. 184-193.

57. A. Mathew, 1988, p. 45, also see Charles Heimseth, 1964.

58. K.N. Panikkar, 1990, pp. 3-32; and 1975, p. 7.

59. For Detailed biographical sketch and his activities see V. Ramakrishna, 1983.

60. For details see, K.R. Suryanarayana, 1952; M.R. Appa Rao, 1972.

61. Proceedings of Revenue (miscls) Department, Government of Madras, G.O. No. 78, Dated May 26, p. 1924.

62. B. Kesavanarayana, 1976, p. 279, Vemuri Viswanatha Sharma, 1916, p. 62.

63. K. Veresalingam, 1954, pp. 341-352.

64. For details see, Pamu Rama Murthy.

65. Y.B. Abbasayalu, 1978, pp. 51-52.

66. Charles H. Heimseth, 1964, pp. 259-262.

67. Chilkamarti Laxmi Narasimham, 1957, pp. 283-286.

68. M.B. Gautam, 1991, p. 2.

69. Manya Sangam (1911) was a later form of an organization called Jagan Mitra Mandali established in 1906, by Madari Bhagya Reddi Verma, (1988-1939), a pioneer Dalit reformer of Hyderabad state as well as in coastal Andhra region see D.Ramulu Naik, 1992, pp. 92-95.

70. M.B. Gautam, *Bhagyodayam*, 1991, p. 16.

71. V. Ramakrishna, 1983, pp. 182-183.

72. *Ibid.*, pp. 189, 197-204, 208-211; for the counter arguments see Atluri Murali, 1988, pp. 3-29.

73. For songs written by Dalits as well as non-Dalit writers see K.P. Ashok Kumar, 1993; Garimella Satyanarayana, 1933, several books were written in prose as well as poetry, such as, Unnava Laxminarayana, 1964; N.G. Ranga, 1933; Nanduri Venkata Krishnamacharyulu, 1935; Mangipudi Venkata Sharma, 1933.

74. Simultaneously, Government of India took up the matter and enquired from provincial Governments as to what had been done and what further could be done for the depressed classes. See *Proceedings of the Home (Misc) Department, Government of India*, G.O. Nos. 1676-1676, dated December 2, 1919.

75. *Ibid.* In addition to aboriginal and hill tribes, the Untouchable communities specified under the jurisdiction of this agency were, Adi-Dravidas, Chakkilliyans, Cherumas, Holeyas, Madigas, Malas, Pallans, Parayans, Semmans, Haddis, Bavuris, Dandasis, Madaris, Koragas, Nagadis, And Valluvans.

76. S. Saraswathi, 1974, p. 157.

77. Gilbert Slater, K. Ramanujachariar and M.C. Raja were members of the First Committee.

78. Y. Vaikuntham, 1982, p. 163.

79. Proceedings of Law (Education) Department, Government of Madras, G.O. No. 275, 1086, Law (Education), July 17, 1921.

80. Proceedings of Law (Education) Department, Government of Madras, G.O. No. 275 Law (Education) February 17, 1923.

81. See the Proceeding of Various Departments of Government of Madras, for Instance, Education Department, G.O. No. 329, March 17, 1919; Local and Municipal Department G.O. No. 380, April 24, 1920; Home (Education) Department G.O. No. 886, August 1920; Law (Education) Department G.O. No. 1086, July 27, 1921; G.O. No. 275, December 16, 1923.

82. Proceedings of Law (Education) Department, Government of Madras, G.O. No. 778, dated May 14, 1921.

83. Proceedings of Law (Education) Department, Government of Madras, G.O No.28, dated January 6, 1922.

84. On the Admission of 6 Panchama children, 50 Caste-Hindu Children were withdrawn from the school. See Proceedings of Law (Education) Department, Government of Madras, G.O. No.778, dated May 14, 1921.

85. Proceedings of Law (Education) Department, Government of Madras, G.O. No. 28, January 6, 1922.

86. L. Eleyaperumal, 1969, p. 180.

87. Indu Raja Gopal, 1985, p. 118.

88. Proceedings of Law (Education) Department, *Government of Madras*, G.O. No. 2017, dated November 21, 1924.

89. Vemula Kurmayya, 1947, pp. 49-50.

90. For details see, A. Satyanarayana, 1990; Carol Upadhyaya, 1988; Nata Duvvury, 1986.

91. Gail Omvedt, 1994, p. 114.

92. By the 1930s, Telugus were the single largest racial group among the Indians living in Burma. As per the *Burma Census Reports 1931*, the Indian population consisted of Bengalis, 1,23, 319; Hindustani (North Indians), 1,25,054; Oriyas, 57, 906, Tamils, 84,327,Telugus, 1,31,72. However, the unofficials estimated between 1.5 lakhs to 2.18 laks. See Adapa Satyanarayana, 1998b; and 2005, pp. 217-255; Harold R. Issacs, 1965, p. 69.

93. G. Ram Reddy, 1989, pp. 263-284.

94. For details of the Communist movement and their activities See Kambhampati Satyanarayana, 1984-90; A. Satyanarayana, 1986, pp. 34-47.

95. P. Sundarayya, 1990, pp. 39-40.

96. Kancha Ilaiah, 1995, pp. 18-19.

97. *Ibid,* further he says, "Ambedkar was almost a banned name within communist discourse, though Ambedkar was never as much Anti communist as he was anti-Congress".

98. For details *Souvenir*, 1976.

99. Gurram Jashua (1895-1971) wrote many poetic kavyams including *Madalassa* (1919); *Chidananda Prabhatam* (1925); *Phiradausi* (1930); *Kandhiseekudu* (1943); *Gabbilam* (1946-50); etc. His Poems on *Satya Harischandra's* burial ground operations are said to be the most powerful expressions of an untouchable's life. For details see Nagalla Guru Prasada Rao, 1959; Yendluri Sudhakar, 1992; Katti Padma Rao, 1994.

100. Jashua's poetic work *Gabbilam* is named after the bat, signifying a dark, ugly bird, which is considered a bad omen. He relates this to the plight of "untouchables". The bat was Jashua's weapon to bring about a social awakening among Dalits, to tell them that they had a right to live with dignity and freedom. See *Jashua's Gabbilam* 1996, p. 71.

101. For details of his activities see M.B. Gautam, 1976.

102. M.B. Gautam, *Bhagyodayam op cit.* p.14; also see Y.B. Abbasayulu, 1979.

103. M.B. Gautam, 1991, p. 15.

104. R.K. Kshirsagar, 1994, p. 180.

105. For details see *Souvenir*, 1976, pp. 1-3.

106. *Ibid.*, p. 2

107. *Ibid.*, pp. 91-93.

108. *Ibid.*, p. 46.

109. R.K. Kshirsagar, 1994, p. 212.

110. Gail Omvedt, 1994, p. 115.

111. Gail Omvedt, 1995, p. 35.

112. Nandini Gooptu, 1993, pp. 277-298.

113. M.B. Gautam, 1991, p. 4.

114. *Ibid.*, p. 5.

115. See Law (General) Department, Government of Madras, G.O. No. 817, March 25, 1922.

116. *Census of India*, 1931, Madras, Part I: Report (Madras, Superintendent of Government Press, 1933).

3

The World of 'Untouchables': A Study of Vemana

Literature often serves both as mirror of reality[1] and of the structures of thinking that constitutes the consciousness of the age they live in. Analytical studies of literature can therefore serve to illuminate an understanding of social relationships in any given period of history.[2] There is no doubt that literature of the transitory periods has a valuable historical importance. It provides a panorama, showing the transition of the society from one phase to another.[3] The seventeenth and eighteenth centuries the constitutes of transitory phase between the disintegration of Indian polity and the advent of the British in India in general and south India in particular. The greatness and grandeur of Telugu literature in this period is characterized by *satakas* of didactic value. This chapter is concerned with the relevance of and symbolism of *satakas* attributed to Vemana, with a view to examine the socio-cultural conditions of the untouchables' life as reflected in Telugu literature in general and Vemana's writings in particular.

'Untouchables'—The Background

The origin of Untouchability is obscure and its development difficult to trace. Untouchability with its manifold manifestations is rooted in the notions of "purity" and "pollution", which is believed to have developed in the later *Vedic* period, when Brahmanic literature emerged in the form of *smritis, samhitas* and *upanishads*. The Rigveda does not show any acquaintance with people with whom contact was even remotely tabooed. In the later Vedic period terms like *Chandala*[4] and *Paulaksa*[5] come into existence and they suggested such people as objects of spite and abhorrence existing at the lowest rungs of the ritual and social ladder. But they were not treated as "untouchables".

According to the *Boudayana Dharma Sutra*, a *Chandala* is an offspring of a *Shudra* father and a *Brahmin* mother.[6] Although not all the Brahminical texts are unanimous on the origin of the *Chandala*, he is represented as an instrument of derivative pollution as well as a transmitter of contagion through contact. Further references to infection from the *Chandalas* through sight, speech or proximity occur.[7] *Chandalas* were forbears of several castes, such as *Nishads, Kaivartas, Dasas, Bidalakaris* etc., who were subsequently treated as "untouchables". His shadow, however, not regarded as polluting then, was a later development. The commensual and connubial taboos in relation to the *Chandala* became severe and absolute. The notion of pollution became a potent reality and it was seen in full play with respect to the *Chandalas*.

The Brahminical 'legal' texts imposed harsh restrictions upon the Untouchables, as a result of the elaborate development of the concepts of purity and pollution as manifest in the *Manusmriti*. The idea of groups having "lower" status than the Shudra in the *Chaturvarna* scheme of social stratification repeatedly appeared in the later Brahminical writings. These references were often characterized by immense contempt, hatred and castigation. By the Fifth Century A.D. many of the stern injunctions of the "theoretical legal texts" seemed to have become a reality. The Fifth Century Chinese traveller, Fa-Hein[8] and the Seventh Century Chinese pilgrim Yuan Chaung[9] observe that the *Chandala*s dwelled outside the village, in separate quarters. The Eleventh Century scholar Al-biruni describes the *Chandala*s and three other groups as illegitimate and were not members of any caste or guild, perform dirty jobs.[10] Legal texts, secular works and most foreign accounts note untouchability as a practice of segregating these sections of society with strict rigidity.

A Brief Note on Telugu Literature and Society

When we look at the situation of Telugu speaking region, even a cursory glance at the history of Telugu literature, particularly the medieval texts, would reveal how literature was mainly confined to zamindar darbars and scholarly gatherings with an emphasis on literary gimmicks such as *satavadhana* and *asthavadhna*,[11] which indulged in depicting *sringaraviraha* (erotica). Until mid-seventeenth century, all the writers, (primarily Brahmins) tried to only to make the language more difficult to display their command over language (Sanskrit or sanskritised Telugu), and to score over their rivals.

There are no literary sources available other than translations of the Hindu epics till fourteenth century A.D. The preceding period was characterized by the waning of Buddhism and Jainism. It is a historical fact that Jainism and literature based upon it were prevalent in the Andhra and Kannada regions prior to Nannaya, the first known Telugu poet (*Aadi Kavi?).* And it is said that the scholars of the Jaina faith also wrote some books in Telugu. But these works must have been destroyed when Jainism was suppressed.[12] Nannaya, must have been acquainted with some of them, because otherwise he could not have become an "eminent" poet all of a sudden to compose a Telugu version of the Mahabharata. Starting from Rajaraja Narendra (eleventh century) all the then rulers, 'generously' donated *Agraharas* (Tax free lands) to poets, who in turn devoted all their 'intellect' to praise their patron and depict some of their affairs with women and also to preserve the Vedic rituals and Varnasrama Dharma intact.

Some scant literary sources reveal that the *Chandala*s were employed as *Talayaries* or village-watchmen.[13] Edarupalli record mentions them as Charmakaras,[14] but not more than that. Fourteenth and fifteenth centuries literature like *Kridabhiramam* of Vallabhacharya refers to the *Chandalas* as a caste but does not categorized them as separate i.e., outside the pale of Hinduism,[15] Proudhakavi Mallana in his *Rukmangada Charitra* mentions that *Chandala*s were prohibited from witnessing religious ceremonies performed by the "high caste". These sources evidently show that *Chandalas* were appendage to the *Chaturvarna* of Hindu society, but their main occupation was as agrarian labour and thus playing a major role in the economic activity of the society,[16] and were thus considered as productive community and their deities such as Ekavira and Mahuramma.[17]

The later medieval period is known as Rayalu-yugam in Telugu literature.[18] Poets of the Prabhanda style, included Allasani Peddana (author of *Manucharistramu*), Nandi Timmana (*Parijatapaharanam*), Ramabhadrakavi, (*Ramabhyudayamu*), Dhurjati (*Kalahasti Mahastyam* or *Kalashastisva Satakam*), Pingali Surana (*Kalapornodayam*) and so on. But none of them took 'society' realistic as a subject. While analyzing the local administration systems under Vijayanagra, T.V. Mahalingam mentions that a seventeenth century inscription refers to eighteen professional association bodies. *Kurantakas* (shoe maker) was one of them and seemed to have formed a recognized part of local assemblies.[19] And the literary references to "untouchables" do not go beyond this.

In the Seventeenth Century, Vijayanagar lost its importance to feudatory courts such as Gandikota, Siddhavatam, Nellore and Gingee, Tanjore and Mathura. Literature flourished through Matli Ananta of Siddnavatam (Cuddapah district), Pushpagiri Timmana at Nellore and Raghunadha Nayaka at Tanjore.[20] In northern Andhra too literature enjoyed patronage at feudatory courts like Pithapuram and Paddapuram.[21] There was a set of poets outside the patronage who made a considerable contribution to Telugu literature in this period. Worth mentioning among them are, Tyagayya, Potuloori Vira Brahmam, Paparaju and Vemana.

Since there was no dearth of patronage, there was no dearth of poets and works as well.[22] Surprisingly no work deals with a social theme. In other words, society is reflected neither as a subject nor as an object. Whatever references about "untouchables" are made, it is in the context of taboos, punishment and perpetuation of their servile status. These

Prabhanda texts depart from the epic and puranic texts in several respects, and though a theme might have taken from the puranas, it's restricted to one or two episodes only. Importance is given to the *Sringararasa* (the erotic sentiment), but they're confined to the classical standard in usage and the narration is subordinate to the description, and the two are not integrated.[23] The only qualitative shift is in the target of audience: while the Puranas target "common people", the Prabandhas are meant solely for the pleasure-seeking upper class—the kings and his nobility. The prime aim of these texts is only to please the patrons and as a result they lost relevance for society at large.[24]

Vemana—Time and Place

Vemana's poetry occupies a distinct place in Telugu literature, both for its literary style as well as for its content and he is considered as a social revolutionary in literary circles.

Scholars, both Indian as well as Western, have achieved very little success with regard to fixing the time of Vemana's birth and death. But based on the evidence of the manuscripts and from the various oral traditions, some critics have placed Vemana in twelfth Century,[25] while William Howard Campbell places Vemana roughly in the middle of the Sixteenth Century.[26] However, most of the critics believe that he lived in the Seventeenth Century. C.P. Brown, for example, says that Vemana born in 1652,[27] while Dubois states that "we were told" that Vemana died towards the end of the seventeenth century.[28] If Vanguri Subba Rao makes a persistent effort to put back the age of Vemana, there is a pronounced tendency in Rallapalli Ananta Krishna Sharma to push it forward.[29] Bandaru Thammayya places him between 1650 and 1750, which is the period agreed upon by most scholars. Lack of adequate sources has become an impediment to accurate accounts of his date of birth, the place he lived and what caused his death. However, since the manuscripts of Vemana literature have been found in different parts of what are now Andhra and Tamil Nadu, it's probable that Vemana wandered through most of the southern regions.[30] But his activities were concentrated in

Andhra Desa. One of the oft-quoted verses, repeated in several manuscripts in different versions, places him in Kondaveedu in Guntur district.

> Home town-Kondaveedu,
> district-Muga Chintapalle; first house; west street;
> Caste-Edde Reddi; what shall I say it is?

However, in 1874, J.D.G. Gribble wrote in a pamphlet that Vemana lived in Cuddapah district. Both the oral tradition as well as some critics maintain that Vemana died in Katarlapalle in Cuddapah district, but Telugu scholar Rallapalli Anantha Krishna Sharma, to cut short that debate, concludes that Vemana spent the best part of his life in Cuddapah and Kurnool districts of the Rayalaseema region. It's doubtful whether the internal evidence of the manuscripts and oral traditions will ever conclusively establish a definite date and place for Vemana.

Another much debated point is the caste of Vemana. Rallapalli says that Vemana belonged to the Kapu caste, Vanguri Subba Rao, on the other hand, affirms that he's a Reddy. And both of them call in Vemana as a witness. This is no equivocation on the part of Vemana, for he is at once a Kapu and Reddy. Till the beginning of the twentieth century these two terms "Kapu" and "Reddy" were used interchangeably.[31] Edgar Thurston,[32] says it is possible that the same person is known under different nomenclature in different regions.

Vemana—The Resurgence

Vemana was dismissed as beneath notice by the Telugu literary world until the first quarter of the Twentieth Century. Until then, no Telugu poet, scholar, critic or even a conscious social reformer made any reference to Vemana either in their works or the debate on reform. It is speculative as to what were the reasons for the conscious negligence of Vemana and his philosophy. Was it his non-Brahmin status or his questioning of the society as a consequence of which he ridiculed the caste system, idol worship etc.? Probably the first available source of information about Telugu poets and writers is the

Biographical Sketches of the Deccan Poets (1829) by Cavelly Ventaka Rama Swami Pundit. It consists of 'memories of the lives of several eminent bards, both ancient and contemporary, who have flourished in different provinces of the Indian peninsula, compiled from authentic documents'. It deals, in all with 108 poets, of whom 46 are Telugu poets, but Vemana does not figure in it too. Later on, Kandukuri Viresalingam's *Andhra Kavula Charitramu* (1899), which includes many minor poets, and even obscure ones, surprisingly, omits Vemana. With some more additions in his revised edition (1917) the total number of poets swelled to 220 but still Vemana was excluded.[33] But this "scholastic" Brahmin negligence in including Vemana was compensated far by western scholars, who recognized him for his enormous popularity among the masses.

The western world's first recorded contact with Vemana's literature occurred when in 1730, a French Jesuit priest Le Gac working in the south India sent the manuscript of 368 poems by Vemana to the French King Louis XV. This manuscript is preserved in the Bibliotheque Nationale, Paris since then.[34] In 1806, another French Missionary, Abbe J.A. Dubois, writing about Hindu society and culture, described Vemana as one of the Indian poets who wrote in "philosophic vein" and goes on to say:

> Amongst the few Hindu works which are written in a free philosophical vein and in which the Hindu religion and its customs are openly criticized, not one that I know of has been written by a Brahmin.... One of the most famous is Vemana... We are told that this philosopher, who was of the Reddy caste, and was born in the district of Cuddapah, died towards the end of the seventeenth century. His writings, from which I have seen several extracts, appear to me to be most interesting, and are distinguished by much discernment and independence.[35]

This description caught the attention of a British Civil Servant in Madras, Charles Phillip Brown, who was interested in preparing a Telugu text, as a teaching guide for Englishmen learning Telugu. In fact, Brown was looking for a poet, "whose writings are particularly useful to those who study the language, the style being simple, and the variety of topics extensive." In 1824, with the assistance of Telugu scholars, Brown started reading Vemana and began collecting, palm leaves and paper manuscripts of Vemana's poems from different parts of Andhra. "This author", Brown said, "is in Telugu literature what Lucian is in Greek – a familiar writer, useful to a beginner, though neither poetical nor classical."

In 1829, the first edition of this collection was published by Brown, entitled *The Verses of Vemana: Moral, Religious and Satirical,* Brown has recounted the difficulties, which he met with in his pioneering work.

> When commencing the study of a language, we are naturally led to enquire for works popular among the natives themselves, but composed in a style easy enough to be comprehended without difficulty by a foreigner. Such an enquiry in the year 1824 regarding Telugu made me acquainted with the verses collected in the present volume. Several manuscripts of *Vema* or *Vemana,* (for both names are used) were put into my hands, which I perused and translated in such hours of leisure as my public employments allowed. They proved to be full of errors of every kind, in orthography, metre, and meaning; no two copies followed the same arrangement, and they varied in extent from two to eight hundred epigrams. After collecting such copies as were to be found at Masulipatam, where I was then stationed, I gradually procured others from Vizagapatam, Nellore, Guntoor, Cuddapah and Madras. I then caused an index to be drawn up wherein nine columns exhibited the places at which the verses appeared in as many manuscripts, which I thus was enabled to collate. The number of stanzas I found amounted to about 2,500; a comparison, however, showed that the total was a little more than 2,000.

> It next became necessary to reduce the verses to some regular arrangement. Each transcriber had evidently selected such as he preferred, and no order was anywhere preserved. I, at length, formed the whole into five tolerably consistent divisions—religious, moral, satirical, mystic and miscellaneous.

Here is an important point that needs to be noted. Out of the 500 copies of this edition, fifty copies were presented to him (Brown) as editor's copies and the remaining four hundred and fifty copies disappeared mysteriously. It took Brown ten years to discover that, with an active connivance of the "high" caste-Hindu *pundits* of the College Board, the missing copies were rolled up as waste paper and tucked away in the lumber-room of the college library.[36] A host of Western rendering of Vemana's work poured in following the translation by Brown. Worth mentioning among them are Dr. G.U. Pope,[37] R.M. MacDonald (1866)[38], Charles E. Gover (1874), J.D. B. Gribble (1875), W.H. Campbell (1898)[39] and Leonel David Barnett (1908).[40]

Major R.M. MacDonald of the Madras Staff Corps,[41] writing in the *Madras Journal of Literature and Science* in 1866, commented at length. He wrote that:

> Dr. Pope observes that the writings of Vemana are extremely popular among the Telugu people. His popularity is, I believe, entirely confined to the Sudras, and even among them, every true believer in Hindooism regards him with much the same feelings as an evangelical curate looks on Colenso. This feeling was very apparent when Vemana was first made a text-book in Government schools. Both teachers and pupils did all they could to evade the order. In some instances the introduction of it into the classes, for which it was prescribed, was postponed under various pretences. In others, the teachers took on themselves to omit certain verses on the ground that they contained profane attacks on their religion. Brahmins, the particular, most cordially detest this author and in

support of their view often point with triumphant scorn to the vulgarity of his style and the libertine character of his matter.

Among all these western scholars, Campbell was a better judge of Vemana than either Brown or Gover. In his article in the *Madras Christian College Magazine*, he wrote:

> Vemana is emphatically a poet of the people. He wrote not for scholars, but for plain uneducated village folk, and he owes his popularity quite as much to the simplicity and force of his style as to the excellence of his teaching. Careless of mere literary fame, he set at naught the canons of classical poetry. He showed his wisdom in so doing. In India classical poetry can never be really popular, for to the great mass of the people it is almost absolutely unintelligible.... Vemana owes much of his popularity to his power of satire. He had a keen eye for the weaknesses and follies of men, and could depict these in all their meanness and absurdity...Vemana was not only, or indeed chiefly, a satirist, he was an earnest reformer who felt that he had a great mission to his countrymen and refused to allow any consideration to interfere with his fulfillment of it... Vemana's theory of the Universe, unlike that of most Indian thinkers, is, in the main, theistic rather than pantheistic. He recognized the distinction between the supreme spirit and the individual self, and assigns to the human will a place and an importance which prevent him from considering men mere puppets in the hands of some superior power...he denounced asceticism with the vigour and earnestness which would have done credit to a Wycliffe or a Luther.

Since C.P. Brown's editions there have been more than hundred editions of Vemana's poems, and a few of them have been translated into English and other Indian languages such as Kannada, Sanskrit, Tamil and Hindi. Some of these editions are merely reprints of Brown's first and second editions, whereas others are based wholly or partly on new poems from the palm-leaf manuscripts. Of these, three editions are worth mentioning. R. Purnacharyulu collected and edited entitled *Vemana Sukti Ratnakaramu* (Musalipatnam, 1913) which was later edited by Nadendla Purushottam Sastrulu with 4,035 new poems of which about 65 per cent occur in Browns's editions. The second important work P.T. Parthasarathi Ayya's,[42] contains nearly 1800 poems and the third one is by Mutyala Narsimha Yogi's[43] which includes a life of Vemana and some of entirely new poems, not found in Brown's editions. Yet, the most voluminous of the collections is by N.Gangadharam.[44] It contains over 5000 poems, of which many are slight variations of other poems.

Vemana—The Reformer

Vemana scoffs at the *Vedas, Puranas* and *Dharmsastras* which teach discrimination and uneven scales of social justice. Hence, Vemana as a social rebel was constantly at war with the upholders of the caste system, and was opposed to the practice of untouchability and represents a non-Brahmin social category. His anti-systemic pronunciations in forceful and sarcastic tones with the potential of fuelling conflicts in the society might have led to the conscious silence and subtle boycott of Vemana's works. So strong and persistent was this contempt for Vemana that, when his works were included in a text book in Government schools in the nineteenth century, both teachers and pupils did all they could to evade the order. There even instances of its introduction getting postponed citing various excuses. In some other cases, the teachers took on their own omitted certain verses on the ground that they contained profane attacks on "their" religion or caste. The Telugu literary authority also represented this attitude and countered the use at Vemana's poetry. Appakavi, an authority on Telugu poetics, ruled that the work of a Ṣhudra poet should be rejected without examination.

Henry Bowers, a member of the 'Committee for the revision of English, Telugu and Tamil school books in the Madras Presidency' of 1872, observed:[45]

> Coming to the Telugu books there is one regarding which there is a general chorus of disapproval among Hindu teachers, and that is—selection from Vemana—the poetical textbook for the third class... the chief objections rest on the satire which it contains on points of Hindu practice and doctrine and on the difficulty which teachers find in explaining the abstruse truths embodied in some of the stanzas. One Headmaster of a large school, an intelligent man and a graduate of the Madras University, has suggested that the book was originally adopted on the recommendation of the Missionaries, that 'it teems with views quite repugnant the Hindu feelings, and is calculated to create an impression that the Government is trying to proselytize the Hindu boys to 'Christianity'. One can well understand the dislike of Brahmans to the book and it is to be remembered that at least four-fifths of our teachers are Brahmans. My own opinion is in its favour of its discontinuance, much as I approve of a good part of Vemana's teaching. But orthodox Hindus have as clear a right to complain of being called on to teach heresy as the clergy at home would have to complain of the introduction of some catechism of dissent into all the National Schools.

Later, in 1921, the Presidency college, Madras instituted a Powell and Morehead Vernacular Prize for 1922 and the subject of the essay was "a critical review of the works of Potana and Vemana with special reference to the Religious, Social and Political conditions of their age" and it was open to all graduate students and the essay must be in Telugu. Perhaps, this was the first re-appearance of Vemana at the university level, after withdrawing his verses from school textbooks. Later on, C.R. Reddy, the Vice-Chancellor of Andhra University, instituted a series of lectures on Vemana by the eminent scholars of the time.

The devotional or *bhakti* egalitarianism is carried forward in Vemans's works to a pitch verging on revolution. In fact, Vemana was not associated with any sect nor he did found one. But in his sarcasm on the inequalities of material possessions he is no less radical and realistic than in his invectives against the disabilities engendered by caste distinctions. His place in Hindu positivism is of the same rank as that of Kabir, Chaitanya and others, if not higher. Vemana also attacked every external aspect of Hindu religiosity. Sometimes it may not be mistaken for socialism of egalitarianism. It has nothing in common with the elements that constitute Vemana's economic philosophy and its general impact and drift towards narrowing down the economic disparities in society, may share in common with some of these theories, but as a system it stands on its own.

In fact, Vemana's poems are his self-portrayals revealing him as a yogi, a social critic and a poet whose knowledge ranged from the esoteric to the common place and who made use of that knowledge to enhance his own teachings. These poems exhibit his deep knowledge about the various sects of the Hindu religion with its multitudes of rituals and practices. The poems also reveal his awareness of the different activities and events involving the peoples of many castes around him. As a social critique he attacked and scorned at man's preoccupation with the rituals, idol worship and caste prejudices. Moreover, Vemana's expressive language has greatly helped in making his poetry so popular. He very rarely resorted to Sanskrit words and expressions, as he found the local *desi* dialect sufficient, powerful and expressive enough to convey his message.

Vemana's philosophical thought is a matter of claims and counter claims. Criticizing the "auspicious times" (*Muhoortham)* fixed by the Brahmin, he says:

If Brahmins bring a husband and wife together
By mad utterances on a 'holy' timing of weather
with a sanction so vouchsafed and careful
How can the wife be widowed face inspite all this bother?

Vemana is never more vigorous than when exposing the evils of the caste system and denouncing caste prejudices. "Why revile a *pariah*?" he questions and asks, "Are not his flesh and blood one with ours; and of what caste is he who dwells within him, "there is in the wide world no viler pariah than he who scorns others, calling them Shudras. After he has perished the hell is his portion."

The trouble men take to talk about caste seems to him utterly vain and ridiculous. Since all castes have had the same origin it is absurd to consider one greater over the other, is how he puts in. So far as birth is concerned all men are equal, for all are brothers. If we draw distinctions, it is the liar and the hypocrite, the cruel and the sensual, who are real pariahs, not those who happen to have been born in a particular family. If Vemana had the power, he would made a speedy end of caste pretensions. "Come", he cries, "set one dish before all men in the world, and make them eat together. Make them all equal, and then placing your hand on their heads, bid them, believe this to be the true way." And it is not only caste distinctions, but also all arbitrary social distinctions, arouse his indignation. His attitude is of that of the great English satirist who made his famous protest thus: "the table of ranks and degrees is a lie and should be flung into the fire." He also recognized the popular attitude and describes it in the most contemptuous terms. Vemana recognizes the popular attitude and describes it in the most contemptuous terms. "When a man has wealth, people look on him as the fairest of the gods, when brought low by want and unable to raise himself, though he be a very Cupic, they look on him as an outcaste" wrote Vemana.

Questioning the meaningless caste distinctions and Brahminical customs, Vemana says:

> You make morsels of food invoke ancestors
> and feed the crows as part of memorial rite
> Turd-eating crows, how can they be ancestors?
> You donkeys!

He was very critical about high-caste traditions and was also against the idea of calling a *Sadhu* (saint), who pretends to be the torchbearer to "Mukti" (freedom) to do rituals. He describes his contempt for it:

He wears saffron clothes for a bliss effect
but Knows well the ways of all guises and dialects,
No bliss would ever follow a shaven head
As no desires for her are shaken by heads being shaven.

Vemana rejected all distinctions based on caste. He distinguishes between the caste one is born into, which is the result of one's past *Karma,* and one's true caste, the caste determined by one's character. Thus, a man is a true Brahmin because of his truth seeking and honest conduct, and not because of his birth. An honest "untouchable" is nobler than a dishonest Brahmin he said. Questioning beef eating as the cause of "untouchablity" he asks:

By slaying grass eating cattle
and eating them,
Men became untouchables
what will be the caste of those
who eat pigs and chicken
which eat everyone's fasces!

Vemana's socio-economic thinking goes further, much ahead of his times. Vemana, perhaps the first Telugu social revolutionary who questioned the inhuman practice of Untouchability, has no patience with the pretensions of the "higher-castes" and denounced the caste system saying:

Why revile a Mala,[46] again and again
Aren't his flesh and blood
same as yours
what is the caste in him
who moves in him?

Vemana was very critical about caste distinctions and declared that "all humans are equal". He says:

You plunge into the water; after you touch a Mala
When you depart to the cremation ground
The Mala burns your body
The filth that touched you then; where did it go now.

Despite of being a social critic, he had his limitations too.

Vemana's perception of women is regressive. According to him women ought to be obedient and virtuous. For instance, he says:

> Wives who disobey their lords
> Are as death, as poison snakes.
> Wives who live to please their lords,
> Wives indeed the best on earth.
> Disobedient wives are not
> wives at all but only gyres?

A good deal of Vemana's satire is directed against women. He speaks so bitterly of the fair sex that it seems as if he doubted the possibility of any woman being capable of truth and fidelity. "In time of wealth a wife looks to her husband. In time of want she will not even rise at his approach, she looks on him as dead though he is still alive." Vemana considered woman to be inferior to man, hence had to be under his control, for "as the track of a ship on the sea, as the path of a bird in the sky, so is the way of a woman."

Thus his ideas sanction a patriarchal social order and his conservative ideas on women denied them freedom of movement and expression in accordance with the norms of the period in which he lived. It is in his references to women that Vemana fails most conspicuously to rise above the false conventionalism of Hindu society. Thus, his advocacy of equality as a social philosopher was limited in scope.

However, Vemana's poetry has been popular with the Telugu speaking people of all sections including the semi-literate, the ascetic and the common folk. He is regarded as popular wit, who spoke the truth. His poetry has thoroughly permeated Andhra social consequences and had a major influence in shaping the language. Perhaps more importantly, his literature laid the foundation stone for the future non-Brahmin and social reform movements in Andhra. It is difficult to determine exactly to what persuasion Vemana belonged, for his ideas do not fit completely into anyone particular thought.

Since the time of Buddha, who rebelled against the Brahminic, priest dominated Hindu religion with its exclusive hierarchical caste system, the elaborate rituals, sacrifices and exploitation of "untouchables" under the guise of their "lower" status. Buddhism, Jainism, Virasaivism etc., all are part of the non-Brahminic tradition which refused to observe caste distinctions and did away with rituals such as image worship, wearing the 'sacred' thread etc. Vemana's thought strongly resembles the teachings of Virasaivism, but does not share the metaphysical interest in Sakti which central to Virasaivism; indeed he only mentions Shakti to criticize its worship.

His belief and thoughts were free from all religious influences and does not fall into any particular sect. It is not that only his philosophy is unique, so too is his poetry. The language is simple, straight forward, and local in dialect. The poems do not contain the emotionality, the religious devotion or the interest in nature which are characteristic of most of the Sanskrit and even vernacular poetry in the country; nor are they merely didactic like the verses in Sanskrit technical or "legal" texts. Criticism, argument, sarcasm, outright scolding and moral and religious teachings characterize Vemana's verses. Many poems are filled with fresh, often striking imagery, contrasts, caricatures and phrasing. Finally there is no doubt that Vemana's literature served the ends of criticism and teaching. Through his literature, he laid-down the foundations, for the social reform in order to "purify" the society, and fought against the social evils of Andhra.

Vemana had no respect for kings and courts or of court poets. Writing poetry to please a patron and to earn a pittance he said, is to demean the call the muse of poet. Only a sturdy spirit, free and untrammeled, he believed, can be a poet with an enduring message. Enraged by Vemana's philosophical thought and his ideology, the traditionalists of his time turned his bitterest enemies. They called him a village lout, an irrelevant wretch, a mad cap.[47] They tried to kill him by ignoring him totally. But Vemana was too potent and powerful to be ignored. His potency lies in his mastery over the common man's language. The source of his strength is to be traced to his stout championship of such human values, as social equality and justice.

It was Vemana who launched a virulent attack against the evil practice of untouchability in the Telugu literary scene. His thought provoking ideas were so striking that, he's consciously ignored by the Brahminical social order of the time. It is only in the early part of the twentieth century that Dalit organic intellectuals like Madari Bhagya Reddi Varma, Kusama Dharmanna and Gurram Jashua provided us some description of Dalit lives, to show us what exactly the untouchable world was. After that, the recent decades, i.e., towards the end of twentieth century have shown that in addition to socially "concerned" scholars and a growing number of Dalit intellectuals have sought directions for the future through a better understanding of their past.

An earlier version of this paper was presented at a National Seminar on 'Social Evils of Andhra Desa during 17th and 18th Centuries', held at Department of History, Osmania University, of Hyderabad on 12-13 March, 1999.

NOTES AND REFERENCES

1. P.C. Gupta, 1985, p. 181.
2. See Chinna Rao Yagati, 1992, p. 128.
3. S.C. Roy Choudhary, 1982, p. 206.
4. *Vajasaneyi Samhita, XXX. 21; Bruhadaranyaka Upnishad, IV.3.22; Chandogya-Upanishad*, V.10.7, cited in Vivekananda Jha, 1975, pp.18-31; also Vivekananda Jha, 1986-1987.
5. *Taitreya Brahmana, III.4.1.14; Vajasaneyi Samhita, XXX.17, Ibid.*, also see Gen'ichi Yamazaki, 1997, pp. 1-19.
6. For an 'Inter-Varna marriages and their progenies' see Chinna Rao Yagati, 2003b, pp. 230-233.
7. Hiroyuki Kotani, 1997, pp. 55-57; also see Cynthia Talbot, 1992, pp. 17-52.
8. James Legge, 1971, p. 43.
9. For details see T. Waters, 1904-05; also see J. Tarakusu, 1966.

10. E.C. Sachau, 1914, pp.101-102; Qeyamuddin Ahmed, 1993, pp. 44-47.

11. *Avadhana* means, very learned person and a Varsastile man and expert in Vedas and other texts. Astavadhana means who can attend to eight matters simultaneously and *Satavadhana* means, who can attend to a hundred issues.

12. See G.V. Sitapati, 1968.

13. *Inscriptions of Andhra Pradesh,* Warangal District no. 87; *Sri Vasavi Kanyakapuranam,* Chapter 46, verse.3, cited in K. Suryanarayana, 1956, p. 265.

14. See *Bharati,* January, 1968, p. 3., *Ibid.*

15. *Kridabhiramam,* verse 73, *Ibid.*

16. David Washbrook, 1996, pp. 68-86.

17. Praudhakavi Mallana, *Rukmaugada Charitra,* I.V.95, also see M. Somasekhara Sharma, 1948, p. 279.

18. Nidadavila Venkata Rao, 1954, *Introduction.*

19. *Epigraphia India., XX p.90; Madras Epigraphical Report,1918,* Paras 84-85; K.R.R. Sastry *South India Guilds* pp. 6-32, Cited in T.V. Mahalingam, 1969, p. 229.

20. K.A. Nilakanta Sastri, 1976, pp. 405-417.

21. P.V. Chalapati Rao, 1994, pp. 128-138.

22. For details see Velchuri Narayana Rao, 1992.

23. Bh. Krishnamurthi, 1995, pp. 77-102.

24. Velcheru Narayana Rao, 1978, pp. 50-60.

25. Charles E. Grover, 1871. He says that "from the absence of reference to Mohammedanism and the Muslim rule, and the close resemblance in style and matter to the Tamil Poets of the tenth century are there about, it is suggested that the proper date of Vemana's life is not later than the end of twelfth century'. If this is to be considered to place him in a particular period, he is wrong. In fact, there are at least three references to Muslims in Vemana's verses. For details see V.R. Narla, 1969.

26. W.H. Campbell, 1898. He says, "it is generally believed that Vemana lived about 250 years ago". Western Scholar, Grierson also states that Vemana lived in sixteenth century.

27. C.P. Brown, 1911 and 1967, Introduction. Brown said that "he lived in the beginning of eighteenth century... Many verses however prove satisfactorily that he wrote in the latter part of the seventeenth century when the Mohammadens were governor of that part of India. These poems have attained very great popularity and parts are found translated into Tamil, Malayalam and Canarese... Of his aphorisms many have become proverbs."

28. Abbe J. A. Dubois, 1953; Vanguri Subba Rao, 1951 and 1957, says that Vemana was born in early fifteenth century; For more complete account of this controversy see N. Gopi, 1980, pp. 94-133.

29. Rallapalli Ananta Krishan Sharma, 1971, says that Vemana lived in early parts eighteenth century.

30. J.S.R.L. Narayana Moorty and Elliot Roberts, 1995, p. 2.

31. Gurram Venkata Reddi and Pochana Rami Reddi, 1988, p. 108.

32. For details see Edgar Thurston and K. Rangachari, 1909, Vol. III, pp. 222-249.

33. This conscious neglect was noticed by the Dalit Poet of the Twentieth Century, Gurram Jashuva (1895-1971), who said:

    Vemana's Poetry is immortal
    Veeresaliagam has surely erred
    by ignoring this great poet,
    In his treatise on Andhra poets.

    For details of Jashuva's Life and Works, see Yendhuri Sudhakar, 1992, Hemalatha Lavanam, 1986.

34. JSRL Narayana Moorty and Elliot Roberts, 1995, Introduction.

35. Abbe J.A. Dubois, 1953.

36. These instances can be found in C.P. Brown, 1866 and 1991. In his own words, "In 1829 I had printed Vemana. As this author satirizes Brahmans they dislike or scorn his volume, and at their desire the College Board shelved it, and it was forgotten. About 50 copies were given me, and 450 disappeared. After ten years, I discovered these rolled up as waste paper in the Library". See Bangore, 1981, p. 40; V.R. Narla, 1969, p. 15.

37. Dr. G.U. Pope in his edition of Abbe Dubois' *Hindu Manners, Customs and Ceremonies* remarked that "nothing can exceed the sweetness and rhythm of Vemana's versification."

38. R.M. MacDonald (1866) felt that "in the whole range of Telugu literature there is perhaps no author whose writings have attracted so much notice among Europeans as those of Vemana."

39. W. Howard Campbell, 1897-1898, pp. 522-537. Even after thirty years of MacDonald's observations, the position was no better, for William H. Campbell, who recorded that "the Brahmins have always been bitterly opposed to his (Vemana's) teaching, and still speak contemptuously of his writings, the common people idiolize him and hold his name in such reverence that a reference to one of his verses is considered quite sufficient to settle any question at issue."

40. For details of these Western Writings on Vemana see V.R. Narla, 1971.

41. R.M. MacDonald was a Director, Public Instruction, Government of Madras, and also been a Chairman of the Committee for the revision of English, Telugu and Tamil school books in the Madras Presidency (1872).

42. P.T. Partha Sarathi Ayya, 1908.

43. Mutyala Narsimha Yogi, 1958.

44. Nedunuri Gangadharam, 1960.

45. Cited in Bangore, 1981, pp. 43-44; Narla, 1969, p. 15.

46. Mala is one of the two major "untouchable" communities in Andhra, Consists of nearly 35 per cent of Scheduled Caste, a population in Andhra.

47. See V.R.Narla, 1969 and 1971.

Vemana in his 50s as a preacher
Source: Gurram Venkata Reddy and Pochana Rami Reddy, *Viplava Yogi-Viswakavi: Vemana Vedasastramu*, Kurnool, 1988 (Cover page).

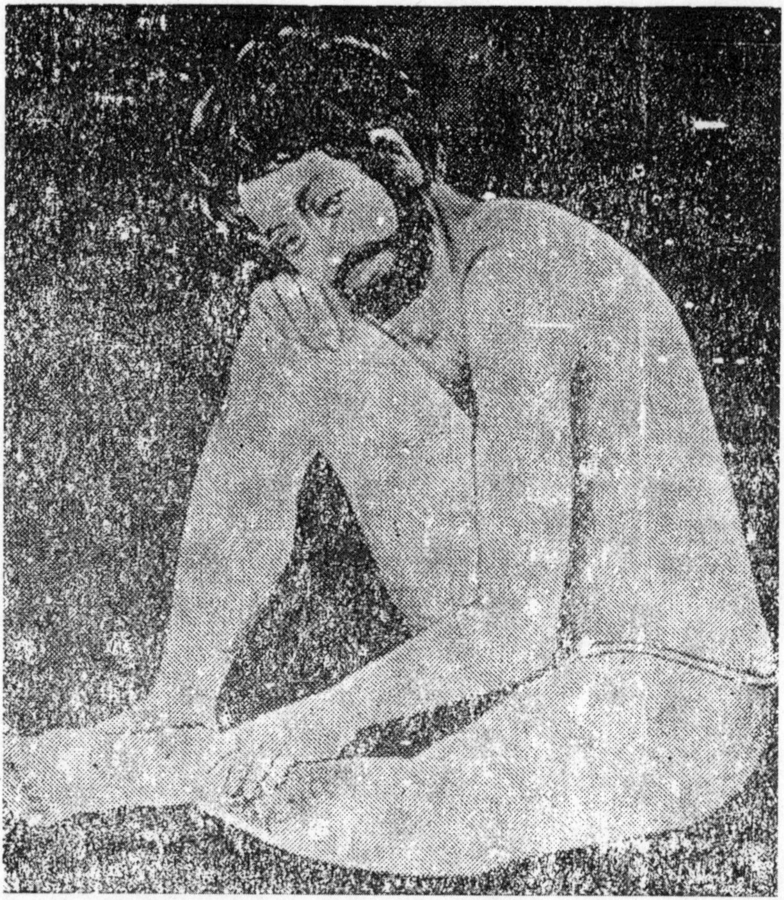

Vemana as a Yogi
Courtesy by Rao Sahib R. Krishna Rao Bhonsle,
M.R.A.S., Zamindar of Tanjavur.
Collected by Vanguri Subba Rao (1922)

Vemana before becoming a Digmabara
This was published in 1917 in a volume published by Vavilla Ramaswami Sastrulu & Sons, Madras. Before that it was published in 1913 by Rayavarapu Purnayachari from Bandar (Machilipatnam).
Source: Tripuraneni Venkalaswara Rao, *Viswadabhirama Vinuravema Vijayawada,* 1981, pp. XCI-XCVI.

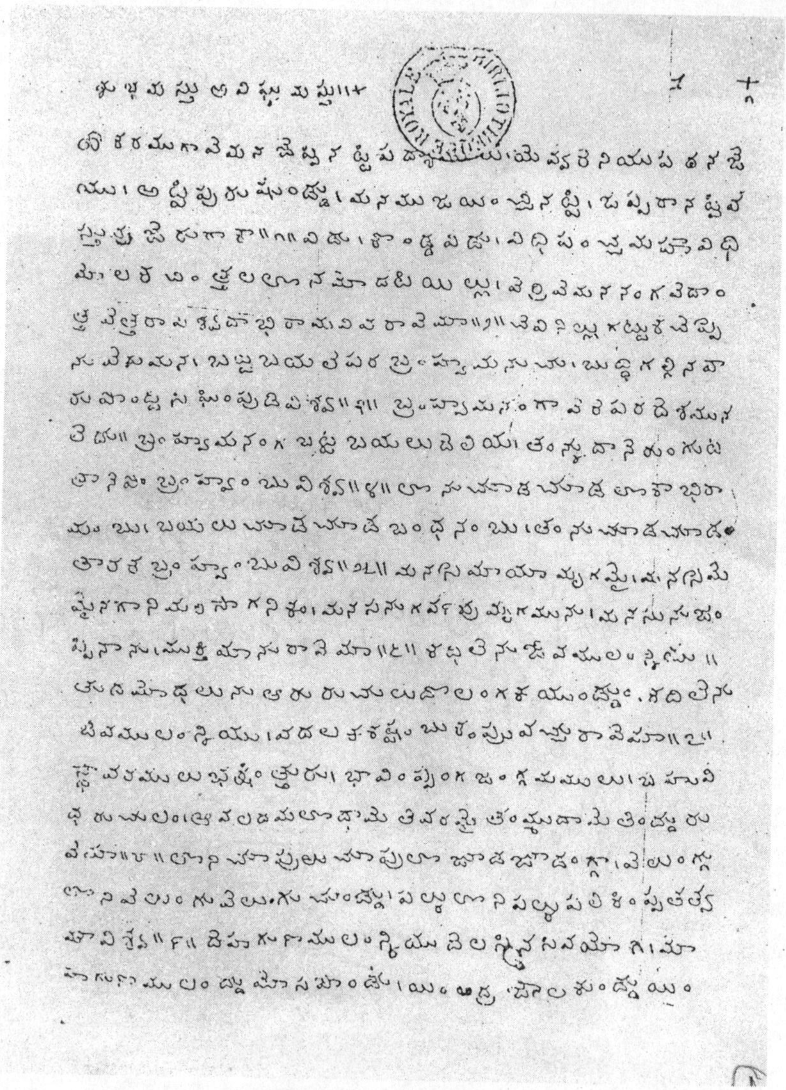

This is the first page of the manuscript of Vemana's Poems preserved in the Bibliotheque Nationale, Paris. Date of Collection 1730 A.D.

4

Dalit Politics: Ideology and Consciousness

Dalit movements have not yet become a part of Indian historiography yet, even though the study is of immense importance in view of their inherent radical democratic identity and its interrelation with contemporary movements. The available studies on Dalit movements suffer from lack of historical and written documentation, leaving scope for ambiguity. This is not to rule out the significance of the few analytical and comparative studies on the subject. The journey from a Pariah, an "untouchable" whose very shadow was considered polluting, to the present day defiant Dalit has been long, troubled and painful. For different communities, jurisdically encapsulated within the official category of Scheduled Castes, receiving recognition as equal citizens of a democratic republic is a project still waiting to be actualized.

Owing to their extremely dehumanized and degraded position in the society, the Dalits have always been a subject of interest for missionaries, anthropologists and social historians. In the early stages, this interest was sporadic and fragmentary in nature and was mostly an outcome of missionaries' travel records and personal accounts, official papers, district Gazetteers, ethnographic notes, census reports and such sources. Some early writings of officials, including Risely, Crooke, Enthoven, Sherring, Thurston, Rose, Russell, and Iyer, have contributed to furnishing a very rich account of the ethnic backgrounds, occupational patterns and customary habits and practices of almost all important communities belonging to different regions during the late nineteenth and the early part of the twentieth centuries.

Many authorities on caste in India were at some level or the other related to census operations. Regular estimations of Dalit populations in selected regions by various governmental agencies provided some account of life and conditions of the Dalits. After a detailed caste-and tribe-wise denotation of the population of India in the1931 census, with a considerable variation in their detailed tabulation and form there was a long gap on Dalit studies during the colonial period. During the post-colonial era there emerged problem oriented studies on Dalits were: Dalit social structure; socio-economic and other disabilities; the impact of a deliberate development strategy of protective discrimination for their uplift; and caste conflict.

The missionaries' yeomen services to ameliorate the condition of the Dalits forced social reformers to change their attitude from Brahmin and Hindu religious reform-movements to a social reform movement. Colonial government agencies could initiate some measures for the uplift of the Dalits. The early negligence meted out to the Dalits by the nationalists was compensated by the neo-nationalists and Marxists, who not only mobilized them but also brought them to their movements besides enslisting them into their cadre base. The classical Marxists being limited to a class perspective, could encompass castes in their perspective in visualizing the prevailing social reality. Neo Marxists or Subalterns could speak only of intermediary classes of the social setting. For them the term "subaltern" includes "the lesser rural gentry, impoverished land lords, rich and upper middle peasants."[1] Socially oppressed, economically exploited, politically marginalized and a landless agricultural labourer, a Dalit did not fall within ambit of their ideological construction. On the contrary, their understanding of the "subaltern" sections of society constitute the "rural gentry and impoverished landlord", direct oppressors and exploiters of the Dalit masses. The Dalitist or Dalit perspective of Indian history can invariably be distinguished from the "subaltern". I prefer to call this trend as the sub-subaltern, which is of course, yet to emerge as a major discourse in historiography.

The main issues dealt in this chapter are the nature of the Dalit politics and their movement, its ideology and perceptions in a broader framework so also the organizational basis, structure, and the different activities undertaken by various Dalit organizations, particularly their methods of creating consciousness and popular modes of mobilization.

A powerful Dalit movement emerged in Andhra in the early decades of the twentieth century, encompassing the coastal region (also known as Circar districts) and Rayalseema[2] region of the Madras presidency and Telangana,[3] the Telugu speaking areas of erstwhile Nizam state. These two regions provided diverse trends in the movement as a whole. While coastal Andhra had the choice between 'autonomy and integration'[4], Hyderabad witnessed a radicalized, but later factionalised Dalit movement. Each gained inspiration and strength from the other. The coastal Andhra movement had a broad rural base, whereas Hyderabad found an active fractionalized Dalit leadership limited only to urban centers such as Hyderabad and Secunderabad. It was during this period (1906-1939), that Dalit leaders rebelled against three aspects of their 'Outcaste' status: the economic deprivation resulting from their status, denial of access to social and civic amenities by Brahmins and persecution based on caste inferiority.[5]

However, an examination of the historical process of evolution of Dalit consciousness, rise and growth of 'Dalit democratic revolution' and a shared identity, reveals a significant break with the earlier reform movements, both in terms of ideology as well as its organizational set up. In a sense, the growth of the Adi-Andhra Mahasabha represented the widening of the principles of the broader non/anti-Brahmin movement and their social radicalism in colonial Andhra, for such movements mounted a serious attack on the notion of caste hierarchy and sought to create popular unity based on rationalism and humanism. Dalit movement also expressed the newfound solidarity among the 'lower' castes and their determination to engage in struggles in order to escape the ascriptive and hereditary fixation of occupation and appropriate the emerging form of newer power structures.

The Dalit movement ideologically fought for structural changes in the society, whereas the other 'upper' caste/caste-Hindu movements such as Kamma and Reddi Mahajana Sabhas aimed only at changes within the existing social structure. In other words, unlike the social reform movements among "upper" castes which were essentially "adjustive" in nature and meant to effect minimal changes, the Dalit transformative movement sought to challenge the established unequal social order, value system and the patterns of dominance. The liberation ideology formulated by the Dalit intellectuals in colonial Andhra was aimed at destroying the caste hierarchy, discrimination, untouchability and so on.

The basic thrust of the movement was to critique the ideology of Brahminical Hinduism and counter the socio-cultural hegemony of the "upper" castes. It also sought to organize the Dalits for achieving socio-economic and political equality. The necessity of organizing themselves into a mass movement was felt by Dalit leaders in the light of growing democratization, their increasing importance and their involvement with various political circles. Organizational strength was important for achieving political power. As a result, they started mobilizing strength from within their organizations to put forth their political demands and to confront and strike squarely at the decaying practice of untouchability.

Initial Inspiration: Formative Phase in Hyderabad

The Dalit movement in Hyderabad dates back to 1906, when Madari Bhagya Reddi Varma (1888-1939)[6] founded an organisation called the *Jagan Mitra Mandali* and started the work towards awakening social consciousness among the 'Untouchables'. He arranged regular *Harikatha Kalakshepams* and during or at the end of which he spoke eloquently, bringing home the point that they (Dalits) were the real and original inhabitants of the country and that others were migrants. He also proposed that the main cause of the backwardness of the untouchables was their ignorance and illiteracy. Its membership was restricted to non-drinkers.[7] The Jagan Mitra Mandali, by its name and activities, was truly a friend to the wretched poor and illiterate masses and tried to educate the "untouchables" about social maladies. Its members believed that Buddha should be venerated and hence his birthday should be celebrated as their main festival. They gave due recognition for Buddha's movement against the Vedic Dharmas, varna system, offering animals to appease deities, and so on. Buddha Jayanti was celebrated every year practically on Vaisakhi *poornima* day from 1913 till 1938.[8] Through their *Harikadhas*, the organization spread the message of untouchables' misery and Hinduism's treachery as the main culprit behind their social disabilities. It also organized inter-dining among all 'untouchables' called *Preeti Bhojanam*. This gave a feeling of oneness, and bought them together to fight for betterment of their brethren.

In 1911 Bhagya Reddi Varma founded the *Manya Sangam* through which he worked for the removal of certain evils like intemperance, sacrificing animals or fowls at the temples, child marriage etc. The primary aims of the *Sangam* were:[9] (1) to impart education to the 'untouchable' children; (2) to discourage child marriages; (3) to disallow non-vegetarian food and intoxicants in marriages and other auspicious functions; (4) to abolish the 'Devadasi' system known as 'Jogin' or 'Murli' or 'Basavi' custom prevalent in the community'.

At the general committee meeting held on 19 January 1913 it elected an executive body,[10] to work towards their objectives. The *Sangam* was formed, with members including a building contractor, a confectionery baker, the superintendent and other employees of the Hyderabad public gardens. It was a disparate group of young men without much education but an enlightened lot, and this gave a sense of the emerging 'Dalit middle class'. They initiated social reforms and admitted their fellow caste members into the group.[11] In addition to Bhagya Reddi Varma, another personality, Arigey Rama Swamy (1875-1973),[12] stood at the centre of Dalit activities in the early period. Madari Adiyya, a son of a butler started another Manya Sangam at Ghandsimendoy. Arigey Rama Swamy founded Suneetha Bala Samajam and carried on his activities in Kummonaguda, a locality in Secunderabad, where he lived. He exhorted his brothren to abandon spurious drinks with a view to eradicate the Jogini system and preached against animal sacrifice and child marriage. Though Rama Swami had faith in *Achal Siddanth* and Brahma Samaj, he firmly believed that the Dalits were separate from Hindus. He formed an Adi-Hindu Jatiyonnati Sabha in 1922, with Konda Venkata Swamy as president and J. Papayya and Arigay Rama Swamy as its Secretaries.[13]

In 1912, Bhagya Reddi Varma organized *Swasti Dal* with the help of 35 Dalit volunteers. The main aim of this Dal was prevention of cruelty to animals, after he was inspired by the activities of the Humanitarian League of which Bhagya Reddi Varma was a fulltime preacher. They worked on similar lines of the Red Cross Society, but their symbol was yellow Swastika, the Buddhist Cross.[14] This band of enthusiastic volunteers did yeomen service during the epidemic days when plague and Cholera broke out in and around Hyderabad. In 1925, when plague broke out, it took a heavy tool in Hyderabad. Swasti Dal volunteers served the desolate, tended to the sick and disposed off the unclaimed dead. Their activities and timely service were recognized and awarded accordingly.[15] These volunteers involved in various activities of local organizations and rendered services to many others, including at the Congress session at Kakinada, and the Cow Conference at Gudiwada.[16]

The development of Dalit consciousness can be seen through their active participation in the above mentioned organizations. Between 1906 and 1916 the activities of *Bhajan Mandals*, *Harikadhas*, spread all over Hyderabad. Bhagya Reddi Varma toured all over the Telangana region and created a sense of revolt in the minds of the "untouchables".[17] With the relentless programmes of *Bhajan Mandals* as well as the activities of Adi-Hindu Volunteer Corp called Swasti Dal and with their close contacts with philanthropic caste-Hindus, the Dalits succeeded to a greater extent in controlling the prevalent social evils like the Devadasi/Basavi/Jogini system and spurious drinks.

The spirit of social service and their convincing eloquence attracted caste-Hindus of the state, who extended their helping hand in their work. Prominent among them were C. Balakumud, a high court judge, Seth Ganashamji, a Jain, Jagirdar, a philanthropist, Dharmaveer and Vaman Naik.[18] In a short time *Bhajan mandalis* sprung up in each *wada* and *basti* in the city, where Bhajans were conducted and speeches were delivered on the basis of pamphlets and tracts issued by the Sangams.

The *Bhajan Mandals* also served as free reading rooms for its members. The *Sangam* regularly celebrated Buddha Jayanti and Jayanti of Nandanar, Chokmela, Narsi Mehta and such other saints.[19] All these organizations worked towards internal social reform. They found that structural change was necessary to bring about some cultural changes among the Dalits. They felt that it was essential to narrow down the social distance between communities among the Dalits themselves by coming together and living an associational life. This required communication of a new thought and values to the masses. They realised that this process of socialization was possible through organizations and thus these associations spread not only throughout Hyderabad but also extended, influenced and interacted with coastal Andhra region.

Adi-Andhra Movement in the 1920 and '30s

The term 'Adi-Andhra' arose in the post-1917 period when the Dalits all over the south, influenced by the 'non-Aryan' theories of the Dravidian movement, began to identify themselves as Adi-Dravidas, Adi-Andhras, Adi-Karnatakas, or 'original sons of the soil', exception in Hyderabad regions where it was a slightly different picture, as the organizations there took up the Adi-Hindu theme. The Adi-Hindu Mahasabha, which at its inception was known as 'Adi-Hindu Jatiyonnati Sabha', came into existence in 1922.[20] The Adi-Dravida

Mahajanasabha when launched in 1890, was known as Pariah Mahajana Sabha.

During this period, 'untouchables' of Madras made couple of representations to the government for the recognition of a new name for them, reiterating the demand they had presented to Montagu at the time of constitutional hearings in Madras. "... we should be designated as Adi-Dravidas or the original Dravidas, thus bringing us into line with the non-Brahmin Hindus who are ... called Dravidians".[21] Then the "Council recommended to the government that the term *Panchama* or *Pariah* used to designate the ancient Dravidian community in southern India be deleted from government records and the term Adi-Dravida in the Tamil and Adi-Andhra in the Telugu districts be substituted instead".[22]

The identity of "Adi" ideology was also spreading among the north Indian Chamars at this time, claiming to be the exploited and conquered original inhabitants. In short, the partly educated Dalits and the radicalization of Dalit movements throughout the south brought an identification with the "Adi ideology" for the entire community.

But for coastal Andhra regions, the decisive year was 1917. A caste-Hindu reformer, Guduru Ramachandra Rao,[23] called a conference in Bazawada, which was labeled as the "First Provincial Panchama Conference" in (4-6 November) 1917 at dramatic hall of Mylavaram Rajah. While Bagya Reddi Varma presided, Sundru Venkayya was the chairman of reception committee of the conference. On the very first day of the Conference in his Presidential Address, after mentioning the atrocities on untouchables and their miserable plight being meted out by the caste Hindus, Bhagya Reddi Varma stressed that the so-called untouchables were the original inhabitants of India. While condemning the term "Panchama" he justified the use of the term "Adi-Andhras".[24] He argued that the term "Panchama" (the fifth order) was nowhere to be found in the *Puranas* or other Hindu scriptures and that they were the rulers of the country. Surprisingly, the very next day, all the banners and sign boards of the venue changed into Andhra Desa First

Adi-Andhra Conference.[25] The delegates rejected the term *Panchama*. Thus, the Dalit movement in coastal Andhra began to be called Adi-Andhra movement.

Major themes focussed on by the Adi-Andhra movement between 1917–1947 were related to the socio-economic uplift of the Dalits as well as the issues of land, education, employment and representation in decision-making bodies and so on.[26] The Dalit movement in Andhra during this period can be broadly divided into two phases: the first phase lasting from 1917-1932 and the second phase from 1932-1946. The first phase, essentially represented self-mobilization of Dalits outside the organizational and ideological framework of the Congress and the Communists, although at the initial stages positive response and sympathy was forthcoming from liberal caste-Hindu individuals. The second phase was characterized by interaction between the Dalit movement and the nationalist and left movements. It also manifested an earnest desire on the part of Dalits to be consciousness of their rights and condemn untouchability, and discrimination, demanded political and minimum level of basic human rights.

At various conferences of the Adi-Andhra Mahasabha, several resolutions were passed demanding: free education; scholarships to meet expenses of books, food and clothing; hostels for boys and girls; blocking government funds and withdrawing recognition to educational institutions that do not admit Dalits children;[27] employment to Dalit youth; establishing vocational institutions and cottage industries for the benefit of the Dalits;[28] to grant government waste lands to them; reservations in government services,[29] punishment to those caste-Hindus who refuse to allow the Dalits to draw water from public wells and tanks, and their entry into public places like temples, chaultries, and hotels.[30] The Mahasabha also urged for unity among various Dalit communities.

Between 1917 and 1937 nearly 15 Conferences were held in different parts of Andhra ventilating the grievances of the Dalits. The geographical spread of these Conferences at provincial, Taluk, town and village levels suggests that the

Adi-Andhra Mahasabha could draw rural masses into its fold. A content analysis of the resolutions passed by these conferences indicates that the Dalits were essentially resentful of the caste Hindu monopoly of socio-economic resources.

Many factors helped to bring about consciousness amongst the Dalits and they consequently made the Dalits participate in the movement in Andhra, particularly during the 1920s and 30s. By then Christian missionaries had already penetrated into Dalit localities. While establishing educational institutions, they undertook amelioration measures in addition to proselityzation. The Madras Government also set up a 'Labour Department' to work for the welfare and educational uplift of Dalits in the presidency.[31] Commercialization of agriculture, major irrigational schemes on Krishna, Godavari rivers, which eroded traditional caste and Jajamani ties that had bound Dalit labourers, led to the development of a mobile labour force that gave opportunities to many Malas and Madigas to move ahead.

Burma was also a major base of the movement.[32] Tens of thousands of Dalit labourers, especially Malas, used to migrate each year for work on the Rangoon docks from the late nineteenth century onwards. Some of them stayed back, even after their contract was over, where they managed to learn new trades. In Burma they got education and earned money, and on return, while a few of them took direct part in the movement,[33] others enthusiastically financed it.[34] Many Dalit leaders later on visited Burma to collect funds for their movements back home in Andhra.[35]

Most of the Dalit leaders who were active in the 1920s were the product of the *Sevasram*, an organization established by a caste-Hindu reformer, Guduru Rama Chandra Rao, at Gudivada at Krishna district in 1912. He invited Dalit activists to work in the *Asram* so that they could train the untouchable cadre in the rural areas. Those included Sundru Venkayya, Kusuma Venkatramayya, Naralasetti Devendrudu, and Kusuma Dharmanna among others.

After the first Adi-Andhra conference in 1917, Dalit activities and organizational base increased strikingly. Many associations cropped up and organized conferences at district, Taluk and *firka* levels. They established Farm Labourers Associations, Field Labour Credit Societies and educational institutions and hostels for Dalit pupils.

Provincial Level Conferences and Local Activities During 1920s

The 1920s was a decade that witnessed the growth of socio-political consciousness. Conferences held at provincial as well as District levels influenced the Dalit youth deeply and made them conscious of their social, political and economic degradation. Later this saw these youth ceaselessly fighting against the prevailing social system. Conferences were held in 1920 at Gudivada with Bhagya Reddi Varma as President and Sundru Venkayya as Reception Committee Chairman; another such meeting was held at Eluru in 1922 under the leadership of Bhagya Reddi Varma and Naralasetti Devendrudu; a the one at Guntur held in 1924 under the leadership of Kusuma Venkataramayya and Nutakki Venkateswarlu; and another one was organized in 1925 at Anantpuram again by Bhagya Reddi Varma as President. Most of the resolutions passed at these conferences were "appeals to the government to appoint a Labour Commissioner to each district; to allow free education to the children of depressed classes; not to assess the *porambok* lands given for the benefit of the depressed classes, till they give satisfactory yields for three years continuously; to remove age limit of sixteen years for awarding scholarship; to appoint Adi-Andhras in the vacancies that would thereafter occur in various departments."[36] The conference condemned the shameful custom of dedicating women in the name of God as *Devadasis/ Jogins*,[37] and also strongly condemned practice of demeaning suffixes/prefixes like *gadu, vore, vole, vose*, etc.[38] after /before the names of the Dalits. There prefixes/suffixes were degrading names identifying the Dalits with their servile status. Because these Conferences also recommended the formation of working committees consisting of leading Adi-Andhras in various villages.

It is pertinent to note that the Justice Party Government of Madras responded favourably to some of the demands with regard to education, employment and political representation.[39] As a measure of providing social justice to the trodden Dalits, the justice party ministry, with the backing of the colonial administration initiated certain concrete measures like, providing free elementary education to the children of Dalits in the local board schools as well as establishing separate schools for them through the newly created Labour Department. The land question raised by the Adi-Andhra Mahasabha was also addressed by the Ministry in terms of ascribing government waste lands to Dalit labourers, and to the rural poor.[40] However, limited the efforts of the justice ministry might have been, they provided a sense of relief to the Dalits. As for as the question of political representation of Dalits was concerned, the Madras Government sought to assure the participation of Dalits in the decision making bodies by nominating some Dalit leaders to the Legislature.[41] Also a close affinity was sought to be forged between the non-Brahmin movement and Dalit movement in terms of containing Brahminical supremacy. But given the lack of organizational coordination and programmatic unity the non-Brahmin leadership of the Justice Party failed to build a cohesive movement with the active support of the Dalits.[42] Yet some of the Andhra Zamindars belonging to the justice party had a personal relation with Adi-Andhra movement leaders.[43]

However, the Adi-Andhra movement during the 1920s was isolated and separated from the mainstream political organizations. Its rural base indicates that the fact that the widespread reach of the movement, the regional movement like the language based separate Andhra movement,[44] and the Congress led national movement like non-cooperation and other allied movements did not attracted any significant following from the Dalits. Although caste-Hindu nationalist leaders exerted an enormous influence over the Adi-Andhra movement,[45] Dalit interaction with the mainstream movements was minimal till the early 1930s. Till then the integration of the Adi-Andhra movement with other movements may be characterized as insignificant. For instance, the participation of Dalit masses in the national movement in Andhra districts during the 1920s was quite negligible, but this considerably increased during the 1930s and the 40s.[46] Majority Dalits were either indifferent or even opposed to it precisely because they were mostly led by caste-Hindu or castiest ideologies unlike communism and thus did not adequately reflect or represent the aspirations of the vast majority of Dalits. Dalit leadership also refused to be dragged and involved in the rising controversies of political or national issues which were unrelated to the Dalits.[47] But this changed radically by the 1930s and the 40s, as many Dalit leaders coopted into all leading political outfits of the time, i.e., Indian National Congress, Communist Party and so on.

Gandhi and the Dalits

Though the autonomous and radical character of the Adi-Andhra movement of the 1920s, fell into a big vacuum in later parts of 1930s, the launch of the Gandhian "Harijan" upliftment programme in the 1930s led to the development of close relations between the Dalits and the Congress. The formation of the Andhra branch of the Harijan Sevak Sangh (HSS) at Vijayawada in 1932 facilitated the participation of the local Congress leaders in the welfare activities of the Dalits in colonial Andhra.[48] In the process, Dalit activists were incorporated into these activities. Two caste-Hindu Gandhian reformers K. Nageswara Rao and M. Bapineedu were its (HSS) President and General Secretary respectively and two Dalits, N. Devendrudu and V. Kurmayya were its Joint Secretaries. These two Dalit leaders were very active in the Adi-Andhra movement of 1920s.[49] The Andhra Rashtriya Harijan Sevak Sangh had established its branches in all Telugu speaking districts of the Madras Presidency and obtained financial assistance from their central organization.[50] This incorporated Dalit leadership had to work under the hegemony of caste-Hindus in Harijan Sevak Sangh, which carried out programmes like cleaning of Dalit localities, setting up educational institutions and separate hostels for them[51] and digging wells for drinking water for Dalits and so on. During Gandhi's

Andhra tour, millions of rupees were collected from the public in the name of "Harijana Biksha" and Gandhi earmarked these funds to each district for providing the needs of the provincial and district Harijan Sevak Sangh branches.

The main thrust of Gandhi's visit to Andhra in 1930s was to campaign against the evil practice of untouchability and secure temple entry for the "Harijans", which had been a burning debate in the Madras legislative proceedings for a long. On 1 November, 1932, Dr. P. Subbaroyan, the Madras Chief Minister, introduced a resolution in the Legislative Council on the right of the "untouchables" to enter Hindu temples and it was seconded by T.A. Ramalingam Chettiyar.[52] But the orthodox Hindu organizations like the Varnashrama Swarajya Sangam condemned the government action on the grounds of undue interference of politics in religion.[53] It was argued that the Legislative Council had no mandate from the electorate to pass a law on this subject and added that temple entry was not related to the question of the uplift of the Depressed Classes.[54] On the top of it, the Governor-General refused to give his assent to the bill passed by the Madras Legislative Council.[55]

Learning about this controversy Gandhi warned that Hinduism would suffer extinction if untouchability continued,[56] and also pointed out that the Dalits themselves did not take part in this controversy. Further, Gandhi, with reference to the Tirupati temple made an appeal that "when the Europeans ascend the hills, why not Harijans?" The temple officials promptly replied that no "Harijan" sought permission to do so.[57] On 17th December, 1933, Gandhi personally led the "Harijans" into two temples in Siddhantam Village-Gudivada Taluk in Krishna district. On this occasion he said:[58]

> I am happy to throw open these two temples for the Harijans. The people who are responsible for this act of mine are pious. God is the same for the pious and the sinner. How do we know whether the Harijans or the Savarnas are sinners? "...Treat Harijans as Brothers. Harijans should be clean. Do not eat dead animals. Don't drink alcohol. May God protect you.

The so-called "Harijan upliftment programme" was carried out in various parts of Andhra districts. Volunteers of the *Sangh* reportedly visited many villages, attempted to convince caste-Hindus to permit "Harijans" to use public wells and the news of such acts like the entry of Dalits into specific Hindu temples, drawing of water from wells and tanks were reported in the local press.[59] However, the Gandhian programme appeared to be more symbolic than real. It could only induct Dalits into the Congress, but failed to inspire many caste-Hindus to change their hearts and work sincerely for social equality.

Gandhi's teaching of tolerance and brotherhood seemed to have been short-lived. The caste-Hindu hegemony in the HSS clearly failed to persuade most of their brethren to follow Gandhian ideals in letter and in spirit. In implementing Gandhian ideals, Congress activists faced many practical problems at the grassroot levels, where orthodox ideas were strongly embedded. For instance, a local official of the revenue department at Bhimavaram in West Godavari district, felt that several members of the Depressed Classes were suspicious about the avowed intentions of caste-Hindu leaders and activities of Congress activists and hence preferred to remain aloof.[60] A local level Dalit association in Krishna district noted that Gandhi might have the interest of uplifting the Dalits at heart, but all caste-Hindus were not Gandhijees. The district Labour Officer of East Godavari mentioned that though few Dalits had visited some temples in Rajahmundry town they could perform their *Bhajans* only in front of the gates, since the temples were closed and admission was denied to them. The only temple in which Dalits were allowed was the insignificant Aanjaneya Temple, where Dalits could perform *Bhajans*. It was claimed to have been maintained by a non-Brahmin and was open from all sides and any person who passed by it could entered it.

The District Magistrate of Krishna District reported that, on 26th September, 1932, nearly 33 caste-Hindus of Bandar, instigated the local Dalits to enter the temple. But the temple priests closed the doors against them. Similar unsuccessful attempts were also made at Bazawada. It was reported that there were also instances of 'purification' ceremonies being held in temples that were open to the Dalits so that the orthodox trustees of these temples would consent to open them to the Dalits. There was a strong feeling in many parts of Andhra against any such concession being granted to them. It was legitimate then that the Dalits were extremely suspicious about the caste-Hindu reformers.

The leadership and activists of Adi-Andhra movement were quite alert and quickly pointed out the fallacies and inadequacies of the Gandhian programme for Dalit liberation. Some of the militant sections of the Mahasabha were pessimistic about the exhortations of Gandhi and his disciples regarding untouchability, discrimination and temple entry. Even prominent leaders of the *Sangh* (HSS) confessed to the inadequacies and lacunae in the actual realization of Gandhian ideals. The literate Dalits who also exposed the hypocrisies of local Congress leadership and caste-Hindu reformers highlighted some of the glaring inconsistencies.

In one of the many such incidents, Dalit activist from Krishna district criticized K. Nageswara Rao Panthulu, a Brahmin politician, who was also a local Congress leader and president of the provincial Harijan Sevak Sangh, for not allowing the Dalits to enter a temple in his own native village. The Dalits asked him either to immediately throw open the temple for them or make his stand public through the press.[61] It was a clear rebuff and indeed embarrassing for the senior nationalist leader. A similar incident of a social discrimination against the Dalits was reported from Elure town too. A prominent caste-Hindu reformer named Mathe Gangaraju, who voted in favour of the Temple Entry Bill in the Madras Legislative Council,[62] on the basis of rumours, petitioned the local police to prevent the attempted forcible entry of the Dalits into temples on the *Ekadasi* day as well as to protect "Hindu society and Dharma". Consequently the Sub-Magistrate passed orders directing the Dalits to complete their religious celebrations and leave the main streets of the town by 9 a.m. Further, they were also directed not to interfere and cause inconvenience to the caste-Hindu processions.[63] In effect, this was meant to ban Dalits from the main streets and confine them to their localities during festival celebrations. This incident confirmed the distrust of the Dalits regarding the sincerity of caste-Hindu reformers.

In yet another instance, the Dalits of Machilipatnam town reported that they were prevented from listening to the *Harikatha* along with the caste-Hindus. When they protested against it, caste-Hindus became aggressive and violent.[64] In the same town, in yet another glaring incident of discrimination involving caste-Hindu trustees of a premier educational institution, a Dalit graduate in their school was denied appointment citing his caste.[65] In a village of Anantapur district, caste-Hindus refused to allow Dalits to draw water from public tanks and threatened them with social boycott and ex-communication if they did so.[66]

However, incorporation of Dalits into the Congress fold through HSS increased gradually, but did not bring any noticeable change in inter-caste relationships. Harassment and victimization persisted despite repeated appeals by Gandhi. While this was the reaction to the Congress 'politics of accommodation and incorporation' the Communist movement (emerged in mid-1930s) on the other hand, attracted the Dalits in masses. The Communists, under the organization of agricultural labourer unions focussed on the economic issues and gave a call for an anti-zamindari struggle that gave an immediate rederessal to their grievances.

Resurgence of Adi-Andhra Movement

In 1935 Ambedkar's announcement of conversion from Hinduism energized some Dalits to resume the Adi-Andhra movement in the second-half of the 1930s. In the same year, the tenth conference was organized at Rajahmundry, East Godavari district with Kusuma Venkataramayya as president and Kusuma Dharmanna as its reception committee chairman. This Conference was inaugurated by M.C.Rajah, one of the leading personalities of the Dalit movement in the presidency.[67] The eleventh conference was held in 1936 and the twelfth at Tallarevu in East Godavari district in 1938 again with Bhagya

Reddi Varma as president and Vundru Subbarao as the chairman of the reception committee. The resolutions included a demand for reserved seats for Adi-Andhras from the panchayat level, sanction against those opposing the presence of untouchable children into schools; job reservations and formation of labour cooperatives and credit banks, demand for waste lands for Dalits among others.

Under the influence of state-level Adi-Andhra conference resolutions, local level organizers organized many district level conferences. The first such conference was held in 1921 at Amalapuram under the leadership of Vundru Tatayya (1850-1930)[68] with the help of Talari Gopala Rao Naidu, the then Assistant Labour Commissioner of East Godavari district. Many Dalit activists such as Nakka Venkata Reddy,[69] Tadepalli Tatayya[70] and others played a major role in mobilizing the masses and local activists to these conferences. Most of the younger Dalit leaders, including Chuttagulla Venkayya,[71] Didla Pullayya,[72] Ambati Gangisetti[73] and many others were influenced by these conferences.

Amongst all the districts of coastal Andhra region, East Godavari was in the forefront, which evidently showed the consciousness of Dalit intelligentsia, as between 1921 and the early 1940s regular district level conferences were held in this district. The first ever district level conference was held at Amalapuram in 1921. Golla Chandrayya (1888-1972) made use of his overseas connections and travelled to Rangoon to collect money for the conferences.[74] Another conference was held in 1926 at Cheyyur, Amalapuram *taluk*, which was presided over by Kusuma Veera Swamy (1885-1964), in which a new executive body was elected with Veera Swamy as president and Pandu Laksmana Swamy (1892-1960) as Vice President, Tadepalli Tatayya (1895-1952) as Secretary. Later, they registered this organization as the East Godavari Adi-Andhra District Association. In 1926 a Conference was held at Neerullipalem in Narasapuram *taluk* with K. Peda Veera Swamy as president and was inaugurated by K.N.Daniel Smith.[75]

Conferences were held at Ramchandrapuram in 1930 with Pamu Rama Murthy presiding over it at Rajolu in 1933;

at Vijayanagaram in 1936 with Kusuma Dharmanna presiding over the function; again at Ramchandrapuram in 1937 with Pamu Rama Murthy at the helm; at Tallarevu with Gottimulla Venkanna and Bhagya Reddi Varma presiding over it; at Eluru in 1938 with Vundru Subba Rao and V.T.Muniswamy Pillai inaugurating it; at Peddapuram in 1939; at Kakinada in 1940 with Eeli Vadapalli presiding it; and another conference at Opata Korangi in 1940 and one in 1943 at Kakinada with N.Sivaraj, another leading Dalit leader of the presidency presiding over it. Conferences were arranged at *taluk* and *firka* levels also.[76] They were held at Korukonda in 1933; at Korangi in 1938 under the leadership of Janipelli Venkata Rao and in the same year at Challapalli with Geddada Brahmayya presiding over it; at Tandavapalli in 1940 with Jala Ranga Swamy at the helm and in many other places including Paddapalem, Rajolu, Chandrapuram and at village level associations in almost all villages such as Tanuku, Relangi, Kanteru, Volamooru, Martooru and so on.

All these villages and taluk level organizations had their executive committees, maintaining regular contacts with their district-and state-level organizing committees. All these associations had a common code of conduct and common demands but with separate constitutions. Unlike the Hyderabad state, the early decades of twentieth century remain those in which the lack of historical written documentation[77] and of efforts to uncover the history of the Dalit movements in coastal Andhra has left a large vacuum in knowledge. But the very spread of conferences at district, taluk and village levels throughout Andhra indicates a broad rural base to the movement.

Expansion and New Activities: Land and Credit

The growing Dalit consciousness gained further momentum after the Labour Department was set up in the Madras Presidency in 1920, which saw many activities such as establishing field labour credit societies, schools and hostels throughout the 1920s and the 1930s.

With the support and encouragement of Talari Gopal Rao Naidu, the then district Assistant Labour Commissioner, Vundru Tatayya established the first Adi-Andhra Credit Society in 1922 under his Presidentship, and Golla Chandrayya as its Secretary.[78] Vundru Tatayya, himself was a small landlord and had a lot of property in Rangoon, hence was the constant source of income for the 'Society'.[79] Golla Chandrayya made a couple of visits to Burma for financial help. These credit societies provided funds to the Dalits, small farmers, and agricultural labourers during the off-season. They also provided scholarships and other financial assistance to the Dalit students from the interest earned from such loans. Soon these credit societies spread throughout the region.[80]

Golla Chandrayya, who convened the first East Godavari Adi-Andhra Mahajan Sabha at Amalapuram, with the help of the Labour Department, arranged 200 acres of land for Appanivanilanka Adi-Andhra Credit Society for cultivation besides offering five acres of land for houses in 1922.[81] He also established credit societies in almost all *Dalitwadas* of Rajolu taluk of East Godavari district.[82] Goda Venkanna established an Adi-Andhra Field Labour Credit Society at Challapalli in 1922 through which he extended loan facilities. He utilized his friendship with the Maharaja of Pitapuram and acquired 100 acres of estate land to the 'Credit Society'.[83] He was an active member of the Adi-Andhra movement and a member of the executive committee of the Adi-Andhra Association of East Godavari district from 1937 to 1942. He convened the Challapalli *firka* Adi-Andhra conference in 1938 that was presided over by Geddada Brahmayya.

In Amalapuram, Ambati Gangi Setti established many 'Credit Societies' and acquired land for these 'societies'. Bojja Apalaswamy[84] established a 'Credit Society' at Kandikuppa and acquired many hundred acres of *Banjar* lands for these societies. He also established another 'Society' at Polamuru Padu of Kakinada taluk and acquired 300 acres of endowment board lands for this 'Society'.

Establishment of Educational Institutions

Against the background of rampant illiteracy, the Dalits set up many models of schools like day schools and night schools aimed at the labouring Dalits, they also opened vocational institutes for women. That apart they also established many hostels for Dalit kids. Adi-Andhra leaders, besides establishing new schools renovated the old schools established by Christian missionaries and 'separate schools' established by the British Government.

In fact, Dalit leaders had been establishing schools since the early years of the 1920s and the prominent one was the one at Ponnamanda in 1922 by Vundru Tatayya. When the caste-Hindu teachers refused to teach Dalit children, Tatayya made use of his earlier Burma connection and brought Dalit teachers. He also financed construction of school buildings at Anatavaram, Allavaram and Mogalakuduru. In the early part of the 1930s Bojja Appala Swamy established a school at Kandikuppa, with himself as a Manager-Headmaster. Another Dalit intellectual who worked in this direction was Jala Rangaswamy. Along with this wife Jala Mangamma, he established schools at Ramadasupeta, Kontamuru, Kolamuru, Rayudu Pakalu and Palacharla. They also established a night school at Kolamuru.

In 1928, Jala Ranga swamy opened the first separate hostels for both Dalit girls and boys. Later, many more such hostels were established by others, with a major one being the one set up at Mandapeta in 1930 by Eeli Vadapalli. He also established the Laxmi Industrial Training School at Rama Chandrapuram. It was said that Jala Ranga Swamy used to beg for food and money to feed the hostel students. His admirers honourably addressed him as "Sevadhurandara", "Mahatma of Adi-Andhra." He also published the *Jaibheem* journal and authored many books, including *Nimna Jatula Charitra* (History of Untouchables).[85]

Hostels established for Dalit pupils included the one at Rajolu set up by Golla Chandrayya in 1936, the Bapuji Harijan Hostel by Pandu Lakshmana Swamy of Rajahmundry; the

Gandhi Memorial Harijan Boys Hostel at Recharlapeta set up by Pachchipala Rama Swamy; the Adi-Andhra Hostel opened by Moka Mirayya at Kakinada, and the Harijan Hostel by Medidi Narayana Murti at Tuni among others. Many hostels functioned even without any grants from the government and also conducted cultural programmes to educate and organise the Dalit students.[86]

Organized Labour Force

During the 1930s, the coastal Andhra region also witnessed vigorous agricultural labour struggles. Dalit labourers were mobilized and became an organized force particularly influenced by the emerging Communist movement. They were attracted the Marxism and Socialist ideals many of them joined in the anti-zamindari struggles led by the Communists. Since the overwhelming majority of the Dalits constituted agricultural labourers with the landlords being Kammas and Reddis, the conflicts became obvious due to their organized force against the oppression at the hands of the landlords. They formed *Ryotu Coolie Sangams* in many villages and also undertook many strikes. Notable among these were the ones in the East Godavari area, which assumed a militant tone in the 1938-39 period, climaxing in a 15 day strike of 10,000 labourers from 13 villagers. But the state machinery unleashed a reign of terror overthem and as a many leaders was killed or put behind the barks.[87] Another struggle at Nadavapalli in 1942 resulted in landlords taking up arms against labourers with the tacit help of the police. Another strike of farm labourers (*Palerla same*) took place in mid-40s in Guntur district. The membership of agriculture labour groups in Andhra region grew up to a hefty 60,000 by 1945-46 compared to 5000 to 15,000 in the other regions.[88]

The Dalits were organized by Communists on class lines. The relationship between the Dalits and Communists could be seen in the presiding over the agricultural labourers conference held at Tekisetti Palem in 1938 by the Dalit leader Vundru Subba Rao, which was organized by the socialists, and conference was inaugurated by B.T. Ranadive.[89]

Dalit Consciousness

The Dalit intelligentsia perceived that the existing structure perpetuated only their exploitation and irrationality which would even make the unconscious ones conscious of this plight. Hence, they tried all possible ways to educate, organize and unite all the Dalits. They organized associations and conferences and established schools and hostels, thereby enlightening them to challenge their "low" status on rational and ideological basis. They employed popular means like conducting *Hari Katha Kalakshepams*, Bhajan Mandalis on one hand and establishment of newspapers/journals on the other.

The emergence of Dalit journalism in the 1930s played a significant role in highlighting caste-Hindu atrocities on them and in creating awareness among the Dalit masses. It may be stressed that journals like *Nava Jeevana*[90] edited by Dalit intelligentsia successfully articulated their issues and kindled Dalit consciousness. The other important Dalit periodicals were *Adi-Andhra* of Didla Pullayya, the *Veera-Bharathi* of Jala Ranga Swamy,[91] the *Harijana* of Vundru Subba Rao, and the *Jeevana Jyothi* of Chuttumalla Venkataratnam,[92] all of which effectively generated consciousness among the Dalits.

In addition to Dalit journalism, the writings of Dalit intelligentsia also played a major role in bringing about a feeling of oneness and self-respect among Dalits to establish an egalitarian society and a vision for their future. The educated and enlightened sections within them provided the direction, programme and leadership for the movement,[93] and people like Bhagya Reddi Varma and Sundru Venkayya provided the leadership. The main programme in the agenda was abolition of untouchability. The counter-cultural movement and ideology propagated by Dalit intellectuals contained critiques and negation of Brahminical Hinduism and undermining of the cultural tradition of the caste-Hindus. These aspects were well represented in the literary and cultural traditions of the Dalits. The literary and cultural sensibilities were projected by the Dalit intelligentsia, like Boyi Bheemanna,[94] Kusuma Dharmanna[95] Jala Ranga Swamy,[96]

Gurram Jashua, Bhagya Reddi Varma and Nakka China Venkayya[97]. They depicted the miseries, pain of "untouchables" and built up consciousness conducive to the struggle for their rights during the 1920s and 30s.[98]

In an effort to create solidarity and identity among Dalits. Boyi Bheemanna coined a new term *Mamalu* which indicated the two main sub-castes within Dalits – the first *Ma* is indicates the Malas and the second *Ma* indicates the Madigas.[99] He deliberately used this term to foster the concept of unity among the Dalits. Gurram Jashua was critical of sub-caste rivalry among Dalits and held that ignorance was the main reason for this.[100] He questioned the very creation of the fifth order, the *Panchama varna*.[101] He also questioned the wisdom of the caste-Hindus in treating the Dalit masses as Panchamas and wondered.

We heard that for the old Brahma
She bore four sons
The wretched lower than the animal who is this
Fifth caste person…Savitri!

Adi-Hindu Movement in Hyderabad, 1920s and '30s

Hyderabad showed a variation of the 'autonomy–integration' process in the specialized circumstances under Nizam's rule, as it was the largest princely state.[102] When the Dalits of the coastal region derived their name from the prefix "Adi", the linguistic regional name, Hyderabad adopted up an Adi-Hindu theme, as the descendants of the original inhabitants who were rulers and owners of this land before the advent of the Aryans.[103] As a result even the names of the other contemporary Dalit movements of the 1920s, organized by non-Brahmins and Dalits, were drawn to an anti-Hindu ideology. Also, both Maharashtra and Madras radicalized and influenced the rest of the country as the strongest initiators of non-Aryan themes. Subsequently, with their regional and low caste identities, Dalit movements began to argue across the country in terms of the Aryan conquest and Brahmin exploitation through religion.[104]

In the later years of 1920s and the '30s Dalits organized many conferences in the Hyderabad state but unlike coastal region with less rural participation. In 1925, Bhagya Reddi Varma organized an exhibition of handicrafts containing paintings, sketches, sculptural works and other novelties prepared by the Adi-Hindu community at Residency Bazar, now known as Sultan Bazar in Hyderabad, and this was opened by Goswamy Rajah Dhanrajgiri Narsingji.[105] The idea behind the exhibition was to prove that the Dalits were in no way less skillful in fine arts and crafts than their so-called upper caste counterparts even though they had no facilities and opportunities to develop their skills.

In 1931, a special political session of the Ninth All-India Adi-Hindu Conference was held at Lucknow, on the eve of the Second Round Table Conference. Bhagya Reddi Varma presided over this with participation from across the country. The most significant and unanimous resolution passed at the conference was the recognition of Dr. Ambedkar as the sole and true representative to speak on behalf of the 90 million of Adi-Hindus (Untouchables).[106] Second important resolution, reiterated the demand for a separate electorate with an adequate weighting to the Adi-Hindus, and this was also adopted unanimously. An interesting event of the conference was some delegates objecting to the suffix "Varma" of Bhagya Reddi Varma's name, as they regarded it to be an Aryan title. Without giving any room for controversy Bhagya Reddi Varma renounced the title and signed all the papers without the Varma suffix.

As a result of the anti-caste radicalism, along with growing consciousness of the Dalits all over the country, the "Adi" ideological identity became a major discourse in the 1920s and the 1930s. The state census indicated a rather vigorous cultural debate. The 1931 census of Hyderabad reported a division among the 'untouchables' with respect to their orientation towards Hinduism.[107]

A similar vigorous debate within the Agra Chamars resembles the arguments of the Adi-Dravida Educational

League is worth mentioning.[108] They argued that the 'untouchables' were in fact, Adi-Hindus, or the original or autochthonous Negar or Dasas of the North and the Dravidas of the South, and that they were the undisputed, heavenly owners of India. All others are immigrants to the land, including the Aryans, who conquered the original populations not by valour but by deceit and manipulation, and that since then the Hindus and untouchables remained poles apart.[109]

In November 1931, the Adi-Hindu (Depressed Classes) political conference of Nizam state was held at Bolaram, a British administered area, since the Nizam government did not permit any conference or meeting of political nature in its dominion.[110]

By the late 1930s Hyderabad Dalit politics was marked by incentive competitive struggles, divisions and arrival of rival Adi-Hindu organizations to the fore, as also the development of rival caste-Panchayats reforms with occasional physical confrontations between them.[111] There were differences between B.S. Venkatarao[112] and Arigay Ramaswamy and later between Venkatarao and Subbaiah too. The differences were more personal in nature than being ideological or political. None of the later Hyderabad leaders was capable of organizing any mass movement.[113] The Adi-Hindu movement of Hyderabad mostly concentrated in the twin cities with less rural base unlike in the coastal region. Gradually the Communists gained a foothold in the rural Telugu regions while the Ambedkar movement attained some significant mass base in the Marati speaking regions of the Nizam state.

Last Phase of the Movement

By the turn of 1940s, the Dalit movement in the coastal region gradually faded away due to several reasons. While on the one hand, the process of accommodation and absorption within the pattern of Hindu reforms reached its zenith under the leadership of the Congress led by Gandhi.[114] There was steady erosion in the Dalit movement base on the other end of the spectrum, thanks to the systematic organization of the landless agricultural labourers by the Communits. As a result, many

Dalit stalwarts like B.S.Murty, Gaddada Mahalaxmi, Vemula Kurmayya, Chuttumalla Venkataratnam, Jala Rangaswamy, Vundru Subbarao, Naralasetti Devendradu and many others, who were active in the 1920s and the '30s, were gradually integrated into the Congress. At the same time, the militancy of lower class Dalits was increasingly being expressed amongst Communist agricultural labour organizations. Many young Dalits, including Guntur Bapaiah, Prasada Rao, M. Sriramulu, Koneru Ranga Rao, R.A. Kotayya, K. Nagabhushanam, K. Mohan Rao, Konada Surya Prakasa Rao and many others joined the movement from early 1940s. These two parties systematically took the Dalits into their respective folds, and the latter formed the main cadre base for them.

The worst retrogressive feature of the development of the Communists at the organizational level, the Communists were unwilling to accept any kind of Dalit autonomy,[115] while at the culture and identity levels they failed to provide any alternative to the Brahmanical interpretation of Indian history.[116] This was because the entire Communist leadership of the 1930s and '40s remained in the hands of either Brahmins or 'high' caste-Hindus.[117] And capping it all was the complete hegemony of the Congress over the Dalits and their movements. In that sense, incorporation of Dalits into the Congress fold through the *Harijan Sevak Sangh* become more and more wide with the opening of its district and local level branches by 1940s, inflicting a serious setback to the Adi-Andhra movement of coastal Andhra.

The death of Bhagya Reddi Varma in 1939, was a severe setback for the Dalit organizations in Hyderabad and coastal Andhra as with his death they lost the last effective leadership. Taking this opportunity, caste-Hindus absorbed them into their respective parties, providing meager concessions and successfully created factions among them. However, Dalit leaders were not completely oblivious of all this. In fact, they formally expressed this apprehension to the Simon Commission too.[118] For instance, there were conflicts between Golla Chandraiah and Kusuma Veera Swamy, president and executive member respectively of the Adi-Andhra Sthayi Sangam.

Subsequently Kusuma Veera Swamy left the organisation, formed another organization along with Pandu Laxman Swamy, and Nakka Venkata Reddy, who formed another organization.[119]

The September 1944 visit of Dr. B.R. Ambedkar energized the young Dalits in Andhra and a branch of the Scheduled Caste Federation was formed under Buldas Swamy. Nandanar Hari and Eeli Vadapalli played a major role in inviting Ambedkar. Ambedkar addressed many public meetings, notably the three, at Rajahmundry, Rama Chandrapuram and Kakinada presided over by Jala Ranga Swamy, Eeli Vadapalli and Pamu Rama Murthy respectively. Gradually, the largest section of the Dalit leadership got absorbed into Congress with its 'Harijan' terminology and its reiteration of Hindu identity. The few who opposed this strongly, mainly Kusuma Dharmanna were discredited by their pro-Muslim stance. Dharmanna in his *Jayabheri*, the mouthpiece for Ambedkarite Group, called upon the Dalits to convert into Islam. In many ways this reformist 'Hinduisation' can be traced to the writings of Boyi Bhimanna, a Dalit Congressman, who was described by many Congress Dalits as their guiding spirit. In the mid-1940s, Dalit employees formed their employees associations, but could not take any steps to organize masses or any form of movement.

However, a host of young educated Dalits stood behind the new leadership. Most prominent among then were B.S. Venkata Rao (1896-1953) who dominated the scene for nearly three decades and known as the 'Hyderabadi Ambedkar'.[120] Earlier in 1922 formed the Adi-Dravida Sangam. With the assistance of M. Govindarajulu and M. Venkata Swamy, he worked for the removal of Devadasi system besides trying to unite the Dalits.[121] He formed the Adi-Hindu Mahasabha in 1927 along with C.S. Ethirajan, K. Rama Swamy, Arigay Rama Swamy and others, and tried to bring a new awakening among the Dalits. He constructed eighteen temples in the Hyderabad state for the Dalits besides a library and a residential area for Dalits at Ghasmandi area, which was later named as Audia Nagar. He led the delegation to the Maharashtra Asprishya

Youth Conference in Pune in 1936, which was presided over by N. Shivaraj and addressed by Dr. B.R. Ambedkar.

Later, as the years rolled on, the Telangana movement dominated the scene on the one hand, while both the groups Depressed Classes' Association (DCA) and Scheduled Castes Federation (SCF) were vying with each other to mobilize the Dalits in the name of Ambedkar. In this political turmoil, the Dalits were a confused lot. The Depressed Classes' Association's pro-Muslim orientation and propaganda gained sustenance from the fact that the Nizam was actually implementing some reforms, including granting waste lands to Dalits, while the Communists were under attack by the Nizam *Razakars*.

Dalit organizations in Hyderabad were split into six groups working simultaneously until late '40s. The Dalit masses were even confused with London announcing the transfer of power in February 1947, and Hyderabad issueing a declaration of independence on 11 June, 1947. This set off increased factionalism and fermentations among the Dalits. By then, Ambedkarites become weak both organizationally and politically. And within this political and factional trauma, the Dalits were being pulled into various directions, but without any objectives. If the coastal Andhra Dalit movement ended in 40s with establishment of Brahmin led Congress hegemony, the movement in Hyderabad broke into pieces due to factionalism and climaxed with the 'police action' on the Telangana movement, coupled with the forceful integration of Hyderabad into Indian Union in 1951.

Every political party, irrespective of its ideological differences, including the communists,[122] used the Dalits only as their cadre base. While a few parties did that to get votes, the Communists were concerned about advancement of their movement. In the process, the Dalits got some marginal benefits and a small section of them also emerged as leaders and writers. It is from this section that the first Dalit Chief Minister of Andhra Pradesh, Damodaram Sanjivayya, was elected in the 1960s. He also managed to become the first

AICC President from the community. Below him there were many M.Ps and M.L.As and district level leaders who became khadi clad Dalit leaders, but could not play any independent, assertive ideological and political role.

Concluding Remarks

An overview of the Dalit politics in Andhra makes it clear that their organizational struggles and activities were the result of different political and socio-economic conditions, of the 1930s, and were mainly outside the scope of Ambedkar's influence. In Hyderabad, the movement was determined largely by the backward political autocracy of the Nizam state, while in the coastal regions, this was mainly due to the agriculture based commercial development. However, these movements shared several features with other regional Dalit movements. They emerged first with sponsorship from either caste-Hindu social reformers and from philanthropic Christian missionaries, and all had an inclination to adopt a 'non-Aryan ideology' and a proclarity to claim to be the original inhabitants of the land.

Within this broad framework, two trends can be traced: the first towards a radical assertion of autonomy from 'Hinduism' as also from the social and political organizations of caste-Hindus, and the second towards integration. To some degree, the "Adi" identity could lead back to integration within Hinduism as exemplified in by the claims Telugu Dalit poet Boyi Bhimanna who said the Dalits were the writers of 'Hindu' scriptures. He was also absorbed into the Congress, worked as its "propagandist", but later with his *Paleru* he asserted his Dalit identity in the 1940s. He claimed that the scriptures "were our literature", the Aryans having taken them from the Dalits. To some extent, this trend towards absorption into Hinduism often led via identification with the Bhakti movement, with saints such as Chokamela as well as with the linkages with other reformist organizations.

The Communist Party, after its formation, acquired a strong base among all sections of the exploited rural toilers in which the Dalits constituted the majority. In addition to the national developments that led to the independence, caste-Hindus succeeded in sowing the seeds of dissension and mutual rivalry among the Dalit leaders. Though attempts were made to resolve disputes, it appeared to be settled superficially with no change at the surface.

The emergence of the Dalit movement was related to specific socio-political upheaval in colonial Andhra as characterized by the growing trend of social reform movements like the Brahma Samaj, the Arya Samaj, and non-Brahmin movements under the leadership of caste-Hindus. At the political level, constitutional reforms such as the Montagu-Chemsford reforms, also gave impetus to self-organisation and political mobilization of Dalits for demanding their share in representative institutions. The rise and growth of the Adi-Andhra movement since 1917, was influenced to a significant extent by the earlier social reform movements, because a number of leaders of the Dalit movement were associated with them earlier. Bhagya Reddi Varma is the best example. Moreover, some of the Brahma Samaj Brahmins from coastal Andhra were instrumental in creating awareness among the Dalits by imparting modern education. Also many schools and hostels exclusively meant for the Dalits were initiated by philanthropists. The Rajah of Pithapuram is a case in point. In fact, many of the first generation Dalit intellectuals and leaders were products of such educational institutions.

There were two stages in the whole movement. The radical assertions of autonomy and self-consciously defined non-Hindu identity forced them to form their own organizations. From 1900 to 1930, they fought against social oppression and economic exploitation but could not stand together to endure powerful pressures of absorption by caste-Hindu dominated political parties and leverage their political power. This was evident due to the lack of strong and dynamic leadership among them after the death of Bhagya Reddi Varma in 1939. The re-absorption into Hinduism included the acceptance of Hindu leadership with a Harijan identity. There were many voices around to make the claims of leading the Harijans and providing an ideology for their advancement without a proper direction. While the Gandhi dominated Congress idealized village centered 'Ram Raj' on the one hand and the communists, imagined an industrialized casteless socialism on the other.[123] But both diverted the vital issues only to transform Dalit movements into splinter groups.

Group rivalries within the Dalit movement coupled with ever increasing influence of power politics among contending political parties were the most decisive factors in bringing a disastrous end to the movement itself. Dalits getting organized in the post-colonial Andhra during the first and second general elections was clear from the election of Bojja Appala Swamy to the legislature on the SCF banner, and B. Subba Rao in 1957 but later lost to the representative of the Congress. Ambedkar's pre-occupation with regions mostly outside Andhra and his involvement in Delhi in the late 1940s, ensured that Dalit influence could not compete with the Congress and Communists for long. Though the independent Dalit movement in Andhra faded away by the late 1940s, it is not unfair to conclude that the movement came to an end by the 1950s under the burden of power politics. Much later, in the late 1960s an attempt was made to revive the movement by K. Rama Swamy and Neredumilli Nagendrudu, but could not get off the ground. Only in the late 80s they could revive and reorganize the militant Dalit movement in Andhra particularly after the Karamchedu massacre.

Parts of this paper has been presented at a Conference on 'Social consciousness and culture in colonial and post-colonial India: New approaches' held at India International Centre, New Delhi (27-28 February, 2006) and at a National Conference on 'Communities and the Nation: Dalits and Adivasis in colonial and post-colonial India' held at Department of History, University of Calcutta (22-23 March, 2006).

NOTES

1. Ranajit Guha, 1984, vol. I, p. 8.
2. Today's Andhra Pradesh's geographically consists of three regions, i.e., Coastal Andhra (fertile wet land region), Rayalaseema, derived from the monarchs (rayas) of Vijayanagara once controlling this region, but later on more known colloquially as "land of stones" because of its less fertile lands and Telangana, (Telugu speaking districts of erstwhile Nizam state). The nine districts of coastal Andhra are Srikakulam, Vizianagaram, Visakhapatnam, East Godavari, West Godavari, Krishna, Guntur, Nellore and Prakasam; while Rayalaseema consists of four districts—Cuddapah, Kurnool, Anantapur and Chittoor, these two regions were a part of Madras presidency during colonial rule.
3. Telangana consists of ten districts—Adilabad, Hyderabad, Ranga Reddi, Karimnagar, Nalgonda, Warangal, Mahaboobnagar, Medak, Khammam and Nizamabad. Telangana and other two linguistic regions (Marathwada and Karnataka) comprised the Nizam state or Hyderabad state.
4. Gail Omvedt, 1994, p. 114.
5. Indu Rajagopal, 1985, p. 118.
6. Originally his name was Madari Bhagaiah. Born on 22 May, 1888, he was a second child to Madari Venkayya and Rangamamba. He worked as a steward for a Goanese Catholic family who educated and later employed him. Their family Guru, a Shaivite and a learned person "conceived as a fact historically, that 'untouchables' were the rulers of the land prior to migration of Aryans to India for their livelihood. Hence the term "Reddi" (derived from 'redu', means ruler) justified as a suffix to his name, became Bhagya Reddy in 1913 "at the annual function of the Arya Samaj where he was honoured by the title "Varma" for his laudable social service.
7. Y.B. Abbasayalu, 1978, p. 32.
8. Interview with Bhagya Reddi Varma's son M.B. Gautam.
9. See *Bhagya Reddi Varma Papers and Collections*.
10. The executive committee consisted of Walthati Seshaiah, President; H.S. Venkataram, Vice-President; J.S. Multhaiah, Secretary; H.S. Shivaram, Treasurer and M.V. Bhagya Reddi Varma as Organizing Secretary.

11. P.R. Venkata Swamy, 1955, vol. I, p. 10.
12. Arigay Rama Swamy (1885-1973), born in 1885 at Ramankola, in Ranga Reddy District, was the son of a *tonga* driver in Secundarabad. He was sent to Baptist Mission School, Secunderabad, but could not continue due to acute poverty, worked as an office boy, carpenter and a ticket collector on the railroads at Bolaram, before he began his social reform activities amongst his brethren.
13. R.K. Kshirsagar, 1994, p. 166.
14. M.B. Gautam, 1991, p. 16.
15. Sir Ali Imam, President of the Executive Council, the Nizam's Government, in appreciation of its activities awarded a certificate to the *Swasti Dal*. The Deccan Humanitarian League awarded a gold medal to Bhagya Reddi Varma and silver medals to volunteers for their meritorious service.
16. K. Chandraiah, 1982, pp. 17-24.
17. M.B. Gautam, 1953.
18. Y.B. Abbasayalu, 1978, p. 32.
19. M.B. Gautam, 1976, pp. 70-71.
20. P.R. Venkata Swamy, 1955, vol. I, pp. 18-40.
21. *Madras Legislative Council Proceedings vol. IV*, (20 January, 1922), p. 2051.
22. *Proceedings of the Law (General) Department* Government of Madras, G.O. No. 817, Dated 25 March, 1922.
23. Guduru Ramachandra Rao, along with Ayyadevara Kalaswara Rao Vamuri Ramji Rao, Madapati Hanumanta Rao, Vellanki Krishna Rao and other caste-Hindus made attempts to introduce some ameliorate measures for the upliftment of the 'untouchables'.
24. M.B. Gautam, 1991, pp. 16-18.
25. *Ibid*.
26. A. Satyanarayana, 1999.
27. *Krishna Patrika*, 15 June, 1921.
28. *Krishna Patrika*, 8 June, 1927, 18 February, 1929.
29. *Krishna Patrika*, 23 February, 1929, 16 Nov. 1929.

30. *Krishna Patrika*, 13 August, 1932, 18 November, 1933, 29 June, 1935, 9 Jan. 1937.

31. For more details see Chinna Rao Yagati, 2002, pp. 84-120.

32. Harold Issacs, 1969, pp. 67-70.

33. A. Satyanarayana, 1998.

34. B.S. Murthy, B.A., B.Ed., (b.1906) is the best example of this. He was educated at Rajahmundry and at Madras, was elected Secretary of Andhra Pradesh, Harijan Sevak Sang from 1940-49, was electoral member of Madras Legislative Assembly in 1937 and Minister for Industries and Labour; later became Deputy Minister in the Nehru Cabinet. He also took part in the national movement and played a major role in establishing Hostels for Dalits.

35. In their usage, Burma is more known as "Rangam" (Rangoon). In many popular Dalit stories the "Rangam" factor is visible. Dalits often fled to Rangoon because of their inability to repay the debt or as a mark of protest against landlords' exploitation. This information is based on the author's interview with many Dalits activists/leaders in coastal Andhra, like Bojja Appala Swamy, Vajrapu Samba Murty, Konada Suryaprakasarao, Ravuri Ekambaram, Yagati Ramulu.

36. Chinna Rao Yagati, 2003c, pp. 117-153.

37. Priyadarshini Vijaisri, 1997 and 2003.

38. The terms are generally used along with the person's name by caste-Hindus with to show the inferior status of a "low" caste person. For instance names of Polayya, Muttaiah, change its form to be called Poligadu, Muthugaḍu. Another variation of making a "low" caste person is through the prefixing of caste names to personal names. For instance, "Madigolla Potayya" (Pothayya of Madiga community) or Malolla Gavarayya (Gavarayya of Mala community). This is very much in prevalence even now.

39. The prime reason may be that many local *zamindars* of coastal Andhra reason were pro-justice party, like the Rajah of Pithapuram (Ravu Venkatakumara Mahapati Surya Rao Bahddar, D.Litt.), who was a great philanthropist and played a prominent role in establishing and endowing Patronage to educational institutions and Hostels for Dalits. The other pro-justice party *zamindars* like those from Gollapalli and Mirzapur also presided over Adi-Andhra Conferences, see *Krishna Patrika*, 31 October, 1936.

40. A. Satyanarayana, 1999.

41. *Krishna Patrika*, 8 January, 1927.

42. For details see, Eugene F. Irschick, 1969.

43. *Krishna Patrika*, 31 October, 1936.

44. In fact the rise and growth of regional and political consciousness and Andhra movement coincided with the rise and growth of Dalit consciousness.

45. For instance, the famous nationalist leadership of the time in Andhra including K. Nageswara Rao, Ayyadevara Kaleswara Rao had personal relations with the Adi-Andhra leadership.

46. Many Dalits joined and participated in the Congress led national movement only after the visit of Gandhi to Andhra in 1932 and after the establishment of Andhra branch of Harijan Sevak Sangh.

47. See Ayyadevara Kaleswara Rao, 1959.

48. *Krishna Patrika*, 11 November, 1933.

49. Naralasetti Devendrudu was the Chairman of Reception Committee of the third Adi-Andhra Conference (1920) and Presided over the Sixth Conference (1926). He was later nominated to the Madras Legislative Council. Vemula Kurmayya was the Chairman of the Reception Committee of the Eighth Conference held at Vijayawada (1929). Later, he was elected in 1937 and in 1946 to the Madras Legislative Assembly and became 'Harijan' Welfare Minister in the Prakasham Ministry from 1946 to 1949.

50. *Krishna Patrika*, 27 October, 1934, 25 May, 1936.

51. As many as 41 night schools and 11 day schools were started for Dalits in 12 districts of Andhra region, and on amount of Rs. 8,637 were spent. See *Krishna Patrika*, 11 July, 1936.

52. Fifty-six members voted for the resolution and 19 remained neutral. See *Government of Madras, Public Department, G.O. 114, Public*, (General) dated 31 March, 1933.

53. See for the representation of the Varnashram Swarajya Shagam, *Government of Madras*, Public Department, G.O. No. 140, Public, (General), Dated 7 February, 1933.

54. Not stopping here, all the caste-Hindus held in protest public meetings against the legislative interference in religion. A Temple Defense Day was observed in Triplicane in Madras. See *The Hindu*, 7 May, 1934.

55. S. Saraswathi, 1974, pp. 166-169.

56. *The Hindu*, 4 January, 1934.

57. *The Hindu*, 2 January, 1934.

58. *Krishna Patrika*, 23 December, 1933.

59. *Krishna Patrika*, 29 October, 1932.

60. M. Venkatarangaiah, 1969, vol. III, p. 539.

61. *Krishna Patrika*, 30 December, 1935.

62. *Government of Madras*, Public Department, G.O., no.114, public (General), dated March 31, 1933.

63. *Krishna Patrika*, January 1, 1928.

64. *Krishna Patrika*, September 27, 1924.

65. *Krishna Patrika*, August 15, 1936.

66. This incident was also shown in a Telugu feature film, "Malapilla". Interview with John Akkidas. Also See *Krishna Patrika*, 4 May, 1938.

67. Interview with Bh. Tirupati.

68. Vundru Tatayya was born in 1850 at Ponnamanda, Rajolu Taluk, East Godavari District. He was one of the outstanding example of the Burmese factor. During his stay at Burma he earned huge property including 330 acres of land in Burma and 150 acres of land in Panamanda (India). He became one of the main financial sources for the movement. He was nominated member of Rajhmundry Taluk Board E.G. district board. He died in 19 May, 1930.

69. Nakka Venkata Reddy (1892-1972) from 1917 he played an active role in Adi-Andhra movement. He trained and encouraged many Dalit activists such as Pamu Ramamurty (b.1905), Geddada Brahmayya (1912-1950), Eeli Vadapalli (1911-1971) and many others. He was an executive member of Adi-Andhra Mahajana Sangam (Regd.) of East Godavari District from 1937 to 1942; see *Souvenir*, 1976, pp. 21-22.

70. Tadepalli Tatayya (1875-1952) was warden of Adi-Andhra hostel of the Pithapuram Rajah (in 1922) and worked as Headmaster in the night school established by His Highness of Pithapuram.

71. Chuttugulla Venkayya (1896-1965) belongs to the Madiga community. He organized the district Arundatiya Association

and was conferred with the title "Good Recruiter" the British for his services to mobilize youth in joining the armed forces during the Second World War (1939-45).

72. Didla Pullayya (1894-1958) of Rajahmundry, was a teacher, started the *Adimandra* journal to mobilize and to create consciousness among Dalits. Initially he was supporter of Justice Party later turned a staunch Congressman.

73. Ambati Gangi Setti (b.1902) played a major role in establishing Field Labour Credit Societies in many villages in the Amalapuram taluk, East Godavari district. He was a prolific speaker, and a Congress follower from the beginning.

74. Golla Chandrayya (1888-1972), started his career as a teacher in Kadali Panchama School in 1908. He played a major role in organizing Dalit Field Labour Credit Societies, and established hostels for Dalits.

75. Dasari Venkata Rao, 1926, p. 10.

76. Nakka China Venkayya, 1935, p. 6.

77. For an excellent detailed documentation of a day-to-day activities of Hyderabad dalit movement see, P.R.Venkata Swamy, 1955.

78. *Souvenir*, 1976, p. 6.

79. Interview with Bojja Appalaswamy.

80. Interview with Boyi Bheemanna.

81. *Souvenir, op cit.*, p. 5.

82. *Ibid.*

83. Goda Venkanna born on 15 June, 1898 at Challapalli, Amalapuram taluk. After completion of his higher grade training, became Headmaster of Adi-Andhra Primary School of Challapalli.

84. Bojja Appalaswamy was born on 19 August, 1913 in Kandikuppa village of East Godavari district. He also established schools, mobilized masses through dramas and other cultural programmes in which Dalit miseries were depicted. He was elected President of Scheduled Castes Federation of Amalapuram Taluk in 1942, and spread Ambedkar's ideas in the state. He was a prolific speaker and for sometime he published *Jyothi*, a fortnightly Magazine. He acted in the much famous drama, *Paleru* written by Boyi Bhimnna and was beaten up by Caste-Hindus several times. He was good Musician, and could play the Harmonium particularly well.

85. R.K. Kshirsagar, 1994, pp. 211-212.

86. Y.B. Abbasayalu, 1979, pp. 12-13.

87. Gail Omvedt, 1994, p. 286.

88. For details see Chinna Rao Yagati, 2003b.

89. *Souvenir*, 1976, p. 50.

90. *Jaya Bheri* was brought from Rajahmundry under the editorship of Kusuma Dharmanna, while *Navajeevana* was started from Madras under the editorship of B.S. Murty in 1939. Interview with Bojja Appalaswamy.

91. Interview with Vajrapu Samba Murty.

92. Interview with Boyi Bheemanna.

93. Interview with Ravoori Ekambaram. Initially he joined the Congress led by Gandhi and actively participated in Harijan Sevak Sangh activities. Later turned into a staunch Ambedkarite, and also authorised a poetical work *Narudo Ambedkaruda*, (Vijayawada: n.d.).

94. Boyi Bheemanna (1911-2005) was a legend of the Dalit intellectuals. He graduated (1936) from P.R. College, Kakinada (B.A.) and B.Ed. at Rajahmundry (1937). He was associate editor for Dalit journal *Jayabheri*. He published nearly 50 words including *Paaleru* (a form boy) (1940), *Kooli Raju* (The labour king) (1947), *Jaana Paduni Jaabulu* (1940), and many more. For details see Haimavati, 1978 and Ganumala Gnaneswar, 1983.

95. Kusuma Dharmanna (1896-1948) was one of the prominent Dalit organic intellectual leader of the Adi-Andhra movement and a prolific writer. His writings including *Nalla Dora Thanam* (1933) *Harijan Satakamu*, (1933) and *Madya Paana Nishedamu* (1930).

96. Jala Rangaswamy, was born in 1904 at Kambala Peta in Rajahmundry. He was a teacher by profession, and worked for Dalit education and established many educational institutions alongwith his wife Jala Mangamma. He writings include *Antarani Vaarevaru?* (Who were untouchables?) (Rajahmundry: 1930); *Malasuddhi (Rajahmundry:* 1930), etc.

97. Gurram Jashuva (1895-1971) would be remembered as a pre-eminent poet who raised his strong voice of protest in verse against caste system, untouchability and socio-economic inequalities. His writings include *Phiradousi*, (1932), *Gabbilam* (Bat), 1941 and many more.

98. The most famous among the writings of Nakka China Venkayya was, *Harijana Keertanalu,* (1935).

99. This argument was renewed again in 1990s among the Dalit intellectual circles. For details see Sarini, 1997.

100. Interview with Boyi Bheemanna.

101. A. Satyanarayana, 1995, pp. 171-175; also see Chinna Rao Yagati, 2003b.

102. K. Chandraiah, 1992, pp. 17-24.

103. In the 8th Session of the All India Adi-Hindu (Depressed Classes) conference held at Allahabad, (16 November, 1930), a total of twelve resolutions were passed at the end of the conference. The sixth resolution says that "This conference demands the representation of the Adi-Hindus (Depressed Classes) in the central and provincial legislatures on their population with adequate weightage commensurate with their position as the descendants of the original inhabitants of this country who were the rulers and masters of this land of their birth before the advent of the Aryans to this country", see *Bhagya Reddi Verma Papers and Collections.*

104. The theme of "Adi" ideology or original inhabitants of the country ('sons of the soil') was growing phenomenon throughout the country. Even the names of most Dalit movements—Adi-Dharm in Punjab, Adi-Hindu in UP and Hyderabad, Adi-Andhra in A.P., Adi-Dravida in Madras are indicated a common claim to being original inhabitants.

105. M.B. Gautam, 1991, pp. 20-21.

106. *Ibid.* p. 32.

107. *Census of India, 1931,* vol. XXIII, Hyderabad State, Part-I, Report, (Hyderabad: 1933), p. 258; also see Chinna Rao Yagati, 2003b and 2003c.

108. Oven M. Lynch, 1969, pp. 14-27.

109. For details see, R.S. Khare, 1969.

110. Y.B. Abbasayalu, 1979, pp. 21-23.

111. K. Chandraiah, 1992, pp. 17-24.

112. Originally his name was Bathula Ashaiah born to parents in the domestic service of the Europeans, was a resident of Ghasmandy,

Secunderabad. His robust and hefty body earned him the colloquial nickname of "Dobba" (Bulky). He was commonly known as Dobba Ashaiah, but later part of his life he was mostly known as B.S. Venkat Rao. He worked in the Public Works Department of Nizam's government, and later appointed as an Asst. Recruiting Officer in the Nizam Sager.

113. This was partly because Hyderabad being an urban areas and gradual deterioration of Bhagya Reddi Varma's health.

114. G. Ram Reddy, 1989, pp. 286-321.

115. Dalit Communist Leaders of Guntur district were interviewed by U. Sambasiva Rao, editor of *Edureeta*, for details see "Experiences of Saapati Samson", *Edureeta*, Supplement, 5 August 1994, pp.1-5.

116. Konada Surya Prakasa Rao was born on 15 February, 1910 at Peda Palaparru, in Gudivada Taluk, Krishna District. Born in a Dalit labouring family, passed his S.S.L.C. in 1930, and later joined the Intermediate at Kakinada College of Pithapuram. He was the first activist of Communist movement, Chief Organizer of agricultural labourers, and President of Krishna District Agricultural Labour Association (1941) and later joined in Scheduled Caste Federation. See, Boyi Bheemanna, 1988, pp.xx-xxvi.

117. Selig S. Harrison, 1956, pp. 378-404.

118. Foe details of oral evidence given by the All-India Adi-Dravida Mahajana Sabha, Madras, and Arundatiya Mahasabha at Madras on 21 Feb., 1929, see *Indian Statutory Commission: Selections from memoranda and Oral Evidence by Non-Officials*, vol. XVII, part. II (London, 1930): p. 87.

119. Nakka Venkata Reddy born on 4 January, 1892 at Mummidivaram Sivarupali Palem in Amalapuram Taluk. He was a teacher-manager at Komana Palli (1909), and was later appointed as teacher in Adi-Andhra school at Mummadi Varam. He had close connections with non-Brahmin leadership of Justice Party and movement. He encouraged and trained many Dalit youth to join the movement, including Pamu Ramamurthy, Eeli Vadapalli. He was also member of executive council of East Godavari Adi-Andhra Mahajana Sabha (Regd.) from 1937 to 1942.

120. R.K. Kshirsagar, 1994, pp. 366-367.

121. Priyadarshini Vijaisri, 2005.

122. The only exception and peculiar feature of Andhra Communists

was that Communist leadership was from non-Brahmin upper castes such as Kamma and Reddi. In other regions of the country, Communists were Brahmins, in other words, they were more popularly known as 'bunch of Brahmin boys'.

123 Gail Omvedt, 1994, p. 134.

5

Aspects of Dalit Culture

Only in the twentieth century, historians and sociologists in India attempted to acknowledge the significance of the mass of "untouchables" to make a detailed study. Prior to this "untouchables" had never been a subject of a scholarly investigation. Whatever references existed prior to the twentieth century were in the form of taboos, punishments and contempt. It was the Europeans who first took the initiative to understand the significance of the world of "untouchables". Later, the Indian scholars undertook this task. Historically, the census reports were responsible for providing exhaustive information about the "untouchables" throughout the country. Other than serving the colonial purpose, these reports explored the innumerable groups and practically for the first time in Indian history dealt about various aspects of lives of these people. In the process, it has made the "untouchables" to know more about themselves. However, interpretations of both Indian and European scholars have their own shortcomings. The Europeans found these institutions to be exclusively different from what they had not known in their own societies. Not being a part of the alien system, they took a comparatively detached view of society, while the Indian scholars were bound by their own prejudices.

But recent proliferations of works on the lives of the "untouchables" by their own people are invaluable. They provide a close insight into their lives and are thus bereft of superficial observations. They had to a great extent explored the unnoticed aspects of the "untouchable" lives and problems ranging from individual to communitarian aspects. These are of a crucial significance, as the Dalits of today, who are conscious of themselves and their plight strive to reconstruct their unrecorded past and identity in terms of their own experiences.

In this chapter, an attempt has been made to look at the Dalit culture from a Dalit perspective, while investigating and interpreting how different is the Dalit culture from the so-called greater culture or dominant culture—Hindu culture. A cultural approach to the study of the Dalits is not only useful but necessary; as such an attempt will help to understand more deeply the cultural manifestations of the Dalits as also how their value system is related to the rest of the cultural systems in the country.

Culture is generally understood as the way of life of a social group; a group's total man-made environment, including all the material and non-material products of group life that are transmitted from one generation to the next. One of the classical definitions of the culture, which most sociological definitions follow is by Edward B.Tylor,[1] who defines culture as the "complex whole which includes knowledge, belief, art, morals, law, custom and any other capabilities and habits acquired by man as a member of the society." After surveying current definitions of culture, Alfred L. Kroeber and Clyde Kluckhohn conclude that the consensus of the most social scientists is that "culture consists of patterns, explicit and implicit, of behaviour acquired and transmitted by symbols, constituting the distinctive achievements of human groups, including their embodiments in artefacts; the essential core of culture consists of traditional (i.e., historically derived and selected); ideas and especially their attached values."[2] In its more recent meanings the word culture denotes "historically transmitted pattern of meanings embodied in symbols, a system of inherited conceptions expressed by means of which men communicate, perpetuate and develop their knowledge about and attitudes toward life."[3]

Little and Great Traditions

The tradition and culture of the suppressed communities representing the majority of Indian population is categorised as the 'little tradition' while the culture of the minority is represented as 'Greater Tradition'. This is because when the Orientalists of the nineteenth century began to interpret Indian culture, they were carried away mostly by the so-called 'Greater Tradition' of the social elite. They further identified it as the creation of Brahmins. Scholars, when they think of Indian tradition mostly refer to the Brahminical tradition.[4] Elements of this tradition are characterized by knowledge of and respect for the Vedas and *Shastras*, emphasis on spiritual activities, extensive ritual competence, concern for ritual purity and other worldliness.[5] The Orientalists held that the Brahmins belonged to the Aryan race, a superior race that also consisted of Germans and Saxons in Europe. They were of the opinion that the whole Indian culture and civilization was an achievement of this particular race. Not only that racial superiority and monopoly of custodianship of culture were also attributed to them. Such an interpretation over the years, strengthened the Brahmanic hegemony over the social structure. The Orientalists like Max Muller observed that the Hindu religion was a contribution of Brahmins, and was "a moribund non-missionary religion."[6]

The British Administrators-cum-historians accepted the textural view of the Brahminical literature, including the *Smritis*, the Vedas and Dharma Sastras. They found them internalised by the whole sections of Indian society. They strongly believed that these texts were accurate guides to Indian culture. For instance, N.B.Halhed's first compilation of translation of the *Dharmasastras* known as '*A code of Gentoo Laws or Ordinances of the Pundits, from a Persian Translation, made from the original written in Sanskrit Language*', was published as early as in 1777 at London. They felt that these translations could together "form a precise idea of the customs and manners of these people." Such an interpretations of the Brahminical texts in nexus with traditional *pundits* led to the view that the Brahmins were the dominant group in society who formed the apex of Hindu social order.

Even the translation of *Manusmriti* by Sir William Jones, was to establish the code of Hindu society. In reality, it was never applicable to the majority of Indian society. Simultaneously, the Indian (more often Brahmin) approach resulted in the acceptance of a view that Indian society is static. For them, Indian society or Indian culture meant only the society represented by the Brahmins or, at most, it extended to the all (*Dwijas*) twice born communities. This did not include the other three-fourths of the population, comprising the Shudras, the Dalits (Schedule Castes in constitutional terms, 'untouchables' in social and religious parlance) and the tribals.

Protest Against Brahmanism

Against the theoretical hegemony of the Brahminist ideology, there were popular protests from the oppressed communities throughout history. These protests inculcated a sense of enthusiasm to fight against their exploitation and oppression. The architects of these movements in different regions articulated their aspirations in the vernacular. The main figures in this larger protest movement were Mahatma Jotiba Phule, Babasaheb Ambedkar, Periyar E.V. Ramaswami Naiker, Ayothi Thass with many others throughout India. At the regional level included Narayana Guru in Kerala, Acchutananda in U.P., Mangoo Ram in Punjab, Devaraya Ingle in Karnataka and Bhagya Reddi Varma in Hyderabad. All of them attacked the system of exploitation at various levels of life—cultural, economical, political and social. They challenged the 'Hindu' ideology that was emerging as a consequence of the elite getting organized actively from the nineteenth century onwards to define Indian society, and trying to transform conceptually the various modules of Indian culture into a Hindu culture.

During the last decades of nineteenth century, which can be categorised as pre-Ambedkaran era, there were strong dissents and protests by Dalits throughout the country. The harbingers of such local organising were the conscious Dalits, who were beneficiaries of colonial measures, especially education. They can be seen as parallel to the social reform movements led by upper caste Hindu reformers during the nineteenth and early decades of the twentieth centuries. Such parallel movements were largely influenced by the non-Brahman movements especially the one led by Mahatma Phule. Thus, throughout the country we could notice local movements organised by educated and conscious Dalits. While in Andhra, the Adi-Andhra movement was led by Bhagya Reddi Varma.[7] In the northern part of Karnataka[8] (erstwhile Bombay presidency) self-respect movement was led by Devaraya Ingle and others. The new rebellious consciousness generated by these leaders led to mass mobilisation across the country during the Ambedkaran era. It was with immense encouragement and strength of these leaders that Ambedkar was able to articulate a subversive ideology for the Dalits as a whole. It should also be noted that the rebellious stance and activities of the early leaders pointed towards the nature of social reforms movements which were divided on the caste-class lines during the nineteenth century. It continued even in the twentieth century.

Earlier, during late nineteenth and early twentieth centuries, Dalits criticized distortions and excrescences in the writing about them. They attacked Hinduism itself by arguing that it was in essence Brahminical, caste bound and irrational. They asserted that Hinduism was not the religion and culture of the majority but an imposed one. As a part of this protest against domination, they rejected the imposed Hindu identity and sought to emphasize their non-Hindu identity. The whole part of early twentieth century witnessed the emergence of neo regional and religious identities. While Mahatma Phule tried to formulate a new theistic religion, Babasaheb Ambedkar turned to Buddhism. In Madras Presidency, non-Brahmin movements tried to claim Saivism as an independent religion. When Narayana Guru formulated 'one religion, one caste, one god' his own follower, Ayyappan, who was more radical, declared 'no religion, no caste and no god' for mankind. In the south the Dalits, either turned to Christianity or Islam or remained within their own ancestral religions. Whatever may be the specificities, the rejection of emerging hegemonic irrational Hindustic culture remained a feature of their resistance. This was a differentiating feature the anti-caste radicals from both Hindu reformers, and halfway houses like Brahma Samaj.

The basic feature of Indian tradition is of its composite character. The selective appropriation of the cultural past that portrays the whole gamut of historical past as an exclusively Hindu experience denies the composite cultural tradition of our society. In this sense, the communal interpretation of history is a falsification and not just a distortion and also denies a significant dimension of our historical tradition.[9] Perhaps, precisely this is the reason, why the Dalit intellectuals are focussing to re-examine their past and trying to re-write it where others may underscore the fundamental difference.

Studies that tend towards a cultural explanation attempt to situate the Dalits in terms of their having or not having a shared value system and its structural relation to the dominant culture. The structuralists, viewing the Dalits from a cultural perspective invariably point to the Dalits' hierarchy and purity concerns shared with the larger society.[10] The conflict and counter cultural theorists, viewing the Dalits from a social-positional or conflict perspective, rightly point to the Dalits egalitarian ethos and the different, even inverted, view of the society.[11] Most of these perspectives do help in some way or the other to explain the varied aspects of the Dalit culture.

Dalit Cultural Interpretations

Broadly, there are three varieties of interpretations can be distinguished, when we talk of Dalit cultural explanations. Michael Moffatt calls them as "outcaste images", "models of diversity" and "models of unity."[12] Moffatt argues that according to "Outcaste images", the Dalits do not have a culture of their own. "They are not detached or alienated from the rationalisations of the system... they possess and act upon a thickly textured culture, whose fundamental definitions and values are identical to those of more global Indian village culture."[13] If it is considered to be true, they are either "cultureless" or "culture free."[14] Although these set of writers[15] do not find a cultural system among the Dalits of the regions which they studied, they consider Dalits having liberated themselves from the oppressive elements of the 'higher' caste culture, and having developed a culture of their own. Some of the early descriptions of the Dalits portray them as a cultureless people possessing more negative qualities such as laziness, drunkenness and lack of thrift than positive values. Such arguments are draws mostly from the traditional Brahmanical texts of dominant Hindus who always referred to Dalits with hatred and castigated them for possessing uncultured and unclean habits.

The second variety of cultural explanation, assumes a fundamental cultural consensus between the Dalits and the rest of Hindu society. In spite of personal dissension between the different elements in the system, concerning their rank in the hierarchical system, this model argues that the different caste groups not only complement each other but also accept the hierarchical value system as their basic value. Even the Dalits who are at the bottom of the caste hierarchy "participate willingly in what might be called their own oppression."[16] Differences between the Dalit culture and Brahminic culture are reduced to the local variations of the "great tradition."[17]

The third and perhaps the most important variety of cultural explanation are the "models of diversity." This school argues and rightly points out that Dalits have their own cultural systems. These cultural systems are sometimes described as 'little traditions' containing elements of a pre-Aryan and non-Brahminic value system.[18] Others claims that, they are 'great traditions' comparable and distinct from the dominant Brahminic culture.[19]

The cultural explanation recognised in the above models are not usually analysed in a comparative perspective or in an evaluative framework. There is no suggestion that the Dalits are at the bottom of the social ladder due to their cultural inferiority. It is generally assumed that power relations in society played a role in determining their dehumanized societal status. Max Weber suggests that the lower castes are strong adherents of the karma, dharma or even the idea of rebirth, etc. He further says that[20] "it is precisely the lowest classes, who would naturally be most desirous of improving their status in subsequent incarnations, cling most steadfastly to their caste obligations." However, recent studies either by Dalits themselves[21] or research surveys[22] suggest that there are major differences between the beliefs and customs of Dalits and caste-Hindus. More surprisingly, there are more similarities among several Dalit communities in various parts of India, than the similarities between Dalits and caste-Hindus of the same region.

Dalit Culture Vs Hindu Culture

The models of diversity raise many questions. How does the Dalit culture relate to the so-called Indian culture? What is the place of Dalit culture within the greater tradition? What theoretical model can be used that will not reduce Dalit culture to the same "deep" ideational structure shared with the rest of caste-Hindu society? How can one view social structure as determined by culture as followed by the structuralists? The classical conflict approach, explains culture, as determined by social structures based primarily on materialistic considerations. To understand and explain Dalit culture, one can take recourse to Dumont's movement and go from structure to the system, [23] using Parson's model of human behaviour that includes cultural, social and psychological dimensions, analytically separable and each with different dynamics.[24] Such an approach would be analogous to a multi-structuralist-funtionalist approach. It is because each dimension pervades the whole system. This point was brought out more emphatically by Lynn Vincentnathan,[25] who considers his approach neo-Parsonian rather than neo-functionalist. These various cultural approaches, such as structural, symbolic and cognitive account for conflict within or between the social, psychological or cultural systems.

However, the structural-functional aspects approach minimizes the importance of the power relations in society and the way in which they affect the social process. When we look at the detailed moorings, and deeper aspects of Dalit culture, we find their culture entirely different from Brahminical culture. The religion of the "untouchables" in its very nature is antithesis to the religious system of the Hindus, and is devoid of the fundamental aspects of Hindu religious system, hierarchical temple structure, authoritarianism of priestly class and domination of male divinities. In other words, in the Hindu religious system, Brahmin priest works as a middleman between God and devotees, where as in Dalit religion this middlemanship is clearly absent. Though a religious system diametrically antagonistic to the Hindu religion existed in the past it was marginalised and integrated into the mainstream as a result of Aryan imperialism. The distinctiveness continued to the modern period, maintaining its original beliefs and ideals in their practice as well as folklore.

The writings and observations of Christian missionaries, Anthropologists, Sociologists and foreign travelogues are invaluable on this score. In 1921, Henry Whitehead, a Bishop of Madras, made an exhaustive account of the rituals and ceremonies of the villages in Madras presidency. Even Whitehead perceived the Dalit religious system as crude animism and distinct, later which came under the influence of *superior* religions of the Aryans.[26] Such observations were a result of non-existence of any sophisticated and subtle metaphysics among the rural masses, where religion was utilitarian in observing their day-to-day problem and also ethnocentric issues.

Worship of Female Divinities

The most striking phenomenon that justifies the alternative religious identity is the existence of feminine element in the Dalit religious system. As against the predominantly male gods of Hindu pantheon, in the Dalit religious system, female divinities figure vigorously. J.H. Hutton notes that in the villages, the goddesses are still the real deity, and protectress of people, rather than the recognised Hindu gods.[27] Lynn Gatwood[28] in her stimulating work makes a clear distinction too. Worship of Devi receives greater intensity among the lower castes and the spouse goddesses are more worshipped among the higher castes she says.[29]

Explaining this phenomenon Whitehead writes, "in the Hindu Pantheon the male deities are predominant and the female deities occupy a subordinate position." This being the prime characteristic of the genesis of the Aryan religions he goes on to argue that the leading feature in the Dravidian cults is the worship of the female. It is possible that the Aryan deities are the gods of a race of worriers, whereas the Dravidian deities are the goddesses of an agricultural people. All over the south Indian villages, deities were almost exclusively female. In the Tamil speaking areas, it is more prominent and that most of these female goddesses have male attendants who are supposed to guard the shrines and carryout the commands of the Goddesses, but their place is distinctly subordinate. In the Telugu speaking areas too there is a male attendant called Poturaju who figures with ambivalent identity; sometimes as the brother and sometimes as the husband of the village Goddess and sometimes merely as an attendant. But one can never see him as an independent god or a deity. Also never a sacrifice is offered to the male god alone, but only in conjunction with one or more of the female deities. This can be observed even today among the Andhra Dalits. The goddesses have wide cosmological jurisdiction extending beyond household spheres like community, health, property, crop and weather. The shrine of the Goddess may range from a 'small brick-building of three or four feet high to a small enclosure with a few rough stones in the centre and 'no enclosure at all which is the more often case'.[30] They worship often not the idols but shapeless stones or weapons, and the idols are argued as products of external intervention.[31]

More importantly, there is less religiosity among the Dalits than any other section of the Indian society. Going to temples, chanting prayers, or performing *sandhyavandanam* (worshipping at dawn) is unknown to them. Until the Missionary sponsored modern education and Babasaheb Ambedkar's theory of reservation, letter-learning was literally prohibited and reading a book was unknown to Dalits. This confirms the fact that religious texts did not at all exist among the Dalits. Neither idol-based worship nor *Pujari* or priest centred temples were known to them. They only worshipped their ancestral Gods, and *Grama-Devatas*, (village goddesses). These village goddesses were without any written histories and without any incarnations, e.g., Mutyalamma, the pearl Goddess, Chinnintamma, the goddess who is head of the house, Gangalamma, Polamma and Sunkalamma. The Poleramma, the goddess who protects the village, Peddamma, the goddesses of chicken pox, were common goddesses of every village in the south. They pray these Goddesses because they secure them and protect them. Nobody knews who their husbands were or how they looked. Dalits or for that matter any commoner could directly communicate to their goddess without any kind of mediation from the priests.

No Purity and Pollution

The concepts of purity and pollution are not relevant to Dalit beliefs. They do not attach any holiness to the place of worship or the 'symbols' placed therein. During the festivals the whole community comes together to celebrate and participate in the festivities.[32] The community is more important than the place of worship or symbols to Dalits. In the so-called 'greater tradition', only men are considered appropriate for conducting rituals and performing the duty of an intermediatory between the divinity and the people. Women perform only menial jobs like cleaning and sweeping. Even the *devadasis* (servants of the deity) were restricted from entering into the *sanctum sanatorium* of the temples.

The Hindu women are subdued and under constant male control. In contrast, a Dalit women lives as an independent and vigorous female principle. Lynn Gatwood, who has effectively brought forth the underlying versions of femininity in Indian cultural patterns, says that an independent, fertile and unblushing female principle may be discovered within the historical and ethnographic complexity of Indian villages. And yet for various reasons, including orientation towards Sanskrit (orthodox) belief systems and the Hindu bias in the treatment of female deities and perhaps even an academic inertia to this goddess and the type of femininity that she represents, she has been generally overlooked. Instead a male-controlled religiously marginal and morally ambiguous goddess has become the sole representative of the female principle.[33]

Gatwood further distinguishes two distinct versions of the female principles . One of which is free from male control and the other necessarily defined by such control. She calls the control free, non-Sanskrit version as the Devi, and the control-defined Sanskrit one as the spouse goddess.[34] The gender inequality and functional separation between the orthodox gods and goddesses also reflects in the hierarchical interaction involved in their worship. There are symbolic differences between the two types of goddesses. The 'low' caste or outcaste women enjoy relative equality and plays an interchangeable role with their husbands in their day-to-day life while the 'high' caste woman plays inferior and gender-specified marital roles.

Gender Equality

In the non-Dalit societies, the roles of man and woman are markedly segregate.[35] A Hindu or 'high' caste woman does little or no extra domestic or caste-occupational work. The spheres of man's and woman's activities tended to be sharply separated, especially in the north and among the communities who observe *purdah*—the custom keeping the women-folk of the family close to the household by restricting their movement and keeping them inside the court yards except on rare occasions, when they must be accompanied by male relatives. Hindu women secluded in this way can have only very limited visits and contacts outside their kinship. High caste women rarely engage in agricultural or caste specific occupational work and nor their husbands do the household work, except exceptionally.[36]

By contrast, in Dalit societies, women-folk work both in the fields and in caste occupations. Their husbands in turn do considerable amount of household work. Household duties are shared is even interchangeable.[37] The most common tasks such as food preparation, marketing, animal-feeding and childcare are performed by both sexes among the Dalits. Dalit women are much more independent economically and socially than their caste Hindu counterparts.

Differences between 'high' and 'low' caste women extend from economic realm to social autonomy and decision making. Dalit women possess a good deal of social autonomy and formal authority. 'Lower' caste women are equipped with necessary knowledge for management of land, if at all they possess any. Along with men they also involve actively in financial, decision making, and legal matters. Such practices ensure their freedom of movement.

In the household sphere too there is mutual cooperation and no rigid division of household duties as in caste-Hindu families. A great number of domestic and non-domestic tasks are interchangeable. Household work is shared by children of both sexes including teenage boys who may be frequently seen cleaning grains, carrying water, cooking and sweeping, all of which are considered as feminine by the patriarchal Hindu societies.[38] Even Dube, describes the customary division of labour in a Hyderabad village says that such division is not a law, strictly binding on the community, but flexible and no censure is attached to interchange of domestic and non-domestic activities performed by either sex.[39]

The lower caste used to pay bride price (a practice loosing its hold) for the anticipated value of her work and fertility to the husband's lineage. This system was in opposition to the dowry system being practiced in a cultural system of the upper caste-Hindus where women are economically dependent without any productive potential. Among the Dalits, marriage is not considered as a sacred or divinely ordained ritual. Divorce is easier and can be initiated by either of the spouse. Widows are not shunned or suppressed.

Remarriages are common. This observation also corresponds to Mandelbaum's study. He notes that Dalit women may divorce easily and widows and divorces frequently remarry.[40] These women are not so isolated from their natal families and can earn wages as field workers. The tendency of the educated and economically better off Dalits to emulate the familiar norms and religious practices of Hindus has also worked towards the misconstruction of an erroneous Dalit cultural identity. So is the serious problem involved in overlooking women as heterogeneous body within specific cultural entities.[41]

Hindu cultural values are unequal and inhuman in nature. The Hindu morality is just opposite to Dalit morality. An ideal woman in the Hindu society is one who does not eat or drink in the presence of older woman and men. Patriarchy is upheld and unquestioned. Womanhood is discussed in terms of devotion to the husband, cooking with strict adherence to ideas of purity and pollution in mind. A woman is not supposed to smoke and drink even if the man is a chain smoker and a drunkard. In Dalit homes, no one talks badly about a woman who smokes or drinks, rather both the wife and husband light their *chutta* (the cigar) with the same matchstick. The whole family sit together for food. Dalit women participate in all activities both in home front, and in the fields equally. Even in the decision making of every family related matter, she has a voice.

Dalit Language

Dalit language, despite its regional variations, is structured by its own grammar. It is flexible and is based on production and is developed orally. Without the written script it is not less sophisticated than standard Brahminical language. Dalits do share and speak symbolic language of hierarchy, purity and pollution, but their meaning is different. The insights of Michael Bakhtin[42] illuminate this point. He speaks of hidden polemic and dialogue in speech acts. While analysis of structuralists focusses on 'grammatical' structure of symbolic language, Vincentnathan puts his analysis on a 'socio-linguistic' or dialogue level where symbols are manipulated to create different Dalit cultural meanings suited to people's intentions and social situations and in response to the expressed meanings of others.[43] Dalit children experience of the language begin with the fixing names of flora and fauna around them. Every living and non-living things around them bears a name. Many of these things do not have standard equivalent words in the caste Hindu language and they cannot understand Dalit ways of making-up new names. These names are not taught through a written word but are orally repeated in communication that is use-based. Mostly, Dalit language is structured around the production process that they are involved in.

Concluding Remarks

The Brahmin-baniya combination along with the sanskritized twice-born thinks that their non-productive ritualistic life is great and the non-ritualistic working life of the Dalits is meaningless. This philosophical make-up moulds the whole society differently. The non-Dalit person think that they are the greatest race and they are better placed. All this was proclaimed so consistently from time immemorial that it went in to Dalit psyche as if it might be true. Thus, the Brahmanism consolidated its own socio-cultural position in the social ladder. If at all there is any cultural similarity of Dalits with any other section of Indian society, is perhaps with non-Brahminized un-sanskritized Shudras but certainly not with Hindu society or Hindu culture.

The foregone descriptions and discussions reveal the fact that there are many cultures in India, and it is wrong to project Hindu culture as Indian culture. Religious practices and beliefs of Dalits shows that the Dalits have never been followers of Hinduism except by those few literate and economically better off Dalits who tried to Brahmanize or Sanskritize themselves. Finally, Dalits are neither culture free nor cultureless as some of the studies would claim. They have their own rich culture that is characterised by progressive and egalitarian features, which, have never been recognised by the representatives of the so called 'Greater Tradition'.

An earlier version of this paper has been presented at Cultural Workshop (of CSSS, Culcutta) on 'Critiques on Culture' held at Bharatpur, Rajasthan, (24-28 February, 2000).

NOTES

1. E.B. Tylor, 1971.
2. Alfred L.Kroebar and Clyde Kluchohn, 1952.
3. Clifford Geertz, 1966, p. 3.
4. It is a point to be noted here is when a Brahmin sociologist M.N. Srinivas conceptualized the process of sanskritization, was originally used for Brahminization. But later on, as the term 'Brahmanization' he felt was a narrow and to make it more broader and perhaps to get out of the castiest components he changed from Brahminization to Sanskritization.
5. Benard S. Cohn, 1994, p. 94.
6. Cited in K.K.N. Kurup, 1996, pp. 21-28.
7. For details see, M.B.Gautam, 1991.
8. Chandrakanth Vagamare, 1994.
9. K.N. Panikkar, 1991, Introduction, and 1997, pp. 73-88.
10. Kenneth David, 1977, pp. 179-226; also see William Houska, 1981 and Michael Moffat, 1979.
11. For details see Robert J. Miller, 1966, pp. 26-42; J.P. Mencher, 1974, pp. 469-493; R.K. Khare, 1984; James M.Freeman, 1986, pp. 153-171.
12. Michael Moffatt, 1979, pp. 9-13.
13. For counter arguments see Robert Deliege, 1992, pp. 155-173. Later this became a debate for some time. For a David Mosse, 1994 for "Comment" and Robert Deliege, 1994, for response.
14. Jose Kananaikil, 1982, pp. 247-268; Clifford Geertz, 1966, pp. 1-46.
15. Kathleen Gough, 1956, pp. 826-853; Gerald D. Berreman, 1979, pp. 155-163.
16. Michael Moffatt, 1979, p. 303.
17. Milton Singer, 1975, pp. 121-159.
18. See Bernard S. Cohn, 1954.

19. Robert J. Miller, 1966, pp. 26-42, Martin Orans (1965) also developed similar ides while studying Santal.

20. Max Weber, 1964, p. 43.

21. For them Dalit is a symbol of change and a revolution, who believes in humanism, rejects the existence of God, rebirth, soul, 'sacred' books that teach discrimination, fate and heaven. See ": Dalit panthers manifesto" in Barbara R.Joshi, 1986, pp. 141-147; also see Eleanor Zelliot, 1996, pp. 267-292. While studying north Indian "Untouchable" communities, R.S.Khare (1984) found that certain segments and is in the process of constructing new ideologies to support the kinds of action necessary for social change. Dalit's examination of classical caste ideology, 'From the bottom up' and their interpretation for the mythic origin of the four varnas, see Premkumar Mani, 1975; Sunderlal Sagar, 1973. For a good translation along with a meaningful inter-pretation of these works see Michael B.Schwartz, 1977, pp. 177-191.

22. Lynn Vincentnathan, 1987 and 1993, pp. 53-82; also see Richard A. Shweder and Edmund J.Bourne, 1984, pp. 158-199.

23. Louis Dumont, 1970, pp. 33-64.

24. Talcott Parsons and Edward A. Shills, 1951, pp. 3-29.

25. Lynn Vincentnathan, 1993, pp. 53-82.

26. For details see Henry Whithead, 1921.

27. J.H.Hutton, 1963, p. 154.

28. For details see Lynn E.Gatwood, 1985.

29. Spouse Goddess here means the wives of the Hindu Gods, i.e. Shiva, Vishnu etc. Lynn Gatwood argues that Devi is a non-Sanskrit Goddess and entirely different and vice-versa from spouse Goddess.

30. Henry Whithead, 1921, p. 16.

31. James Theophilius Appavoo, 1998, pp. 111-121.

32. *Ibid.* 117.

33. Lynn Gatwood, 1985, Introduction.

34. *Ibid.* p. 1.

35. For details Kathleen Gough, 1956, pp. 826-853.

36. David G.Mandelbaum, 1970.

37. Helen E.Ullrich, 1977.
38. For more details of this aspect see Mary Scarle-Chatterjee, 1981.
39. See S.C.Dube, 1963 and 1955.
40. David G.Mandelbaum, 1970.
41. For details of this aspect see, Priyadarshini Vijaisri, K., 1997 and 2004.
42. Michael Bahktin, 1978, pp. 176-196.
43. Lynn Vincentnathan, 1993, p. 54; also see Gopal Guru, 1997.

6

Change and Continuity in Nomenclature

This chapter studies the concepts or labels that are struck on Dalits; how and why those constructions were made and how Dalits made attempts for its deconstruction and simultaneously, reconstruction of their own identity. An examination of the varied terms arouses a curiosity as to how and when the system of untouchability came into existence and what were the factors that helped its continuation; perhaps, in no other country such a dehumanizing system has survived so many political and economic changes as untouchability in India.

The identification of Dalits and their struggles with those of African Americans, Vietnamese, Cambodians and Africans indicates the internal identity of the oppressed peoples, which is more explicitly stated in their respective manifestos. The only difference of Dalits from those of other oppressed lot else where is the problem of untouchability, a peculiar phenomenon peculiar to India. Social stigmatization and perennial poverty are the basic features of the Dalits. Segregated by the society, they are marginalized by the polity, and oppressed by the power mongers. Acts of brutality and terror continue to be part of the atrocities perpetuated on Dalits; the more they become conscious of their rights and begin asserting themselves they are being tortured so that they do not raise their voice on the existing social norms. But when one looks at their history, probably they are the only lot continuously being used and abused by the rest of the society. Throughout history, they were labelled as untouchables, impure, Outcastes and polluted. These labels change from time-to-time and place-to-place depending upon their purpose. By deconstruction of these articulated labels, Dalits keep on reconstructing their own identity with a collective conscience. But their conscious liberation, quest for identity still lied ahead. The road that struggle takes invariably has important consequences extending far beyond the "untouchable" minority. In spite of twentieth century changes and 58 years of political Independence nothing much has changed. The Dalits are still concentrated at the bottom of the two hierarchies i.e., caste and class, that define so much of Indian life.

The constructions of a label or a nomenclature to identify the untouchables have undergone many a change and each time it appears with a new nomenclature with a salient dimension to their identity. The Hindu doctrine of creation exemplified in the *Chaturvarna* scheme of social stratification, does not clearly account for the origin of untouchables, because all those who belong to the four varnas are above the pollution line. However, by implication, those who are below the pollution line are fifth *varna*, hence called *panchamas*. The identity of the Dalits was defined in the context of the doctrine of creation and its context was essentially religious. Legitimized by the theory of *karma* and reincarnation, the *panchamas* deserved to be untouchables.[1] These nomenclatures were crystallized and transformed multi-dimensionally in particular contexts and given times.

Untouchability with its manifold manifestations is rooted in the notions of purity, pollution, which is believed to have developed in the later Vedic period, when the Brahminic literature emerged in the form of *Smritis, Samhitas* and the *Upanishads*. The Rig-Veda shows no acquaintance with people, with whom contact was even remotely tabooed. In the later Vedic period texts refer to the *chandala*[2] and the *poulkasa*[3] as manifest objects of spite and abhorrence. They existed at the lowest ritualistic and social ladder, but were not treated as untouchables. According to *Baudayana Dharma Sutra*, a *Chandala* is an offspring of Shudra father and a Brahmin mother.[4] The notion of pollution become a potent reality and was seen in full display with respect to the *Chandalas.* Although the Brahminical texts are not unanimous on the origin of *Chandala*, he was represented as an instrument of derivative pollution as well as transmitting contagion through contact. Further, the references to infection from the *chanadala* through sight, speech and proximity occur. These are *Nisada*, the *Kaivartha*, the *Dasa* the *Bidalakari*, the *Malaga*, and so on. The commensal and connubial taboos in relation to the *chandala* became severe and absolute. Subsequently, several castes were began to be treated as "untouchables."

Below mentioned three tables reveals that the manner in which the proliferation of untouchable population, may be one angle. These three tables speaks for themselves of three varieties: *anuloma* children; *pratiloma* children and the children of the *mixed-varna*.

Tables of Inter-Varna Marriages and Their Progenies

(a) Anuloma Children

Authority	*Parentage*		*Child*	*Reference*
	Father	*Mother*		
1. Baudhayana dharmasutra	Brahmana	Kshatriya	Savarna	1.9.1-5
	Brahmana	Vaisya	Ambastha	
	Brahmana	Shudra	Parasava/Naisada	
	Kshatriya	Vaisya	Savarna	
	Kshatriya	Shudra	Ugra	
	Vaisya	Shudra	Rathakara	
2. Gautama-dharmasutra	Brahmana	Kshatriya	Savarna/	Mitra 195:158
	Brahmana	Vaisya	Murdhavasika	
	Brahmana	Shudra	Nisada/Bhujjya	
	Ksatriya	Vaisya	Kanaka	
	Ksatriya	Shudra	Parasava	
	Vaisya	Shudra	Ambastha/Mahisya	
			Dausyanta/Yavana	
			Ugra/Karana	

(Contd.)

Authority	*Parentage*		*Child*	*Reference*
	Father	*Mother*		
3. Vaikhanasa-smartasutra	Brahmana	Kshatriya	Savarna/Nrpa	Mitra 1965:158
	Brahmana	Vaisya	Ambastha	
	Brahmana	Shudra	Parasava	
	Kshatriya	Vaisya	Madgu/Mahanarma	
	Kshatriya	Shudra	Ugra	
	Vaisya	Shudra	Cucaka	
4. Arthasastra of Kautilya	Brahmana	Kshatriya	Savarna	AS.III.7
	Brahmana	Vaisya	Ambastha	*Ibid.*
	Brahmana	Shudra	Nisada/Parasava	*Ibid.*
	Kshatriya	Vaisya	Savarna	*Ibid.*
	Kshatriya	Shudra	Ugra	*Ibid.*
	Vaisya	Shudra	Sudra	*Ibid.*
5. Sasvatakosa	Brahmana	Ksatriya	—	
	Brahmana	Vaisya	—	
	Brahmana	Shudra	—	
	Kshatriya	Vaisya	—	
	Kshatriya	Shudra	—	
	Vaisya	Shudra	Ugra	
6. Manusmrti	Brahmana	Ksatriya	Murdhavasika	SK. 1984
	Brahmana	Vaisya	Ambastha	MS.X 8
	Brahmana	Shudra	Parasava/Nisada	*Ibid.*
	Kshatriya	Vaisya	Mahisya	
	Kshatriya	Shudra	Ugra	
	Vaisya	Shudra	Karana	
7. Amarakosa	Brahmana	Ksatriya	—	MS. X 9.
	Brahmana	Vaisya	—	AK. II. 102
	Brahmana	Shudra	Ambastha	
	Kshatriya	Vaisya	—	
	Kshatriya	Shudra	—	
	Vaisya	Shudra	—	
8. Vasisthasmrti	Brahmana	Kshatriya	—	Vasistha
	Brahmana	Vaisya	Ambastha	XVIII.8
	Brahmana	Shudra	Nisada	Vasistha
	Kshatriya	Vaisya	—	XVIII.9
	Kshatriya	Shudra	—	
	Vaisya	Shudra	—	

(b) Pratiloma Children

Authority	Parentage: Father	Parentage: Mother	Child	Reference
1. Baudhayana-	Shudra	Brahmana	Candala	1.9.1-5
dharma-sutra	Shudra	Kshatriya	Ksatta	
	Shudra	Vaisya	Magadha	
	Kshatriya	Brahmana	Suta	
	Kshatriya	Kshatriya	Ayogava	
	Kshatriya	Brahmana	—	
			—	
2. Gautama	Shudra	Brahmana	Vaidehaka/	Mitra
dharma sutra	Shudra	Kshatriya	Pulkasa	1965:160
	Shudra	Vaisya	Valdahaka/	
	Vaisya	Brahmana	Ayogava	
	Vaisya	Kshatriya	Ksattri/	
	Kshatriya	Brahmana	Magadha	
			Magadha/	
			Dhavira	
			Suta	
3. Vaikhanasa-	Shudra	Brahmana	Candala	Mitra
smartasutra	Shudra	Kshatriya	Pulkasa	1965:161
	Shudra	Vaisya	Vaidehaka	
	Vaisya	Brahmana	Magadha	
	Vaisya	Kshatriya	Ayogava	
	Kshatriya	Brahmana	Suta	
4. Arthasastra of	Shudra	Brahmana	Candala	AS. II. 7
Kautilya	Shudra	Kshatriya	Ksatta	*Ibid.*
	Shudra	Vaisya	Ayogava	*Ibid.*
	Vaisya	Brahmana	Vaidehaka	*Ibid.*
	Vaisya	Kshatriya	Magadha	*Ibid.*
	Ksatriya	Brahmana	Suta	*Ibid.*
	Ugra	Ksatta	Svapaka	*Ibid.*
5. Sasvatakosa	Shudra	Brahmana	Candala	SK.345
	Shudra	Kshatriya	Ksattri	
	Shudra	Vaisya	—	
	Vaisya	Brahmana	Vaidehaka	
	Vaisya	Kshatriya	Magadha	
	Kshatriya	Brahmana	Suta	
			Candala	

(Contd.)

Authority	*Parentage*		*Child*	*Reference*
	Father	*Mother*		
			Ksatta	
			Ayogava	
			Vaiodeha	
			Magadha	
			Suta	
6. Manusmrti	Shudra	Brahmana	Candala	SK.276
	Shudra	Kshatriya	Ksatta	MS. X 12.
	Shudra	Vaisya	Ayogava	*Ibid.*
	Vaisya	Brahmana	Vaideha	*Ibid.*
	Vaisya	Kshatriya	Magadha	MS.X.11.
	Kshatriya	Brahmana	Suta	Ibid.
7. Amarakosa	Shudra	Brahmana	Candala	AK. II. 10.4
	Shudra	Kshatriya	Ksatta	
	Shudra	Vaisya	—	AK.II.10.3
	Vaisya	Brahmana	Vaidehaka	AK.II.10.2
	Vaisya	Kshatriya	Magadha	AK.II.10.3
	Kshatriya	Brahmana	Suta	
8. Vasisthasmrti	Shudra	Brahmana	Candala	Vaisitha XVIII 1
	Shudra	Kshatriya	Vaina	Vaisitha XIII 2
	Shudra	Vaisya	Antyavasayin	Vaisitha XIII 3
	Vaisya	Brahmana	Ramaka	Vaisitha XIII 4
	Vaisya	Kshatriya	Pulkasa	Vaisitha XIII 5
	Kshatriya	Brahmana	Suta	

(c) Mixed-Varna Children

Authority	*Parentage*		*Sons*	*Reference*
	Father	*Mother*		
1. Baudhayana-dharmasutra	Ugra	Ksattri	Svapaca	
	Vaisya	Sudra	(Ambastha + Brahmana)	
			Rathakara	
2. Vaikhanasas-	Brahmana	Brahmana	Napita	Mitra

(Contd.)

Authority	*Parentage*		*Sons*	*Reference*
	Father	*Mother*		
martasutra	Candala	Brahmana	(Adultery) Svapaca	1965:158, 162
3. Arthasastra of Kautilya	Ambastha	Vaidehaka	Rahakara Vena	
4. Manusmrti	Ksatta	Ugra	Svapaca	Mitra 1965:158-60, 162.

Source: These are compilations from the below mentioned Brahminical texts.
Boudhayana Dharmasutra, Kasi Sanskrit Series no. 104, Banaras. 1934.
Jha, Gangavath (ed.) *Makusmriti* 2 vols, Calcutta, 1939.
Kulakarni, Narayan Nathji, (ed.), *Sarvakosa or the Anakartha Samuchchaya of Sasvata*, Pune (n.d.).
Mitra, Veda, *India of Dharma sutras*, Delhi, 1965.
Sastri, T. Ganapati, *The Arthasastra of Kautilya* 3 vols, Trivendrum, 1925.
Sharma, Pandit Vishnu Datta, (ed.), *Aurarakusa*, Bombay, 1929.
Vasistha Smriti, See in V.G. —— (ed), *Smrtinam Samuchchaya*, Anandasvama Sanskrit Series, No. 48.

As mentioned in the above tables, it is clear that the *chandalas* were not one single homogeneous class, but the offspring of five different varieties: *(a)* the offspring of a *sudra* father and a Brahmin mother; *(b)* child of an unmarried woman; *(c)* offspring of Brahmin's union with *sagotra* woman; *(d)* offspring of ascetics who abandoned ascetism and made return to the household or material life and *(e)* an offspring of barber father and Brahmin mother.[5] Segregation was the natural corollary to the ardently preached and widely shared belief in pollution and several terms such as *antya* (the last or at the end), *bahya* (outside, pale of Chaturvarna hence became outcaste), *antyaja* (born at the end), *antavasin* (one who lives in the end) testify to the current practice. Perhaps, all this meant a conscious perpetuation of an old state of affairs and created a definite barrier to free mixing in future. Most often, these generic terms developed into a specific caste name, as it happened in the case of *Nishada* (an offspring of Brahmin father and Shudra mother),[6] and *Antyavasin*. Thus, use of words *Antyaja* and *Antyavasin* is significant. Firstly, it shows that they were living in separate quarters and secondly they were pushed to the corner by the victorious invaders. This was even recorded by the Chinese pilgrim Fahien, (contemporary of Chandra Gupta – II), who lived in India between 405 AD and 411 AD. He stated that the *Chandalas* lived apart from others... i.e., "in separate quarters".[7] The next Chinese traveller, Yuan Chaung, who visited India in 629 AD, reiterated that "these people were forced to live outside the city..."[8] *Purusha Sukta*, a part of the Rigveda states, "from the face of *Virat Purusha* were born the *Brahmins* (thinkers), from his hands the *Kshatriyas* (kings), from his things the *Vaishyas* (traders) and from his feet the *Shudras* (servants)",[9] a mythical and an unbelievable lie. This hymn reveals although irrational and unscientific, about the genesis of the Chatarvarna. However, none of the *Vedas* has references to the untouchability. But there are references to *Asuras*, *Dasas* or *Dasyas* and *Raksasas* with hatred and contempt. The concept of *panchamas* referred to in the *Narada smriti*, speaks of the slaves as the fifth class or fifth order. This label was struck on them by the Brahmins–the self-appointed value givers and norm setters of the time.

By the time of medieval period, the clear-cut growth and practice of untouchability was witnessed. In the beginning of the eleventh century, Alberuni visited India and left some valuable accounts. He observed that the Shudras followed by a section of people, Antyaja or outcaste (outside the *Chaturvarna*), were engaged in eight varieties of crafts and vocations. Those were sailor, fishermen, jugglers, basket makers, weavers, shoe-makers and hunters of birds and wild animals.[10] Nevertheless, it is considered that prior to Muslim invasions of the thirteenth century was a determining period for the status and occupational duties of untouchables.[11] During *bhakti* movement that swept India from the eighth to the eighteenth centuries untouchables were honoured as saints and poets. Nandanar (700-900), a Shaivate saint from Tamil Nadu and his contemporary Tiruppan, became one of the twelve Vaishnavite *Alvars*. The first expression of the concern for the Dalits came from the Bhakti period during the fourteenth-fifteenth centuries in the form of religious reforms. The Hindu reformer, Ramananda, preached equality and chose his disciples, even from among the untouchables. One of his twelve disciples, Rai Das, was a Chamar from Banaras. He found a sect/association of Chamars known as Raidasis or Ravidasis, who followed the teachings of Ramandanda. The *Bhakti* movement also gave rise to the poet saints of Maharashtra, among who were Chokhamela and his entire family, the Mahars of fourteenth century, who fought against untouchability.

The Bhakti tradition rejected the authority of the Vedas, Brahmin priesthood and ritual practices, but failed to recover the lost identity. The revolt continued in various forms till the eighteenth century. However, each of revolting group was reabsorbed into Hindu fold. Perhaps, the last saint poet in this stream was Narsi Mehta, from Gujarat, who coined the term "Harijan". The term Harijan literally means children of God. There is considerable debate on the meaning of the term. In fact, the term initially was used only to refer to the children of *Devadasis*, the female temple dancers. Symbolically speaking, they were children of God and *Devadasi* (*deva* means God and *dasi* means servant) were dedicated to the services of god/goddess and the sexual union between the agents (priests and nobility of the village) and the servants of the god was mystified and even invested with an aura of divinity. However, the children of Devadasi had a stigmatized identity among the general population because of their ambiguous paternal identity.[12] The term "Harijan" surfaced again, when M.K. Gandhi picked it up in the early twentieth century and popularized the term. But, it was totally rejected by the conscious "untouchables" as in this terminology, the Dalits perceived another attempt to subtle segregation from the rest of society.[13]

In the modern period, European visitors to India noted the existence of despised groups, and the Tamil word *Pariah* lent its name to the English vocabulary as a synonym for an Outcaste from society. For them, Pariah meant a person of low caste, or of no caste or a socially outcaste.[14] The Tamil *Pariah* is derived from Paraiyar, the plural form of *paraiyan* in Tamil means 'hereditary drummer', but its common usage refers to a low caste of southern India below the Shudras. The word *Pariah* occurs for the first time in a poem of Mangudi Kilar, a second century (A.D.) poet. It is not found in any earlier Tamil literature or in any ancient inscriptions. Towards the close of nineteenth century, Gopalkrishna Ghokhale, often described the state of Indians as the *pariahs* of the British Empire.[15] In course of time, it acquired so much pejorative connotation that it began to convey the opposite of all that is holy and respectable.[16]

At the first association of the untouchables was formed in 1892, the suggestion to designate it as Paraiya Mahajana Sabha was suggested. However, the same association, in a memorandum presented to Lord Chelmsford and B.S. Montagu in 1917, requested them to help them in their efforts to attain social elevation by issuing orders to the effect that they should be designated as Adi-Dravidas, or the original Dravidians in all government communications. Accordingly, government designated them as Adi-Dravidas.[17]

With the advent of the British, their policies though originally not intended to uplift the Dalits, benefited them like a blessing in disguise. The benefits can be called unintended positive effects of a policy that was not specifically geared to a specific purpose. Simultaneously, through the census, the efforts of British colonial government tried to collect systematic information about the many aspects of the natives and society, thereby giving an opportunity to the Dalits not just to know about themselves but also about their counterparts in the rest of the country.

The 1920s witnessed some major changes and challenges to the Dalits as a new set of self-conscious identities, with greater assertiveness by the Dalit radicals with a claim that they were the original inhabitants of the land, and the "sons of the soil" began to gather momentum by then. This culminated with an "Adi" ideology that came to be prefixed to their regional identity. While those from the Telugu speaking areas called themselves as Adi-Andhras, those from Tamil speaking Dalits named as Adi-Dravidas, and from the Kannada-speaking regions as Adi-Kannadas. But in Hyderabad, Telugu speaking Dalits called themselves as Adi-Hindus and a large section of them gave a militant, anti-Brahmin interpretation to this. For them the word Hindu did not mean the follower of a particular religion. As early as in 1917, the first provincial Adi-Andhra Mahasabha claimed that the so-called *Panchamas* were the original sons of the soil and that they were the rulers of the country.[18] U.P. too, began to organize the Dalits on the basis of an Adi-Hindu identity under the leadership of the untouchable ascetic, Acchatananda, who argued that the untouchables were in fact Adi-Hindus, or the original or autochthonous Nagas or Dasas of the north and the Dravidas of the South of the subcontinent and they were the undisputed, heavenly owners of Bharat. And that all the rest were immigrants to the land, including the Aryans, who conquered the original populations.[19] Similar arguments persisted among the Dalits of Punjab, who organized themselves into the Adi-Dharm movement.[20]

During the 1930s, emerged a new set of British official euphemisms for the Dalits, such as the "Depressed Classes", the "Exterior Castes", and the "Scheduled Castes". In 1930, the Indian Statutory Commission defined that in origin, these castes seemed to be partly functional comprising those who followed occupations which were deemed to be unclean or degrading, such as scavenging, leather works and partly tribal i.e., aboriginal tribes absorbed into the Hindu fold and transformed into an imposed caste.[21] The term 'exterior castes' appeared for the first time in the census of 1931. This term for the Hindu castes, hitherto known as Depressed Classes, was originally suggested by C.S. Mullan, the Census Superintendent for Assam, and was adopted in the 1931 census report as the most satisfactory alternative to the unfortunate sections of population as the label "Depressed Classes" is so depressing. But it was criticized as being the same term as outcaste. Outcaste correctly interpreted seems to mean no more than one who is outside the caste system and is therefore, not admitted to the Hindu society. But, in practice, the exterior castes also meant those who were cast out from the Hindu social body for some breach of caste rules. The term outcaste or outcast was in some cases synonymous with exterior caste and had derogatory implications of obliquity attaching to the latter term had unjustly coloured the former, a taint that was not conveyed by the substitution of the word exterior.

The instructions of the Government of India for conducting the census 1931 concluded with a rejoinder saying "the Government of India also desire that attention should be paid to the collection of information leading to a better knowledge of the backward and Depressed Classes and of the problem involved in their present and future welfare." It also explained that the "depressed classes as castes, contact with whom entails purification on the part of high caste Hindus. It is not intended that the term should have any reference to occupation as such, but to these castes, which by reason of their traditional position in Hindu society, are denied access to temples, or to use separate wells, or not allowed to sit inside a school building but have to remain outside or suffer similar social disabilities. These disabilities vary in different parts of India and are much more severe in the south of India than elsewhere. At the same time, the castes are listed for a definite area, though perhaps the lists for India as a whole will not coincide."[22]

The question of preparation of lists for each province was discussed at a meeting of the Superintendents of Census operations in January 1931 before the census took place. It was decided that each province should make a list of castes who suffered disability on account of their low social position and on account of being debarred from temples, schools or wells. No specific definition of the Depressed Castes was framed and no more precise instructions were issued to the Superintendents of census operations because it was realized that conditions varied so much from one province to another and in some provinces from district to district, as it was felt unwise to tie down the Superintendents of census operations with too many meticulous instructions. The general method prescribed was local inquiry into what castes were held to be depressed and why so and then framing of a list accordingly.[23]

The census of 1931 has played an important role, at least in case of Dalit history for more than one reason. All census reports preceding to the 1931 suffered greatly in terms of accuracy and were termed as estimations. Every new estimate, either increased their number or added to the conflicting statements. For instance, the commissioner, in 1921 gave what he described as *minimum* number of the Depressed Classes in various provinces making a total of 52,680,000.[24] This figure according to him must be taken as "low estimate", as it did not include all those who should have been included. He confidently approximated the number of Depressed Classes between 55 and 60 million. Of the 52.6 millions for which the census Commissioner gave actual figures, less than 43.5 million were to be found in British-India. This figure fairly agreed with the 42 million as given the figures of the Depressed Classes by the Franchise Committee of 1919. This was not too at variance with 44.5 million estimated by the Nair Central Committee of 1929 as the figure of Depressed Classes, but it varies considerably from the Hartog Committee's figure of approximately 30 million.

The governmental agencies estimate these numbers for various purposes. For instance, the data prescribed by the Seventh Quin-Quinnial Review was meant for the educational uplift of the Dalits. The data ascertained by the Home Department was intended for partial implementation of the resolution moved in the Imperial Legislative Council for ameliorating the conditions of the Dalits. All these numbers remained as approximate figures and not accurate. So, the 1931 census decided to procure some more definite figures to be obtained than the estimations hitherto employed. However, they found it difficult to arrive at a definite numbers of the Dalits.

The following tests were introduced to consider a person a member of Depressed Class: (1) Whether the caste or class in question can be served by barbers, water-carriers tailors, etc., who serve the caste-Hindus; (2) Whether the caste or class can be served by a clean Brahmin; (3) Whether the caste pollutes a high caste Hindu by contact or by proximity; (4) Whether the caste or class is one from whose hands a caste Hindu can draw water from; (5) Whether the caste or class in question is debarred from using public conveniences, such as roads, ferries, wells or schools; (6) Whether the caste or class is debarred from the use of Hindu temples; (7) Whether in ordinary social inter-course a well educated member of the caste or class is equal as the high caste; (8) Whether the caste or class is merely depressed on account of its own ignorance, illiteracy or poverty and but for that not subjected to any social disability and (9) Whether the group is depressed on account of the occupation being followed for which it is not subjected to any social disability.

The above mentioned tests were conducted by the Census operators to find out the exact number of the Depressed Classes. Though these tests were not altogether free of difficulty, they however, clearly pointed to the cases of disability as the crucial testing element. It was at least clear that the above mentioned forms of backwardness were not intended to enter into the definition process. The insufficiency of any single test to identify the "untouchables" provoked a variety of responses on the Franchise (Lothian) Committee.[25] However, majority of the Committee members, adhering to the denial of access to temples and causing pollution by touch or approach as generally accepted tests of untouchability, reiterated its conviction that the Depressed Class should include only untouchables and not those Hindus who are only economically poor and in other ways backward but not regarded as "untouchables".[26] Finally, all those untouchable groups were listed or scheduled in 1935 for giving effect to the provisions for special electoral representation in the Government of India Act of 1935. These scheduled groups of communities, later known as Scheduled Castes, adopted by the Indian Constitution, legalized the term to use in its all official purposes.

Though the concept Dalit is comparatively more recent in origin, although is not very recent in coinage as some of the scholars suggest.[27] But some recent theological research shows that the concepts such as the *Dalit, dal, dalah* etc., have been extensively used in the Hebrew language too.[28] But, the concept of *Dalit* came vogue in 1972 in Maharashtra with the formation of Dalit Panthers movement. For the Dalit Panthers, the Dalit is a symbol of change and revolution, who believes in humanism, rejects the existence of God, rebirth, the concept of soul, the sacred books that teach discrimination, fate and heaven. They rejected religion and priesthood because these have made them slaves.[29] The Dalit literally means trampled, squeezed, crushed or broken, or reduced in to pieces. Therefore, the Dalit is the most secular identity that a person could possess. It denotes more of a class, than a caste. And today it's being increasingly used as synonym for the ex-untouchables. However, initially it was used only to denote a particular community called Mahars and later on it began to denote all the Scheduled Castes. Namadeo Dhosal, a powerful Mahar poet and one of the founders of the Dalit Panther movement, widened its scope to include all the Scheduled Castes, Tribes, and landless labourers and the economically exploited lot. But again, it was applied only to the Scheduled Castes, as distinct from Tribal and OBCs.[30]

In the background of Dalit Panthers movement, the Dalit sahitya movement emerged and the term was legitimized and reinforced with each passing day. Though the expression of Dalit is largely used in Andhra and Maharashtra and Tamil Nadu regions, it is yet to gain popularity in the rest of the country. Thus, the whole gamut of Dalit identity is the product of a long historical process, rooted in a collective conscience. The Dalit can be a collective identity, ignoring political differences to bring about the desired revolution, or a democratic revolution. However, the contradictions are still present. On the one side, the Dalit bourgeoisie is prone to capture and monopolize all the advantages of protective discrimination to themselves, while on the other, external forces are coopting the Dalit intelligentsia and are creating conflicts (divide and rule) within the strong radical Dalit movement whereever it is emerging, we shall see in the next chapter.

An earlier version of this paper has been presented at a national seminar of 'Dalit Postgraduate and Research Students' held at Indian Social Institute, New Delhi, (23-25 January, 1999), and at a seminar on 'Dalit Identity in the New Millennium' held at Dr. B.R. Ambedkar Centre for Biomedical Research, University of Delhi, (25 June, 2000).

NOTES AND REFERENCES

1. T.K. Oommen, 1994.
2. *Vajasaneyi Samhita*, XXX. 21; *Taitreya Brahmana*, III. 4.7; *Chandogya Upanishad*, V. 10.7; V. 24.4; cited in Vivekananda Jha, 1975, pp. 28-31.
3. *Brahadaranyaka Upanishad*, IV, 3.22; For details see Vivekananda Jha, 1972.
4. *Baudhayana Dharma Sutra*, 1934, pp. 6-14; also see Chinna Rao Yagati, 2003, pp. 230-233.
5. Vanamali Chakarvarti, 1921, pp. 75-76; Vivekananda Jha, 1986-1987, pp. 1-36; also see B.R. Ambedkar, 1969.
6. T. Ganapati Sastri, 1925, Vol. III, p. 7; also see Vivekananda Jha, 1974, pp. 67-71; S.J. Tambiah, 1973, pp. 204-205.
7. James Legge, 1971, p. 43.
8. For details see T. Waters, 1904-05.
9. R.T. H. Griffith, 1976, p. 603.
10. Qeyamuddin Ahmed, 1993, pp. 44-47; also see E.C. Sachau, 1914, pp. 101-102.
11. Eleanor Zelliot, 1988, pp. 169-171.
12. For a Similar Views of Untouchable Voices, see Horald R. Issacs, 1965.
13. Chinna Rao Yagati, 2002, pp. 84-120.
14. A.S. Hornby, 1985, p. 608.
15. Cited in Trilok Nath, *Politics of the Depressed Classes*, (Delhi: 1987), p. 5.
16. M.C. Rajah, 1925, p. 30.
17. For details see Madras Legislative Council Proceedings, 1921-22, Vol. IV, pp. 2047-2052.

18. For details see M.B. Gautam, 1991.

19. R.S. Khare, 1984, p. 85.

20. Mark Juergensmeyer, 1982 and 2000.

21. *Indian Statutory Commission, Report*, Vol. I, (Calcutta: 1930), p. 37.

22. J.H. Hutton, 1933, pp. 471-501.

23. *Ibid.*

24. *Census of India, 1921*, Vol. I, Part - I, Paragraph 193.

25. For details see, *Indian Franchise Committee, 1932*, Volume I (London: 1932).

26. *The Government of India, (Scheduled Castes) Order, 1936.*

27. T.K. Oommen, 1994.

28. See, James Massey, 1994. Despite many disagreements, one might have with the way in which author argued, still it is a thought provoking work.

29. Gangadhar Pantawane, 1986, pp. 79-87.

30. Eleanor Zelliot, 1996, pp. 267-292.

7

Sub-Caste Consciousness and Submerged Realities

The policy of reservation, in India, has been a bone of contention and conflict in different circles ranging from academics, politics to the general populace. What is perhaps significant is that, in recent times the conflict has witnessed a shift from one between the reserved and non-reserved categories to the reserved communities, as manifest in the contemporary Indian society.

Reservations are available only in government institutions both in admission and appointments, which are being shrinking day-by-day, as a matter of policy. And to the extent that these opportunities are not likely to survive since the government is not making a regular recruitment but has started giving jobs on contract basis. The whole gamut of politicization by endorsing sub-divisional reservation by various governments raises fundamental issues.

In the post-colonial period, in the 1950s and the 1960s, in Punjab which has about thirty per cent of its population was Dalits, the MLAs found their new voice in the Legislative assemblies. Cutting across their party lines, the Punjab MLAs started insisting on punishments to atrocities, more and separate budgetary allocating and occasionally staged walkouts in unison for the Dalit cause. The Zail Singh's Government saw the danger and in 1975 split the Scheduled Caste list into two, sowing the seeds of divisional politics. The 30 per cent strong powerful Dalits split into Ad-Dharmi Ravidasi group and Mazhabhi Balmiki groups into a virtual political slavery. This split incited the dominant sub-castes fight among themselves and the Dalits could never assert again in Punjab.

This formula worked again in Haryana. Fearing the rise of Bahujan Samaj Party, the Bhajan Lal's government in 1994 split the SC list into two. The twenty per cent strong Dalit population never had say since then. The groups led by Chamar and Balmiki castes were made to sit at loggerheads over the distribution of benefits, only to end into cohesion and conflict, at the end only to divert the funds. The BSP could not show the promise it did in Uttar Pradesh and Punjab and the sub-caste loyalties were whipped up sufficiently. Unable to grapple with the BSP's growth, the Rajnath Singh's Government in Uttar Pradesh, just before assembly elections in 2002, tried the same trick, to split them into Dalit and Ati-Dalit groups. It was too late in the day as the Dalit vote consolidation towards BSP was complete by then, as result BJP lost. Latest is the case of Andhra.

In this chapter an attempt is made to look at the differential development of Dalit communities within a historical backdrop along with the reasons for the emergence and consequences of the neo-social movement in Andhra. More specifically the struggle between the Malas and the Madigas in the region primarily resulted out of the distribution of reservations among the Dalits in accordance to their proportionate population and in the light of the state of their development in various spheres such as education, employment and governance. The first section of this paper deals with the early attempts at Dalit education in India in general and Andhra in particular. Secondly, brief note on the nature of educational development among various Dalit communities in Andhra and the role of education as an agency for societal development during the post-colonial period. Thirdly, identify the nature and ideology of this unique form of reservation movement led by the Madiga Reservation Porata Samithi (MRPS), simultaneously reflecting on the implications of this movement on the reservation policy and the Dalit movement.

State of Dalit Education

Education has the potential of transforming the socio-economic fabric of society. The works of many social scientists like Brookover,[1] Havinghurst and Neugarten,[2] Inkeles[3] and many others emphasize the function of education in bringing about social change and economic development. On the other hand, Bowles[4] argues that educational system perpetuates economic inequality along with social segregation. They further emphasize that education, like any other social institution, has been involved in the oppression.[5] In other words, the role of education, in any given society works like a double-edged weapon. While at the micro level it works as an agency for development, at the macro level it also involves in segregation and oppression.

Inequality is the structural feature of the traditional Hindu value system. As such education imposes cultural values in the interests of the 'upper' castes. The reproduction of culture through education, it has been recognized, is shown to play a key role in the reproduction of the whole system.[6] For the 'upper' castes, education was a means of social control for perpetuating their hegemonic dominance and exploiting the 'lower' castes. Thus education, since times immemorial till the end of the nineteenth century, was limited to a few privileged castes. In pre-colonial Indian society education had a religious content. In contrast, the modern education system introduced by the British was theoretically open to all and its contents were secular. It is in this period that an initiative was taken to extend education to the communities that were subject to taboos on access to any form of knowledge.

The policy of protective discrimination developed in stages since the Woods Dispatch of 1854. One of the crucial aspect of the Woods Dispatch was that, it threw open education to all castes. Eventually the Dispatch of 1857 discouraged the idea of separate schools for the 'lower' castes.[7] The caste-Hindus expressed resentment at the policy of the government and raised serious concern that 'low-born' children would be taught along with their children.[8] However, the government reconsidered its earlier decision and the Education Commission Report of 1883 recommended the establishment of separate schools wherever necessary.[9] The number of Schools established under this scheme in the Madras presidency was considered to be quite large. By the turn of the twentieth century the Presidency had 2,934 institutions 'intended chiefly for Panchamas'.[10] In 1893, the Madras Government sanctioned a series of proposals, which are widely hailed as the *Magna Carta* of Panchama education.[11] Some of these special measures, included: setting up special training schools; establishment of special schools by the Local Boards and Municipalities in all possible 'untouchable' hamlets. However, the policy of "separate schools' could not be worked out properly due to the prejudice and contempt of the executive staff, who mostly belonged to the higher/upper castes.

Despite the special measures, the growth of Dalit education was very slow compared to the literacy level of the general population. In addition to the prejudices of caste-Hindus and their non-cooperation with colonial policies, the socio-economic condition of Dalits was also responsible for the slow growth of their education. Before 1901 the Dalit literacy rate was half of one per cent. By 1931, it was just less than two per cent.[12] Again in 1931 the government decided to admit 'Exterior Castes' (as the Dalits were called then) pupils in all aided schools. Many schools were closed down[13] and caste-Hindu pupils were withdrawn as acts of boycott against this move of the government.

The nineteenth and early twentieth centuries social reform movement, espoused education, as a means of enlightenment. However, progress in this direction was limited to the 'twice-born'. In reaction to the Christian Missionaries' attempts to ameliorate Dalits, caste-Hindu social reformers admitted the Dalits, only as marginalized Hindus.[14] Schools became an institutional form of reiterating the Dalit status as under-privileged and unequal. No concrete and collective social movement for the Dalit education was taken up by the caste-Hindus enlightened section which was subject to legislation was only possible during the post-colonial period.

Post-Colonial Situation

The Constitution of India upholds the principle of equality[15] and condemns any form of discrimination. On account of social disparity among caste groups few special provisions have been made in the form of reservations for Dalits in educational institutions.[16] The Policy of protective discrimination was intended to reduce the vast inequalities between the privileged and under-privileged sections of the Indian social fabric. Its explicit purpose was to enable the Dalits, to educate themselves and seek employment so that they may be free of their traditional shackles. The implementation of reservation policy for more than five decades has raised many questions than it can answer. This process of protective discrimination was being contested both vertically and horizontally. In other words, the policy of reservations triggered unprecedented resentment and violent opposition both from outside and within the beneficiaries of this reservation policy. On the one hand, skeptics have repeatedly argued that the statutory protection on caste basis runs the risk of not only perpetuating the caste consciousness but also aggravating caste tensions.[17] Various concessions and relaxation of rules to accommodate the Dalits in different public sectors of employment (although these are shrinking day-by-day) in educational institutions has raised further controversies. It is now being seriously contended from several quarters that the entry of poorly qualified candidates from these castes has led to general lowering of standards besides affecting the work performance and morale of those who have qualified on 'merit'. Secondly, perhaps more importantly, the increasing demand for reservations within reservation, social tensions between the major sub-groups among the Dalits is recently articulated in organized social movements. This dimension of intra-caste conflict is perceived in Maharashtra between Mahars and Matangas and in Andhra between the Madigas and the Malas. The later is focussed as a case study in this paper.

In comparison to any other part of the country, in Andhra, the social tensions have assumed serious proportions and the demand for reservations within reservation is sought to be justified by the so-called deprived groups among Dalits. For instance, Malas have been accused of being 'cunning' as 'deliberately depriving' the Madigas of the advantages of the reservation facility. It is true that the Madigas of Andhra are relatively backward in terms of being benefited by the reservation opportunities. Such rationalization of the conflict points out the need to address this problem in juxtaposition to the Dalit movement in Andhra. What is disturbing about the nature of protest is that the counter affect of the propaganda, carried on by the aggrieved, might hamper the fragile unity of the Dalit movement as whole.

Social Status of Dalits

There are as many as 59 communities or sub-caste/jatis among Dalit populace in Andhra Pradesh[18] (See Table I). Amongst these heterogeneous communities, the Madigas[19] and the Malas[20] are by far the largest of these castes. They make up about 80 per cent of the Scheduled Caste population of the State. In terms of geographical spread of these two communities, there is a regional dimension. The Malas constitute a majority in coastal Andhra districts and about 75 per cent of Malas live in the region. While about 60 per cent of the Madigas inhabit Rayalaseema and Telangana regions.[21] These two major 'untouchable' communities are traditionally opposed to each other, each claiming for a higher status in the traditional hierarchy. Due to their differences in terms of social and economic status and the nature of job a degree of pollution within the Dalit sub-castes is observed. The term Mala is etymologically derived from "maila" meaning dirt.[22] The service rendered by the Malas include grave digging,[23] acting as messenger on occasions of death, birth and puberty, occasions which are identified with 'temporary' pollution. [24]

In addition to these village services, during the colonial period, their duties mainly extended to calling landowners to pay revenue; serving as guides and messengers for government officials and arbitrating boundary disputes. Their multifarious jobs, for instance the *Talayari* or *Bariki* (village servant), were integrated into the new administrative set up especially revenue department. This recognition provided new status to Malas in comparison to their counterparts who were more or less untouched by the administrative changes and continued performing "unclean" jobs.[25] The Malas of eastern Andhra and certain parts of Telangana pursued weaving as their chief occupation,[26] but gradually lost this occupation during the phase of industrialization. For majority of the Mala population the prime occupation was agricultural labour. They live by working on fields as labourers and get a few pots full of rice in return with which they have to support their family.[27]

By the turn of the twentieth century, more particularly during the post-first World War period, growing agricultural commercialization gave a new impetus to the farm labour force. Commercialization of agriculture eroded traditional caste and *jajmani* ties, which had bound the Dalit labourers and aided the development of mobile labour force with opportunities for many Dalits to move ahead.[28] The Malas were the first ones to make use of this benefit as they formed the bulk of landless agricultural labour force in rural society. The colonial period offered new employment opportunities to the labouring population. Thousands of Dalit labourers travelled every year from the east coast of India to work at the dockyard of Rangoon in Burma. This 'Burma factor' played a vital role in their economic development[29] and it would be of great interest to note that some of them even invested for education of their brethren back home.[30]

The Madigas form the most ostracized section of the 'untouchables' of Andhra.[31] They numerically form the highest sub-caste/*jati* among the Andhra Dalits. Although there is no documentary evidence but traditionally they are placed under the Malas due to their association with leather and unclean works. Although earlier inscriptions mentions that the Charmakar belong to an artisan group,[32] it is factually difficult to explain the process by which they were reduced to the degraded status of 'untouchables'.

The prime occupation of the Madigas is the curing and tanning of hides and the manufacture of leather articles. The process of tanning with lime, salt and Tangedu (cassia auriculata) bark is rough and simple. This scientific knowledge of converting the dead skin into fine leather is passed from one generation to another. In addition to their traditional and customary occupations, Madigas are expected to perform certain duties for caste-Hindus. They include: to supply sandals for the ryots; leather belts for bulls and all other necessary items for agriculture. They were also expected to clean the streets and undertake decoration work with *pachchathoranam* (garland green mango leaves) during the village festivals and on all the occasions of officials' visit the Madigas have to notify their entry into the villagers through Dandora/Chatimpu with *Dappau* (a traditional leather instrument associated with the Dalits). For all these services they often were paid meager and negligible remuneration; often in kind which usually consisted of cheap grains and vegetables.[33]

The third largest sub-caste/*jati* comprises of the Adi-Andhras. The Adi-Andhra is a generic term and the sub caste is basically offshoots of the Malas and Madigas.[34] They are descendents of the educated and conscious 'untouchables' of early decades of twentieth century. Influenced by the non-Aryan themes of Dravidian movement they started identifying themselves as "Adi-Andhras", with a claim that they were the original inhabitants of the land, based on the theory of "sons of the soil."[35] Until 1921 Census they were invisible in official enumerations. Significantly in 1931 census they emerged with striking strength of 665,000 under this category (see Table II). Though the term "Adi-Andhra" was popularized from 1917, it was only in 1922 that the Madras Government accepted the requisition of the Dalits to delete all the earlier terms such as 'panchama', 'pariah' from the government records, and replace the term "Adi" prefix along with a language based regional identity such as "Adi-Andhra" or "Adi-Dravida."[36] The fourth group among the Dalit population of Andhra is the Relli, preponderant in the three northern coastal districts of Srikakulam, Vizianagaram and Vishakhapatnam.[37] Their primary occupation specifically consisted of selling seasonal fruits.[38]

Among these four sub-castes/*jati* of ex-untouchables of Andhra, the Adi-Andhra is a predominantly, self-conscious, assertive and relatively developed group while on the other hand, the Rellis, numerically a minority, are backward at the socio-economic fronts. The Rellis have not actively involved in the present day movement of reservation with in reservation. The Madigas responded at a comparatively latter phase to the opportunities offered within the colonial context, specifically modernization and education. Hence, their access to benefits of modernization and subsequent job opportunities through reservations has not been in par with other advanced communities. This was perhaps due to their pre-occupation with their skilled trade of producing leather goods. As mentioned earlier, and as evident by the census figures, most of the Madigas were dependent on their traditional occupation, but during the phase industrialization and introduction of modern technology they were gradually transformed into manual labourers. However, the constraints of the nature of their traditional occupation along with the exigency of agricultural economy tied these communities within the village boundaries. This ultimately kept them away from the process of modernization. The Malas, on the other hand, who formed bulk of agricultural labour force through intensive commercialization of agriculture, were exposed to the process of modernization. Increasing demand for labour resulted in providing better wages, and on access to nearby towns at regular intervals as construction workers during off-season (of agriculture), were exposed to various avenues brought about by the replacement of traditional structure. Thus, they availed certain benefits conferred by the colonial governments' policies. On the other hand, the Madigas remained backward and were unable to utilize the benefits that effects consequently their share in the civilization have tended to remain marginal in comparison. This dichotomy of progress along with the failure of the Dalit movement to strongly redress sub-caste grievances was the primary cause for the Mala-Madiga conflict. In recent years there has been a widespread social movement to break down the total reservation available for the Scheduled Castes, to reallocate the reservation among the different sub-castes (groups) in proportion to their population.

As mentioned earlier the majority of Dalit population is composed of landless agricultural labourers. It is observed that the population of these two communities. Madigas and Malas, although scattered throughout the State, the Madigas are thickly populated in the regions of Telangana (Telugu speaking areas of erstwhile Nizam domain) and Rayalaseema, where in coastal Andhra region the Malas form the majority. Due to lack of adequate irrigation facilities, both the Telangana and Rayalaseema regions remain backward whereas coastal Andhra is endowed with better irrigational facilities. Consequently, the Telangana and Rayalaseema regions are less developed than coastal region. Hence, the Malas of coastal region have been able to avail the benefits of various welfare measures of the colonial policies of educational opportunities and consequently, acquired the qualifications to utilize the Constitutional safeguards and reservations during the post-colonial phase more in comparison to Rayalaseema and Telangana Madigas.[39] Thus, the regional backwardness has vitally contributed in perpetuating disparities between the communities. In addition to this, the role of missionaries was another crucial influence in the region. Though the educational institutional established by missionaries were spread throughout the state, relatively more schools and colleges were established in the coastal region, perhaps with the support of the colonial government. As a result, the Malas were nurtured by the beneficial educational facilities and were better suited for various sectors of employment much in advance than their counter parts in the other regions of the state. The forwardness and relative development of the Malas can be attributed to these factors. On the contrary, the Madigas in the absence of such facilities, in the Nizam's domain, remained relatively backward, gradually led to the sense of deprivation among them.

This conflict necessitates a critical examination of the nature of ideology and programme of the Dalit movement of 1920s and 1930s.[40] The Dalit movement during the colonial period did articulate at different levels more forcefully in literature regarding the existing prejudices, among these 'untouchable' communities, which were dangerous for its healthy growth.[41] Prominent among leaders who adhered such issued were Boyi Bhimanna,[42] Gurram Jashuva,[43] Bhagya Reddi Varma,[44] Kusuma Dharmanna[45] and many others. In an effort to create solidarity, Bhagya Reddi Varma asserted and coined the term "Adi-Andhra" and consciously put to use to denote unity of all 'untouchable' communities. He opposed and rejected the derogatory term "panchama" used by the caste-Hindus. Boyi Bhimanna, a legendary Dalit intellectual, poet and writer, coined the term "mamalu" which indicate the two main sub-castes of Dalits (*Ma*=Malas and *ma* = Madigas together *Mamalu*). This term was deliberately used by Boyi Bhimanna to foster unity among the 'untouchable' communities. In addition to this ideologically deployed neologism, Dalit intellectuals attempted to trace the common ancestry of Dalits. However, these efforts were not successful in generating solidarity among the Dalits. It is because a programme for working towards a practical change remained ineffective and unsatisfactory. Crucially the course of the Dalit movement in the Nizams' region fostered by sub-caste rivalries left very little hope of healing differences.[46] So also lack of an efficient development plan to take cognizance of economic and social realities led to a serious disparity in the process of development.

Formation and Emergence of MRPS

The Madiga Reservation Porata Samithi (MRPS) was founded by a few self-conscious assertive Madiga youth on 27 July, 1994 at Edumudu village in Prakasam district.[47] The rationale for the origin of the movement was the seething discontent among the Madigas over their relatively backward status. The immediate factor was their contempt about the monopolization of resources and reservation facilities by the Malas. They complained that though the Malas relatively lesser in number than the Madigas benefited more by the reservation policy. As a result, they initiated a movement to fight for justice, popularly known as "Madiga Dandora." The term "Dandora" refers to their traditional profession. Traditionally the *drum* (Dappu) was used to make several announcements in the village. Earlier the term "madiga" was considered as defiling and used abusively by the caste-Hindus. The striking thing that the Madigas did was to proclaim their movement and all related activities, by adding prefixes such as "Madiga Dadora Rally", and "Madiga Dandora Meeting". In addition, they started suffixing their caste name to their name to assert their identity and to identify with their own caste men. For instance the leaders of MRPS, named themselves as Krishna Madiga[48] or Krupakar Madiga.[49] This tradition was spread over to the rank and file of MRPS across the state. These leaders were successful in communicating effectively and provided necessary information to their Madiga brethren. By explaining their history, culture, the position of reservation facilities and their position in society made them conscious of their status. This provided a platform to the Madigas to unite and organize themselves. Another important dimension of the success was that it was not identified or loyal to any political organization, at least in the beginning. The MRPS leadership instilled confidence among the Madigas by rejuvenating consciously and positively an earlier demeaning caste identity. Thus, elevating Madigas to a self-conscious position making them proud of their 'new' identity. This is exemplified by one of the song of Madiga Dandora; "as 'untouchables', we were seen as degraded but with the emergence of 'Dandora' we are called with dignity."[50] This facilitated mobilization and organization of the Madigas to fight for their demands for categorization of the existing reservation policy according to proportionate population.

The MRPS leadership has explicitly expressed that their demand for a reasonable share in the Scheduled Castes (SCs) reservation was justified as Madigas were not benefited out of the reservations and have remained backward. On the contrary it was argued that the Malas have availed benefits disproportionate to their population. Their contention is that all the sub-castes of SCs should receive benefits in proportionate to their population. They further declare that there are certain sub-castes or *jatis* like the Rellis, who are more backward than the Madigas. Therefore, such backward groups among the SCs should be ensured their due share. This logical exposition of the 'Dandora' leadership for the classification received wider acclaim. After securing support from the grass root levels by organizing meetings, *rallies* and *padayatras*, the MRPS was successful in mobilizing one lakh Madigas (and their supporters) from all over the State. They proceeded to Hyderabad, the State capital, to demonstrate their strength and to present their demand. Finally, the State Government appointed a one man Commission on 10 September, 1996, headed by a retired Judge of A.P. High Court, Mr. Justice Ramachandra Raju to enquire into the issue of Dalit reservation in the State and demands raised by the MRPS.

Justice Ramachandra Raju Commission

The terms of reference of the P. Ramachandra Raju Commission were as follows: "the Commission will go into all specific aspects of reservation in employment and admissions into educational institutions now available to SCs and examine; whether a disproportionately large number of benefits have gone to any particular sub-caste of Dalits and if so, indicate all such as are necessary and required to be taken to ensure that the above benefits are equitably distributed among the various sub-castes of SCs."[51]

The Commission received representations from various caste associations, government offices and other sources. It collected statistics of various sub-castes/*jatis* and their population and representation in the government employment and educational institutions. The Commission submitted its report on 28 May, 1997. It felt that these disparities did exist availing the benefits of reservation by various sub-castes in the State. The Commission observed that one particular sub-caste, the Malas, was enjoying the benefits of reservations, disproportionate to their population but could not provide ample reasons for the same. The Commission has recommended that all the fifty-nine sub-castes should be classified into A, B, C and D groups for the purposes of reservation for procuring admission into educational institutions and employment accordingly. The recommendation of the Commission to classify Scheduled Castes into four groups is shown in the Table III.

The Commission has recommended that the classification should be based on 1981 census,[52] indicating socio-economic conditions of various groups.[53] Table III reveals the manner in which the sub-castes/*jatis* were classified, along with their population and allocated reservation proportionate to their population. According to the Commission, the Relli and Madiga communities have not been able to reap the benefits from the present reservation policy. So the Relli group is categorized under Group A with one per cent reservation. The Madigas were categorized under Group B with seven per cent of reservations, followed by the Malas under Group C with 6 per cent and Adi-Andhras under Group D with one per cent of reservation.

Immediately, the MRPS has demanded the implementation of Commission's recommendations. To evince further pressure they organized a 'Maha Padayatra' to cover a distance of 1014 kilometers in 53 days to reach the State capital and to begin their agitation. They commenced their 'long march' from Naravari Palle, a village in Chittoor district, the native village of Chief Minister Chandra Babu Naidu on 14 April, 1997, after taking the blessings of the parents of the Chief Minister.[54] The MRPS leadership selected five volunteers from each district to participate in this long march, dressed in dark blue uniform and holding sticks, the *padayatra* was led by Krishna Madiga, trek about 20 kilometers a day in two spells. They used to visit the Madiga colony/locality in every village where arrangements for their food and stay were made. They interacted with the people and educated them about their demands before they resumed their journey. At every village, their caste men received the team warmly with beating of the traditional *drums*. In support of this *padayatra* Madigas organized several *rallies* and *padayatras* at local level to mobilize their brethren from various districts. The government dramatically denied permission to the MRPS *rally* to march into Hyderabad city, because it was alleged that the Dandora's strategy was to siege the house of the Chief Minister on 6 June. In the meanwhile, the MRPS approached the High Court, which directed the police to permit the MRPS to enter into the outskirts of the city and directed the Dalits to conduct their activities peacefully.[55] The MRPS leadership upheld this *padayatra* and identified it with the "Long March" of Mao, compared with Gandhian non-violence to 'educate, organize and agitate' as enunciated by Dr. Ambedkar for the social justice envisaged by Jagjivan Ram.[56] The Madigas who were drawn from various districts decided not to leave Hyderabad until government accepted and declared an order for the classification of reservations on the lines of the recommendations of the Commission. They also made a fresh demand to extend such classification to political reservations and social welfare schemes as well.

Cabinet Sub-Committee

Before accepting the recommendations of the Ramachandra Raju Commission, the Government of Andhra Pradesh appointed a Cabinet Sub-Committee[57] on 2 June, 1997 to examine the recommendations. The Sub-Committee in its meeting on 2nd June 1997 discussed the limits of implementation within the framework of the Constitution and more particularly of its legal tangles.[58] The Sub-Committee gave its green signal to the government on the issue. Followed by it the government finally issued an Order[59] classifying the SCs into four categories, as recommended by the Ramachandra Raju Commission, without any changes. Finally, the Madigas left Hyderabad only after their leaders declared that if the Government did not concede to their demand for the extension of classification to political representation and welfare programmes, they would resort to an indefinite fast, and would resume agitation with more vigour. The Government, thus, virtually met the demand put forth by the Madigas, and the Chief Minister Chandra Babu Naidu contended "no group should grudge the government for the step because it was taken only to ensure social justice to the groups lagging behind."[60]

The Malas' Response

In response to the Madigas success the Malas reacted against the classification, blaming the government, for its insidious policy of creating a divide among the Dalits. In turn, they united themselves into an organization called 'Mala Mahanadu' under the leadership of P.V. Rao, a government servant.[61] The Mala Mahanadu made an appeal in the High Court challenging the legality of the Government Order on classification. It alleged that the Ramachandra Raju Commission hastily prepared the report based on the statistics of 1981 census and that the State Government did not consult either the National Commission for SCs and STs or the Union Government before the G.O. was issued. Consequently, a single Judge of the High Court temporarily suspended the G.O. on 21 July, 1997. The Mala Mahanadu demanded that the government withdraw the G.O. When the Government did not concede, they organized a protest *rally* and planed the 'seizing of state Secretariat' on 11 August, 1997 as a sign of their strength. The *rally*, however, turned violent, as a result one youth died. The G.O. was then referred to a larger bench. On 18 September, 1997 a full Bench of the A.P. High Court delivered a judgement suspending the G.O. on the grounds that the government should have consulted the National Commission for SCs and STs before taking the decision to effect the categorization. Article 338 (9) of the Constitution states that "the government shall consult the SC and ST Commission" on all major policy matters concerned the Scheduled Castes and Scheduled Tribes. The State Government held that the categorization was not a policy matter and alternatively that the word "shall" need not be interpreted as a mandatory.[62] Whatever may be the technicalities of interpretation, the court laid down a sound principle in insisting that Article 338 (9) was a mandatory provision. But Article 341 makes it clear that the list of SCs, declared by the President can be modified only by the Parliament.

The Mala Mahanadu, in their campaign, has taken a strong objection to the picture that was presented by the Madigas, especially cunning and scheming Malas were the root cause of unequal access to reservations. It was also rightly argued that what is seen as a Mala-Madiga difference is in fact a regional difference that cannot be caused by a horizontal sub-division of total reservations that is available for the SCs. Further, it argued, there is a relative preponderance of the Mala community among the Dalits in coastal districts, were educationally more developed and on the other hand the Madigas were concentrated in backward regions of Telangana and Rayalaseema. The Mala Mahanadu also argued that the Madigas had a vocation that normally provides a job for each and every family member, irrespective of their age. Though the profession may not yield adequate income, but usually their children get into the job before they knew the consequences. By the time they realized the implications it would have been too late, thus, they continued to remain backward. On the other hand, the Malas had no vocation, except in remote areas in older days, and have had to compete with others as agricultural labourers. At this juncture, the opportunities and facilities provided by the missionaries through their educational institutions, that also provided lodging and boarding along with free education played a major role. As the Malas had no family vocation, they tended to send their children to missionary free boarding schools or social welfare hostels in the post-colonial period. It is observed that nearly 70 percent of the literate Malas were products of this system. Various missionary associations such as St. Joseph, St. Ann's, St. Anthony, St. Teresa and many more dozens of missionaries can be seen in coastal districts serving these communities. However it needs to be noted that the missionaries did not harbour any prejudices for sub-caste division among the Dalits.

The entire history of Dalit movement in Andhra reveals the fact that the Malas, particularly from coastal regions, were the most assertive community that fought for self-identity and social development of the 'untouchables' communities. But they did not restrict their struggles for the Malas alone. Dalit writers, poets, organic intellectuals were largely drawn from the Mala community.[63] But it is true that they did fail to realize the need for bringing about Madigas within the main fold of the movement in large numbers.

Later Development of the Movement

The MRPS immediately demanded that the government make an appeal in Supreme Court and the government has made a special leave petition. The MRPS pressurized the government to take necessary steps for the rectification of the said G.O. and its speedy implementation. Later on the issue was divided into two political camps. The Telugu Desam Party (TDP) settled down with political alliance with the Madigas, with a electoral promise to fulfill their demands. This created a split in the MRPS movement with the formation of a new organization called Madiga Athmagaurava Porata Samiti (MAPS), opposing the MRPS under the leadership of Krishna Madiga. Similarly Mala Mahanadu also faced the same problem, and was supported by the Congress.[64] Thus, the two movements in a strategy to mobilize support for realization of their demands have themselves been politicized by the parties. It is important to note that the support was extended to these parties neither on any ideological differences for the welfare of Dalits, nor the parties have committed to solve the Dalit problems once for all.

In the meantime, the State Government obtained a certificate of appeal from the High Court, filed an appeal in the Supreme Court and simultaneously sought the opinion of the SC and ST Commission. The Commission asked for more data, which was furnished by the State Government. After giving a hearing to all parties, the Commission advised the State Government against the categorization. According to the article 338 (7) that allows a State Government to reject a recommendation of SC and ST Commission, provided the reasons for the same are explained to the Legislative Assembly. Using this provision the Government issued another G.O. classifying the SC reservations.[65] This was challenged by the Mala and the Adi-Andhra communities, but a five-judge bench of the high court, by a majority of four to one, upheld the Act, overruling the other objections the previous bench had expressed. Against that the petitioners appealed to the

Supreme Court, for which leave was granted by the High Court, and in the apex court they have succeeded. A five-judge bench of the Supreme Court, in E.V. Chinnaiah Vs State of Andhra Pradesh, has unanimously held the Act to be unconstitutional, in a judgement. The Supreme Court said two things. Firstly, apportionment of the reservations made to SCs or STs to subgroups within cannot be done by the State Legislatures and only Parliament has the competence to do so; and secondly, even Parliament does not have the competence to do so since the Constitution has intended that the SCs and STs are an indivisible, homogeneous entity.[66]

Concluding Remarks

Reservation are available only in government institutions both admission and appointments, which have being shrinking day-by-day, as a matter of policy.[67] And to the extent that these opportunities are not likely to survive since the Government is not making a regular recruitment but has started giving jobs on contract basis. The whole gamut of politicization by endorsing sub-divisional reservation by the Government raises fundamental issues. It needs to be noted that the government took no time to appoint a Commission and this one man Commission took barely 8 months to submit its report. Eventually the Cabinet sub-Committee gave its green signal in a record time, barely five days! Had the government shown similar concern, sincerity and speedy implementation in filling the backlog vacancies in accordance with Constitutional guarantees, this kind of problem will not recur in the state or in its neighbourhood. One wonder when Dalits would cease being drawn within the deceptive ploy of caste-Hindu politicians, the notorious "cow headed Tigers."[68]

The intra-caste agitation among the Dalits of Andhra, though disturbing, calls for urgent enquiry into the nuances of the contemporary Dalit movement. This development, as is evident, is a blow to the very survival and unity of a broader Dalit organizing. But it needs to be taken into cognizance that the Madigas demand was culmination of their discontent and disbelief in Malas 'benignity'. Though the Madiga Dandora's claim is a logical and just demand the nature of their agitation is fundamentally a matter of concern. Madiga leadership could have contemplated alternative strategies; resorted to a strategy wherein the Malas also could have deliberated to harness support from among all the sub-castes. Such tactics necessitates more space and time for deliberations but it would have wider social appeal with crucial implications for the Dalit movement. Absence of such initiation for cooperation has sown a deep sense of resentment and antagonism among the Dalits.

What is of crucial necessity is the examination of the insidious role of the ruling party. One would wonder if a combined effort for a much broader and genuine demand would have received the immediate approval by the State Government. Innumerable issues ranging from violation of Dalit human rights, atrocities, unemployment, health, and basic needs have hardly caught the notice of the 'benevolent' State Government. Such selective benevolence mocks at the very intention of the government's agenda of ensuring justice. It is at this juncture that a selfless and honest effort with foresight should be made by all sub-castes to ensure that they would not become a prey to the dangerous and perverse nature of the selfish political parties.

And finally though the entire fifty-nine heterogeneous communities were classified into four groups, neither the Ramachandra Raju Commission nor the Government have explained on what grounds such a classification is legitimate. The classification facilitates 'leading' community(s) from each group to get into higher educational institutions (note this, not into 'super specialty courses'), those already enjoying better status can utilize employment avenues. This classification can facilitate only the dominant assertive and conscious communities of each group who have already been benefited than the rest. Since neither the Commission has recommended nor the government has taken any special measures or schemes to elevate those most backward communities who are clubbed into each group, as no group is homogeneous in any sense be it at the social, economic or cultural level. It is likely that this classification will create and witness a similar situation that prompted the need for classification. The whole gamut of social movement, though could unite and create a consciousness among the sub-castes in isolation, will not yield any concrete and expected results if it is not concerned with the more marginalized communities with in the classification.

**An earlier version of this paper has been presented at a seminar On "Equal Opportunities, Affirmative Action and the Scheduled Castes: Challenges and Prospects" organized by Dr. Ambedkar Chair/CSSS/SSS, Jawaharlal Nehru University, New Delhi. (23-24 October, 2003).*

Table–I
List of the Total Scheduled Castes in Andhra Pradesh, 1976

1.	Adi Andhra	20.	Dom, Dombara, Paidi, Pano
2.	Adi Dravida	21.	Ellamalawar/Yellamma lawandlu
3.	Anamuk	22.	Ghasi, Haddi, Relli Chachandi
4.	Aray Mala	23.	Godagali
5.	Arundhatiya	24.	Godari
6.	Arwa Mala	25.	Gosangi
7.	Bariki	26.	Holeya
8.	Bavuri	27.	Holeya Dasari
9.	Beda Jangam, Budga Jangam	28.	Jaggali
10.	Bindla	29.	Jambuvulu
11.	Byagara	30.	Kolupulvandlu
12.	Chachati	31.	Madasi Kuruva, Madari Kuruva
13.	Chalavadi	32.	Madiga
14.	Chamar, Mochi, Muchi	33.	Madiga Dasu, Mashteen
15.	Chambhar	34.	Mahar
16.	Chandala	35.	Mala
17.	Dakkal, Dokkalwar	36.	Mala Dasari
18.	Dandasi	37.	Mala Dasu
19.	Dhor	38.	Mala Hannai

39.	Mala Jangam	50.	Mundala
40.	Mala Sale/Netkani	51.	Paky, Moti, Thoti
41.	Mala Sanyasi	52.	Pambada, Pambanda
42.	Mang	53.	Pamidi
43.	Mang Garodi	54.	Panchama, Pariah
44.	Manne	55.	Relli
45.	Mashti	56.	Samagara
46.	Mashti	57.	Samban
47.	Matangi	58.	Sapru
48.	Mehtar	59.	Sindhollu, Chindollu
49.	Mitha Ayyalvar		

Source: The Scheduled Castes and Scheduled Tribes orders (Amendment) Act, 1976, (No. 108 of 1976) dated 18th September, 1976. See *Census of India*, 1981, *Series-I India part IX, Special Table for SCs/STs*, p. 9.

Table-II
Population of Selected 'Untouchable' Castes in Madras Presidency 1921-1931

(in Thousands)

Caste	*1921*	*1931*
Cheruman	248	215
Holeya	92	50
Madiga	737	612
Mala	1,493	838
Parayan	2,387	1,117
Thoti	154	2
Adi-Andhra	–	665
Adi-Dravida	50	1,619
Adi-Karnataka	–	1

Source:Census of India, 1931, Vol. 14, Madras, Part I, p. 349.

Table–III
New Classification of Scheduled Castes into Neo-Reservation Policy

Name of the Group	*Sub-Caste in the Group*	*Population of the Sub-Caste**	*Percentage in Total SC Population*	*Percentage of Reservation Recommended*
Group A (Relli Group	Relli, Bavuri, Chandala, Dandasi, Paky and six other sub-castes. (Total 11)	1, 33, 689	1.67	1 (One)
Group B (Madiga Group)	Madiga, Arundhatiya, Chamar, Mochi, Dakkal, Godari, Jaggali, Jambuvulu, Matangi, Chindollu and eight other sub-castes. (Total 18)	37, 37, 609	46. 94	7 (Seven)
Group C (Mala Group)	Mala, Adi-Dravida, Bariki, Chalavadi, Ellamalawar, Gosangi, Holeya, Mahar, Netkani, Manne, Mundala, Pambada and eleven other sub-casts. (Total 24)	32, 63, 655	40. 99	6 (Six)
Group D (Adi-Andhra)	Adi-Andhra, Mashti, Mitha Ayyalwar, Panchama, Pariah. (Total 6)	7, 13, 824	8.96	1 (One)

Source: Justice Rama Chandra Raju Committee Report.

* According to Census 1981.

NOTES

1. Wilbur B. Brookover, 1955, pp. 313-328.
2. Robert J. Havinghurst and Bernice L. Neugarten, 1964, pp. 258-265.
3. Alex Inkeles, 1974, pp. 151-174.
4. Samuel Bowles, 1972, pp. 219-251.
5. This aspect has been elaborated in Chinna Rao Yagati, 1999b.
6. Pierre Bourdieu, 1973, pp. 71-112; also see S. Bowles, 1973, pp. 137-153.
7. For more details see Chinna Rao Yagati, 2002, pp. 84-120.
8. *Dinavarthamani,* 28 March 1874. For details see the Reports of Native Newspapers of the Madras Presidency for the year 1874.
9. Proceedings of Education Department, Government of Madras, G.O. No. 68 (Education), Dated 1 February, 1893.
10. Of them 6 were run by the Government, 491 by the Local Boards and 1,612 were aided institutions. For details see Robert Nathan, 1908, p. 136.
11. Proceedings of Education Department, Government of Madras, G.O. No. 676, Dated 2 December, 1919.
12. Indu Rajagopal, 1985, pp. 118-141.
13. L. Eleyaperumal,1969, p. 180.
14. Chinna Rao Yagati, 1999a, p. 14.
15. Article 14 (provision for Equality) of the Indian Constitution.
16. Article 15(4), 16(4) and 16(4a) of the Indian Constitution.
17. Uma Ramaswamy, 1984, pp. 1214-1217.
18. For the list of total Scheduled Caste communities, see Table I..
19. For details see Edgar Thurston and C. Rangachari, 1909, vol. IV; Census of India, 1961, *Ethnographic Notes on Madiga, Jambuvulu, Jaggali, Arundhatiya, Chalavadi, Chamar, Mochi or Muchi, Samagara and Chambhar in Andhra Pradesh*, vol. II, part V-B (12), (Hyderabad, 1967). T.R. Singh, 1967 and 1969.
20. Edgar Thurston and C. Rangachari, 1909, vol. IV; Sydney Nicholson, 1926; K. Ratnaiah, 1991.

21. A. Satyanarayana, 2003a, p. 9.

22. The Malas are the *Pariahs* of the Tamil Country. Edgar Thurston and C. Rangachari, 1909, vol. IV, pp. 329-331.

23. *Ibid.*, p. 349.

24. Chinna Rao Yagati, 2003b, pp. 39-40.

25. *Ibid.*, p.41-42.

26. *Ibid.*, p. 40.

27. *Vartadarshini*, 22 December, 1894.

28. Gail Omvedt, 1994, p. 114; also see N. Duvvury, 1987, pp. 1-38; Dharma Kumar, 1968; A. Satyanarayana, 1990.

29. Cited in Harold R. Issacs, 1965, p. 69.

30. Chinna Rao Yagati, 2003c, pp. 117-153; also see Pamu Rama Murty, 1974.

31. They are the counterparts of the Chakkiliyans of the Tamil speaking regions and the Chamars of northern India. Edgar Thurston and K. Rangachari, 1909, vol. IV, p. 292.

32. Best example is the Edarupalli record *Inscriptions of Andhra Pradesh* Warangal Districts, no. 87, cited in K. Suryanarayana, 1956, p. 256.

33. For more details see Edgar Thurston and K. Rangachari, 1909, vol. IV; Chinna Rao Yagati,2003b, p. 41.

34. S.R. Sankaran, 1998, pp. 14-15.

35. Y. Chinna Rao, 1999e, pp. 84-95; also see Chinna Rao Yagati, 2003b, Introduction.

36. Proceedings of Law Department, Government of Madras, Law (General) Department, G.O. No. 817, Dated 25 March, 1922.

37. For more details see Mangalagiri Prasada Rao, 1993. Essays by Sonu Gokul Das and Erramsetti Potu Raju contains good information.

38. It has been alleged that they were also professional petty thieves in the region particularly in Locharla, Sundarada villages of Vizianagaram district and Pulti-Mamidi Palle of Srikakulam district, but so far we have no documentation available to support the argument.

39. C.V. Ranga Rao, 1998, pp. 34-39.

40. For details see Gail Omvedt, 1994; Chinna Rao Yagati, 2003b; A. Satyanarayana, 1999.
41. For details see P.R. Venkata Swamy, 1955.
42. For an autobiographical account Bhimanna, see Hymavathi, 1978.
43. Katti Padma Rao, 1994.
44. M.B. Gautam, 1991.
45. Chinna Rao Yagati, 2003c, pp. 117-153.
46. For instances of Mala Madiga conflict at the leadership level see P.R. Venkata Swamy, 1955.
47. G. Venkata Siva Reddy, 2002, pp. 324-342.
48. Manda Krishna was a former radical from Warangal district, who later settled in Ongole.
49. Krupakar was a former activist of a pro-naxalite student organisation, a capable and dedicated organizer.
50. Audio record songs of "Madiga Dandora" have many of this kind.
51. S. Ray, 1998, pp. 14-15.
52. Especially to categorize/classify the SCs in 1997, taking the Census Reports of 1981, instead of 1991.
53. *The Hindu*, 6 June, 1997.
54. *The Hindu*, 7 May, 1997.
55. *Eenadu*, 5 June, 1997.
56. G. Venkata Siva Reddy, 2002, pp. 324-343.
57. The Cabinet Sub-Committee consisted of Ministers Tammineni Sitaram, Chandra Sekhara Rao, Kistappa and the Secretary of Law Department and the Chief Secretary of Social Welfare Department.
58. *Eenadu*, 3 June, 1997.
59. G.O. No. 68 and 69, Dated 6 June, 1997.
60. *The Hindu*, 6 June, 1997.
61. *The Hindu*, 29 August, 1997.
62. K. Balagopal, 2000.

63. For details see *Souvenir*, 1976; R.K. Kshirsagar, 1994; Kota Bhaskara Rao, 1996.

64. *The Hindu*, 4 February, 1998.

65. G.O. No. 116, Dated 10 December 1999, Social Welfare Department, Government of Andhra Pradesh.

66. K.Balagopal, 2005, p. 3128.

67. In Andhra Pradesh, instead of filling the vacancies, TDP government resorted to giving 'contract' jobs in various colleges and universities. This is more particularly in the phase of LPG, i.e., liberalization, privatization and globalization.

68. Kusuma Dharmanna, "Samyavadanni Sahinchani Hinduism", Presidential Address, at Adi-Andhra Conference at Vizianagaram, 1936, (Reprinted in *Nalupu* (November 1992—January 1993) in 3 parts.

8

Sub-Subaltern Perspective of Alternative Strategies for the Societal Development

The challenge facing the Third World countries, more specifically Asian societies, today is how to bring about development that is responsive, equitable, sustainable and accountable, and that gives people greater control over their lives. And people centred developmental efforts have been launched to meet this challenge. The 1980s witnessed a prolific growth of Non-Governmental Organizations (NGO) as agents of development throughout the Asia. There are varieties of NGOs, with distinctive identities. Some of them are part of government's service delivery systems, while some are small independent service organizations, and yet some others are experimenting with a range of new options.

This chapter is an attempt at studying the evolution and the nature of NGOs/Voluntary Organizations (VOs), their rise and growth and how they have succeeded in meeting needs of people. The philosophy of the NGOs for social change is also being discussed from the perspective of Dalits and Tribals.

India has a long tradition of voluntary services for the upliftment of the under-privileged sections. But initially, it had colonial heritage with traditions of charity. Organizations originated as a result of an impulse from the West like the Scout movement, the Red Cross, the Rotary Club, the Lion's Club and so on. This type of voluntary service is oriented to the service of the victims of the state and civil societies. But it has been generally apolitical. Voluntarism normally is either revivalist or millenarian in its character. Revivalist organizations have basically a religious framework. The Divine Life Society, Rama Krishna Mission, the traditional Christian Missions fallen into this category. Tribal upliftment associations, women welfare associations and welfare associations for oppressed castes, subordinated and marginalized communities, whom I would prefer to call as sub-subaltern sections of society come under the category of welfare or service oriented activities. They are secular in nature. It is this category of voluntarism that will be dealt in this chapter.

The principle goal of these voluntary organizations is amelioration of exploitation of specific groups. Their ideology is narrow in the sense that they do not realize the necessity of locating the issue of victimization at a broader context. They only take cognizance of the apparent facts without any critical outlook. For instance, atrocities on Dalits. Nobody questions why the atrocities occur what and are the reasons for such victimization. As a result, remedies to eradicate such institutional abuses are not proposed. This is something like giving medicine to the patient without proper diagnosis. This voluntarism is based on perception that every society in the world has victims who need to be cared for. But by not questioning the structures of power and dominance, the framework remains essentially conservative. What NGOs need is an ideology for structural change which unfortunately most of them do not have at present.

As mentioned earlier, we have varieties of NGOs in India performing various functions with different ideologies. By the end of the 1970s most voluntary organizations were directly working in the field of promoting innovation and experimentation. However, the 1980s witnessed the emergence of greater initiatives on the part of voluntary organizations to influence government policies and programmes at different levels in the country.

During the 1980s as a response to NGOs/VOs initiatives the Government started promoting Government sponsored

NGOs (GNGOs) as an alternative to independent and semi-independent NGOs. For the first time, in its Seventh Five Year Plan (1986-91), the Government allocated a larger share of resources for NGOs involved in rural development. In 1984, Foreign Contributions Regulating Act adopted by the Government, ensured NGOs receiving foreign aid registered with the Union Home Ministry. They were to report to the government all the funds received from overseas and how those funds were utilized. In 1985, government offered income tax exemptions to funds donated for rural development. It was a significant development. In the same year, eleven central ministries earmarked funds for NGOs working in rural areas. But all such NGOs were expected to register themselves and adhere to a code of conduct. However, in September 1986, over 500 NGOs 'unanimously' rejected the proposal of NCVA and the NGO code of conduct at a national convention. As a result, Government had to postpone any further action on this. These developments finally ended up in convening consultative groups at Central and State Government levels for Central Government dialogue. The 73rd and the 74th the constitutional amendments were intended to create mechanisms of local self-governance and devolution of power in rural and urban areas. This gave leg-up to voluntary organizations to make their contributions to local communities. There were also the emergences of independent research initiatives that constantly monitored government's policies and programmes and make independent criticism of the same.

A voluntary organization or an NGO performs usually one or some of these activities: organize and mobilize people and advocate on their behalf, provide relief, charity and welfare services; increase people's voice in the decision-making process engage in developmental work in economical, ecological and infrastructural areas; facilitate social awakening; promote formal and informal education, undertake community developmental activities in urban and rural areas and so on.

With this broad perspective, voluntarism that initially aimed at charity and relief or at best social reforms and social welfare, has moved into the areas of development and social justice. Originally voluntarism sprang out of religiosity and generosity and aimed at providing charity, solace and comfort to the needy. As long as their activities were legal, constitutional and non-violent and aimed at bringing about changes without disturbing the social or political structure there was no problem from the state. On the other hand any organization or groups of activists, who strived for a structural change, or followed violent methods, were unlawful, unconstitutional and punishable. Nexalite activities were one such relevant example.

The post-emergency period saw a mushrooming of voluntary agencies in the country. Though the number of agencies increased their functions practically remained the same, but with some minor differences. Practically, all undertook concrete development programmes while a few others mobilized people to demand their rights and justice. Some expanded their existing programmes while others preferred to experiment and work with new ideas.

Located in a western understanding of reality, the efforts of NGOs so for have failed to tackle the cause of social backwardness. Even today the root cause of any inequality in the country is socio-cultural and not entirely economic. And the NGOs working on the Western model of development have failed to see this point. For example, in the mid-1980s in the Dharwar District of Karnataka, NGOs were working among the Dalits. They planned to empower young school dropout girls by teaching them sewing. Later, these NGOs arranged training and bank loans for these girls to buy sewing machines. But their problem was not not-properly knowing tailoring, but their inability to get clothes to stitch due to problem of untouchability. Later, the social welfare department of the State Government began to supply the cloths for school uniforms to these girls stitching as a part of its programme of supplying free uniforms to children attending government schools. Here too, there was a voice of protest by the parents of caste Hindu children. Later, the entire programme was discontinued due to the "non-availability of the funds." This means that any socio-economic upliftment programme aimed at the Dalits requires an understanding of reality. Dalits have to transcend the hostility of the rest of the society. The point here is that despite their well-meaning and good intentional works these NGOs failed to understand the fundamental nature of Indian society before going full steam with an action programme.

Certain NGOs working in the Tribal areas have attempted to maintain the exclusiveness of tribal culture to the extent of redicule. Tribal culture ought to be preserved. There is no difference of opinion on this. However, their integration into the mainstream is also very essential for their economic development. A case in point is the NGOs working among the tribals of Biligiri Rangana Betta in southern Karnataka. The NGOs got these people organized to reserve the forest for them and also organized them against the government schools which were teaching them to unlearn their own culture. When a study team went there to asses the situation, women in synthetic *saris* were very vocal about their demand and came out on record that they never visited a town. Later, in the absence of the NGOs these women admitted to the visiting team that they visited the near by town once a week to buy items like soaps and hair-oils and also to see the latest Kannada movies. They also sang the film numbers for the team. These women told the study team that they wanted to send their sons to school so that when they grew up they could manage to get jobs in the nearby towns. However, NGOs in the name of preserving tribal culture were organizing these tribals and prevented them from outside contact. How these tribals would survive economically, without any contact with the outside world? In contrast to the government officials who visited the tribal areas, the NGOs whom these women knew for a long thrashed their statement and the parting statement of these women was "probably the NGOs know our interest best".

This is partly the reason why their impact and effectiveness remain nominal despite the increase in the number of voluntary organizations and agencies and improving their techniques and methods. The benefits of development have not reached where it should have been. Ideologically, some among them profess to be apolitical, but have tended to become puppets in the hands of the politicians. Others have worked for tribal and Dalit causes in isolation. As a result, Dalit and tribal communities have continued to exist with sub-human status. There has not been any tangible change in their lifestyles, even after fifty-eight years of 'independence'.

Of late, the government has been encouraging VOs to render services in numerous fields. This had led social welfare and people participatory programmes and developmental activities to be collaborative effort between the government and VOs. Since the First Five Year Plan, the Government has been reiterating that any plan for socio-economic regeneration should take into account the services rendered by these agencies and the State should extend maximum cooperation in strengthen their efforts. Voluntary social service organizations are capable of yielding valuable results in channeling private effort for the promoting of social welfare.

The constitution promises numerous social welfare schemes for the sub-subaltern groups. It is believed that awareness about such schemes among them by NGOs and pressurizing the government to adopt them will positively integrate the Dalits and tribals into mainstream socio-political and economic life. It's through the quiet influence of voluntary workers, steadily engaged in acts of selfless service that the voice of reason can prevail.

Development projects which have mostly benefited the upper castes and influential families in rural areas have been following on elitist pattern, thus hampering the benefits of development efforts from being percolating down to the socially lowest and poorest of the society. This is an outcome of the nature of development proposed within a system that itself perpetuates injustice and legitimizes social discrimination and acts of an impediment to democratic developmental efforts. It is here that NGOs have a crucial role to play. They can introduce subtle changes in the concerned areas by creating awareness and by influencing the developmental process by making it accessible to sub-subaltern groups.

Another decisive role of NGOs should be to represent the grievances and demands of the marginalized groups at a larger level. Such activities have potential of bringing forth the urgent need for structural changes in the society. Structural changes are fundamental for development to reach out to all sections of society. Such a goal would rejuvenate the pristine identity of voluntary groups, which in the past have played a remarkable role in reviving self-confidence and instilling fervour to fight against social evils. Their valuable experiments and factual resourcefulness ensuring the inevitable and reliable source of knowledge for social organizations and governments interested in pursuing welfare oriented measures for ameliorating the sub-subaltern communities. This will give the necessary reorientation to governmental policies. One of the most crucial roles of NGOs is to begin from where the government ceases to act. It can facilitate awareness, social consciousness besides educating people.

Voluntary agencies are required to or expected to have three important functions if they wanted to be serious in effecting structural changes. Firstly, they should take up literary activities. Literacy provides awareness in people. Increasing or extending reservation policies to the sub-subaltern groups is not the urgent need. There is no meaning in fighting for reservations when most of them are rural based agricultural labouring communities. The younger generation of them is mostly employed in petty works like cattle-grazing, and is the helping hand in earning their daily bread. So, it is next to impossible for them to go to schools for education. For such a section of the society, schools should go to them. This is rather an immediate need. Successive governments have failed in providing educational facilities to the majority of the rural Dalits and tribals.

Secondly, since education has been made a fundamental right, it is the duty of the government, to provide education without any discrimination; NGOs/VOs can make these sub-subaltern people aware of their constitutional right, and play a significant role in making them aware of its significance. Sub-subaltern groups do not realize the significance of education as it does not provide them any immediate results. NGOs/VOs can come forward to make them aware of their right besides making them understand the significance of education. But this can be possible only by relieving the children of their caste jobs and duties.

Thirdly, and perhaps most importantly, when the right to education becomes a fundamental one, one can go to the courts for its enforcement when it is violated. There comes the importance of Public Interest Litigation (PIL), through which, one can seek legal remedies not only for the violation of one's rights but for the violation of the right of others. As sub-subaltern and tribal groups, find difficult to approach courts, VOs/NGOs can play an important role by approaching the courts on their behalf of for its enforcement.

These voluntary agencies also can play, yet, another important role in preserving the extinction of tribal and Dalit cultures, due to rapid developmental processes. They can do constructive work by documenting and conducting surveys of tribal and Dalit folk arts, cultural 'utsavs' and art and cultural forms of *Veeragadhas*, *Jambapuranams*, *Tholubammalatalu*, *Chindulaṭalu* and so on. To ensure the continuity and there traditional art forms of sub-subaltern groups, NGOs/VOs should work toward developing and encouraging a culture-specified projects and integrate the public educational system with cultural traditions of these sub-subaltern groups.

Most often, agencies professing to work for these sub-subaltern groups have make them as scapegoats to get more funds from a variety of sources. Recent studies, evidently shows that even the Dalit employees who were working in several of these organizations have not been paid properly. Also, as long as these activists and agencies are apolitical they cannot ensure any social injustice and social transformation. Empowerment of the sub-subaltern groups is possible only if they are included in the development process through massive participation. Without the participation of lower classes and lower-middle clases, development is not possible. Lack of awareness and participation will mould the Dalits, tribals and other marginalized groups into cogs in the new technology. They may loose their identity and humanity.

An earlier version of this paper published in Social Action, vol. 49, No. 1, 1999, pp. 55-62.

APPENDIX

Major Dalit Communities: Brief Notes on their Location and Status

Adi-Andhra: Adi-Andhra means the oldest inhabitants or settlers of Andhra. This caste appeared only in 1931 Census, drawn heavily from Mala and Madiga communities of Andhra Pradesh, thanks to Adi-Andhra /Dalit movement of Andhra Pradesh, which fought for their self-identity and compelled the then government to use "adi" prefix to their regional identity, justifying their claim that they were the original inhabitants and 'sons of the soil'. Information available about these communities in *Census of India, 1931, Vol. XXIII: H.E.H. The Nizam's Dominion, Hyderabad, Part I: Report*, (Hyderabad Deccan, 1933); *Census of India, 1931, Vol. XIV: Madras, Part I: Report*, (Madras: 1932). This caste is found in Andhra Pradesh, Kerala, Madras, Mysore, Orissa and Pondicherry.

Adi-Dravida: On the same line of the above, these Adi-Dravidas (were) are "untouchables" of Tamil speaking areas of erstwhile Madras Presidency. This caste is found in Andhra Pradesh, Kerala, Madras, Mysore and Pondicherry. Information is available about this community in *Census of India, 1931, Vol. XXVIII, Travancore, Part I: Report*, (Trivandrum: 1932).

Adi-Karnataka: are mostly drawn from Holeya and Balagai communities of ex-untouchables. Adi Karnatakas are devided into six sub-groups, namely the Kula Sale, the Muri, the Magga (weaving), the Hagga (rope making), the Morasu and the Gangadikar.

Arunthatiyar, Arundhatiya, Arunthathiyar, Arundhatiyar: is a Scheduled Caste in Andhra Pradesh, Karnataka, Maharashtra, Tamil Nadu and Kerala. The Madigas, the Madaris and the Pagadais are also occasionally describes themselves as Arundhatiyas, or Arundhateyulu. Because the Madigas of Andhra Pradesh believe that Arundhati (the mythical Hindu character) took birth in this community and therefore they associate themselves with her name.

Arwa Mala, Arwamala: is a Scheduled Caste in Tamil Nadu and Andhra Pradesh. The Arwamala are also known as Tamil Malas and Dher. The Telugu people call the Tamil language as 'Aravam', so the Malas of Tamil speaking are known as Arwamalas.

Chalavadi, Chalvadi: is a Scheduled Caste in Andhra Pradesh, Gujarat, Tamil Nadu, Maharashtra, Karnataka and Rajasthan. They are also known as Channayya in Maharashtra.

Chandal, Chandala: is a Scheduled Caste in Andhra Pradesh, Kerala, Tamil Nadu, Karnataka, Orissa and Rajasthan.

Charmakar, Chamar, Chambhar, Chamgar, Charamkar: is a Scheduled Caste in Andhra Pradesh, Bihar, Gujarat, Jammu and Kashmir, Kerala, Madhya Pradesh, Tamil Nadu, Maharashtra, Karnataka, Orissa, Punjab, Rajasthan, Uttar Pradesh, West Bengal, Delhi, Himachal Pradesh, Tripura and Dadra and Nagar Haveli. Their community name is derived from the Sanskrit word Charmakara, meaning leather worker. In Uttar Pradesh and Himachal Pradesh, the Chamar are also known as the Raidas. In Bihar, they are also known as the Charmkar, Harijan and Ravidas. In Chandigarh, they are also called the Joatia Chamar, Reghar, Raigar, Ramdasi and Ravidasi. In Tripura, the Chamar are also known as the Rishidas and Muchi. In Goa, they are known as the Chambhars and Hadis.

Dakkala, Dakkalwar: is a Scheduled Caste in Andhra Pradesh, Gujarat, Maharashtra and Karnataka. Also called the Dokkala and Dakkals.

Dandasi: is a Scheduled Caste in Andhra Pradesh, Orissa and Tripura; Denotified Tribe in Orissa. The Dandasis are traditionally village watchmen or guarding villages at night.. Their community name, Dandasi, comes from the danda (stick) and *asi* (sword) that were carried by their men.

Dhor, Dohor: is a Scheduled Caste in Andhra Pradesh, Gujarat, Madhya Pradesh, Maharashtra, Karnataka and Rajasthan. A community of tanners, their community name derived from *dhor,* meaning cattle. In Karnataka, they are synonymously called Dhor Kakkayya or Kankayya. In Maharashtra they are notified as the Dhor Kakkayya and Kankayya.

Dom, Dome, Doom, Dum, Dumna, Dumne: is a Scheduled Caste in Andhra Pradesh, Bihar, Gujarat, Jammu and Kashmir, Madhya Pradesh, Tamil Nadu, Maharashtra, Karnataka, Orissa, Punjab,

Rajasthan, Uttar Pradesh, West Bengal, Delhi and Himachal Pradesh; and also a Denotified Tribe in Andhra Pradesh, Tamil Nadu and Orissa.

Domar, Domban, Dombar, Dombara, Dommar, Dumar, Dommara, Dombari, Dombo: is a Scheduled Caste in Andhra Pradesh, Gujarat, Kerala, Orissa, Madhya Pradesh, Tamil Nadu, Maharashtra, Karnataka and Uttar Pradesh; a Nomadic Tribe in Andhra Pradesh, Gujarat, Maharashtra and Mysore.

Ghasi, Ghasia, Ghasiya: is a Scheduled Caste in Andhra Pradesh, Bihar, Gujarat, Madhya Pradesh, Maharashtra, Orissa, Uttar Pradesh, West Bengal and Tripura; and a Denotified Tribe in Bihar, Tamil Nadu and Orissa. The word Ghasi means, fish killer.

Godagali: is a Scheduled Caste in Andhra Pradesh, Kerala, Tamil Nadu, Karnataka and Orissa. The word Godagali is derived from the Telugu word *godugu,* meaning umbrella. They were umbrella-makers.

Godari: is a Scheduled Caste in Andhra Pradesh and Orissa.

Gosangi: is a Scheduled Caste in Andhra Pradesh, Kerala and Karnataka. Also referred to as the Gosika, Gosikollu, Gosangollu or Gostika. It is believed that they are called Gosangi because of their occupation as caretakers of cattle.

Hadi, Haddi, Hari: is a Scheduled Caste in Andhra Pradesh, Bihar, Gujarat, Maharashtra, Karnataka, Orissa, Rajasthan, Uttar Pradesh and West Bengal.

Holeya: is a Scheduled Caste in Andhra Pradesh, Kerala, Tamil Nadu, Maharashtra and Karnataka.

Jaggali: is a Scheduled Caste in Andhra Pradesh, Tamil Nadu, Karnataka and Orissa. Also known as Joggali, and they are referred to differently in different languages such as Madiga in Telugu, Muchi in Oriya, Godari in the rural dialect and also as Chamar. They sometimes also call themselves Jambava and claim descent from Jambuvan of Ramayana fame.

Jambuvulu, Jambavulu, Adi Jambavulu: is a Scheduled Caste in Tamil Nadu and Andhra Pradesh. They are also known as Chakkiliyan, Arundhatiyar, and they prefer to be referred to as Adi-Jambavulu after the name of their deity, Jambavamurthi.

Kolupulvandlu: is a Scheduled Caste in Andhra Pradesh, Maharashtra and Karnataka.

Madari: is a Scheduled Caste in Gujarat, Madhya Pradesh, Tamil Nadu, Maharashtra, Karnataka, Orissa, Rajasthan and Delhi; a Nomadic Tribe in Andhra Pradesh, Assam, Gujarat, Jammu and Kashmir, Kerala, Madhya Pradesh, Tamil Nadu, Maharashra, Karnataka, Rajasthan, Uttar Pradesh, Himachal Pradesh and Tripura.

Madasi Kuruva, Madari Kuruva: is a Scheduled Caste in Andhra Pradesh.

Madiga Dasu, Mashteen: is a Scheduled Caste in Andhra Pradesh.

Madiga, Madgi: is a Scheduled Caste (also the largest community amongst the SCs in A.P.) in Andhra Pradesh, Tamil Nadu, Madhya Pradesh, Maharashtra, Karnataka, Orissa and Pondicherry. The Madiga of Andhra Pradesh are also referred to as Arundhatiya, Jambavalu, Jambhavanthulu and Adi Andhra.

Mahar, Mehar, Mahara, Mehara: is a Scheduled Caste in Andhra Pradesh, Assam, Gujarat, Madhya Pradesh, Maharashtra, Karnataka, Orissa, Rajasthan, West Bengal and Dadra and Nagar Haveli. In Maharashtra they also notified as Taral, Dhegu and Megu, and call themselves Neo-Buddhist or Buddhist, after their conversion to Bhuddhism in 1956 under the leadership of Dr. B.R. Ambedkar.

Mala Dasari, Mala Dasu: is a Scheduled Caste in Andhra Pradesh, Tamil Nadu, Maharashtra and Karnataka. The Mala Dasaris are priests to the Vaishnavite Mala.

Mala Hannai: is a Scheduled Caste in Andhra Pradesh, Karnataka and Maharashtra.

Mala Jangam: is a Scheduled Caste in Andhra Pradesh, Maharashtra and Karnataka. The Mala Jangam offer priestly services to the Saivite Malas (due to heavy influence of Vira Shaivism of Basavesvara). The Malas who converted to Lingayat sect or opted to be a Jangam, became mala jangam.

Mala Masti: is a Scheduled Caste in Andhra Pradesh, Maharashtra, Karnataka and Pondicherry. They are known variously as Mala Machachathi, Mala Machachatiollu and Mastiollu.

Mala Sale (Netkani, Netkani): is a Scheduled Caste in Andhra Pradesh and Karnataka. In Andhra Pradesh, they are a community of weaving.

Mala Sanyasi: is a Scheduled Caste in Karnataka, Maharashtra and Andhra Pradesh.

Mala: is a Scheduled Caste in Andhra Pradesh, Tamil Nadu, Kerala, Maharashtra, Karnataka, Orissa and Pondicherry.

Mang: is a Scheduled Caste in Andhra Pradesh, Gujarat, Madhya Pradesh, Maharashtra, Karnataka, Orissa and Rajasthan.

Mang-Garodi, Mang-Garudi: is a Scheduled Caste in Andhra Pradesh, Gujarat, Madhya Pradesh, Maharashtra, Karnataka and Rajasthan; also a Denotified Tribe in Gujarat and Maharashtra.

Manne: is a Scheduled Caste in Andhra Pradesh, Maharashtra and Karnataka.

Mashti, Masthi: is a Scheduled Caste in Andhra Pradesh, Maharashtra and Karnataka.

Matangi: is a Scheduled Caste in Andhra Pradesh. They are also known as Madiga Bhogam Vallu, Basavi, Basavirandru, Matammavallu and Yellamma vandlu. They claim to be the descendants of Matanga Maharishi, the son of Adi Jambava.

Megh, Maghwal, Meghval, Menghvar: is a Scheduled Caste in Andhra Pradesh, Gujarat, Jammu and Kashmir, Madhya Pradesh, Maharashtra, Karnataka, Punjab, Rajasthan, Delhi and Himachal Pradesh.

Mehtar, Mehtor: is a Scheduled Caste in Assam, Andhra Pradesh, Bihar, Gujarat, Madhya Pradesh, Maharashtra, Karnataka, Orissa, Rajasthan, West Bengal and Tripura. The term Mehtar, meaning a prince or a leader, is an ironic title given to the people who are traditionally engaged as sweepers and scavengers and are known by different names in different parts of the country, like Bhangi, Hari, Lalbegi (those who are the followers of the patron-saint Lalbeg) and so on.

Mitha Ayyalvar, Mithulu Ayyavaru: is a Scheduled Caste in Andhra Pradesh. They are a community of priests and spiritual guides (gurus) to the Dalit communities in Telangana region of Andhra Pradesh. They are also known as Nithya Ayyavar.

Mochi, Muchi, Mochigar, Machigar: is a Scheduled Caste in Bihar, Andhra Pradesh, Gujarat, Madhya Pradesh, Karnataka, Maharashtra, Orissa, West Bengal, Rjasthan, Himachal Pradesh and Delhi.

Naikda, Nayakada Nyaka, Nayak, Naik: is a Scheduled Caste in Rajasthan; a Scheduled Tribe in Andhra Pradesh, Gujarat, Maharashtra, Mysore, Rajasthan and Dadra and Nagar Haveli; also a Nomadic Tribe in Madhya Pradesh, Rajasthan.

Paidi: is a Scheduled Caste in Andhra Pradesh, Karnataka, Orissa and Tamil Nadu.

Paky, Paki: is a Scheduled Caste in Andhra Pradesh and Pondicherry. They are also called Thoti and Moti. The name Paky is derived from paki, meaning a bird.

Pambada, Pambala, Pambanda: is a Scheduled Caste in Orissa, Karnataka, Kerala, Tamil Nadu and Andhra Pradesh.

Pamidi: is a Scheduled Caste in Andhra Pradesh.

Panchama: is a Scheduled Caste in Andhra Pradesh, Tamil Nadu, Karnataka, Kerala and Orissa. This is an another generic term, used by the caste-Hindus under the scheme of Chaturvarna scheme of social stratification. A number of endogamous communities like the Mala, Madiga, Paky, Chachoti, Relli, Thoti, Mala Masteen, and many others are encompassed in the generic category of Panchama.

Pano: is a Scheduled Caste in Andhra Pradesh, Orissa, Karnataka and Tamil Nadu.

Samban: is a Scheduled Caste in Andhra Pradesh, Karnataka, Tamil Nadu, Kerala and Pondicherry.

Sapari, Sapru: is a Scheduled Caste in Andhra Pradesh, Karnataka, Tamil Nadu and Orissa.

Sindhollu, Sindhuvallu: is a Scheduled Caste in Andhra Pradesh, Karnataka and Maharashtra.

Thoti, Toti: is a Scheduled Caste in Andhra Pradesh, Tamil Nadu, Kerala, Karnataka and Pondicherry; and a Scheduled Tribe in Andhra Pradesh, Karnataka and Maharashtra.

Vavuri, Bavuri: is a Scheduled Caste in Andhra Pradesh. They are known as Khodalo.

Yellamalawar, Ellamalwar, Yellammalawandlu: is a Scheduled Caste in in Andhra Pradesh, Karnataka and Maharashtra.

Bibliography

Abbasayalu, Y.B. (1978), *Scheduled Caste Elite: A Study of Scheduled Caste Elite in Andhra Pradesh*, Hyderabad.

Abbasayalu, Y.B. (1979), *Sociology of Depressed Groups*, Hyderabad.

Ahmed, Qeyamuddin (ed.), (1993), *India by Alberuni*, New Delhi, (second edition).

Ambedkar, B.R. (1969), *The Untouchables: Who were they and why did they became Untouchable*? Sravasti, (first published in 1948).

Ananta Krishan Sharma, Rallapalli, (1971), *Vemana, (Sir R. Venkataratnam Endowment Lectures)*, Waltair, (first published in1929).

Ananta Krishna Iyer, L. and H.V. Nanjundappa (1928–36), *The Mysore Tribes and Castes*, 4 vols., Mysore.

Ananta Krishna Iyer, L. (1909–12), *The Cochin Tribes and Castes*, 2 vols., Madras.

Ananta Krishna Iyer, L. (1933–41), *The Travancore Tribes and Castes*, 3 vols., Trivandrum.

Andrews, C.F. (1912), *The Renaissance in India: Its Missionary Aspect*, Edinburgh.

Annett, E.A. (1920), *Conversions in India: A Study of Religious Psychology*, Madras.

Appa Rao, M.R. (1972), *Brahmasri Raghupati Ventataratram Naidu*, Kakinada.

Appavoo, James Theophilius (1998), "Dalit Religion" in James Massey, (ed.), *Indigenous people, Dalits: Dalit Issues in Today's Theological Debate*, Delhi.

Arbuthnot, Alexander J. (ed.), (1881), *Major General Sir Thomas Munro, Governor of Madras: Selections from His Minutes and Other Official Writings*, 3 vols. London.

Arbuthnot, Alexander J. (1855), *Papers relating to Instruction in Madras Presidency*, Madras.

Ashok Kumar, K.P. (ed.), (1993), *Dalita Geetalu*, Hyderabad.

Asirvadham, E. (1935), "The Depressed Classes and Christianity", *National Council of Churches (India) Review*, December.

Bahktin, Michael (1978), "Discourse of Typology in Prose" in Ladislav Makejkha and Krystyna Pmorska, (eds.), *Readings in Russian Poetics: Formalist and Structualist Views*, Annarbour.

Balagopal, K. (2000), "A Tangled Web: Subdivision of SC Reservation in AP", *Economic and Political Weekly*, Vol. 35, No. 13.

Balagopal, K. (2005), "Justice for Dalits among Dalits: All the Ghosts Resurface", *Economic and Political Weekly*, (July 16).

Bangore (1981), *Vemana – C.R. Reddy*, Visakhapatnam.

Basu, A.N. (ed.), (1952), *Indian Education in Parliamentary Papers*, Bombay.

Baxi, Upendra (1986), "Activism at crossroods with signposts", *Social Action*, Vol. 36, No. 4.

Berreman, Gerald D. (1979), "The Brahminical view of Caste", in his *Caste and other Inequalities: Essays on Inequalities*, Meerut.

Bhaskara Rao, Kota (1996), *Dalitula Dandora*, Vijayawada.

Bhattacharya, S. (1982), "Presidential Address," *Indian History Congress*, (Modern section).

Bheemanna, Boyi (1988), *Paleru*, Hyderabad, (19th reprint).

Billlington Harper, Susan, (2000), *In the Shadow of the Mahatma: Bishop V.S. Azariah and the Travails of Christianity in British India*, Cambridge.

Bourdieu, Pierre and Jean Cloude Passeron (1990), *Reproduction in Education, Society and Culture*, (tr. Richard Nice), London, (second edition).

Bourdieu, Pierre (1973), "Cultural Reproduction and Social Reproduction", in R. Brown (ed.), *Knowledge, Education and Cultural Change*, London.

Bowles, Samuel (1972), "Schooling and Inequality from Generation to Generation", *Journal of Political Economy*, No. 80, (May-June).

Bowles, Samuel (1973), "Unequal Education and the Reproduction of Culture", in J. Karabel and A.H. Halsey (eds.), *Power and Ideology in Education*, New York.

Brookover, Wilbur B. (1955), *Society of Education*, New York.

Brown, C.P. (Tr.), (1911), *The Verses of Vemana, (693 verses)*, Madras, (reprint).

Brown, C.P. (Tr.), (1967), *Verses of Vemana* (1215 verses), (in Telugu original with English rendering), Hyderabad.

Brown, C.P. (1866), *Some Account of the Literary Life of Charles Phillip Brown*, London.

Brown, C.P. (1991), "Essay on the Language and Literature of the Telugu's", *Madras Journal of Literature and Science*, (first published in 1840).

Burditt, J.F. (1893), *Work among the Depressed Classes and the* Masses, Bombay.

Campbell, W.H. (1897-98), "Vemana—A South Indian Poet", *The Madras Christian College Magazine*, Vol. XV.

Carmichael, A.W. (1903), *Things as They Are: Mission Work in Southern India*, London.

Carson, Penelope (1988), "Soldiers of Christ: Evangelicals and India, 1784-1833", unpublished Ph.D. Thesis, University of London.

Carson, Penelope (1990), "An Imperial Dilemma: The Propagation of Christianity in Early Colonial India", *Journal of Imperial and Commonwealth History*, Vol. 18, No. 2.

Catholic Archives Society (1989), *Directory of Catholic Archives in the United Kingdom and Eire*, Darlington Carmel, (Second edition).

Chakarvarti, Vanamali (1921), "A Short Note on the Hinduisation of the Aboriginals: The Swelling of the Chandala Caste", *Indian Antiquity*, Vol. XLI.

Chalapati Rao, P.V. (1994), "17, 18 Satabdala Sahityam: Samajika Rajakiya Bhumika", in D. ChandraSekhra Reddy, (ed.), *Telugu Sahityam: Charitraka Nepadhyam*, Hyderabad.

Chamberlain, Jocob (1897), *In the Tiger Jungle and Other Stories of Missionary Work among the Telugus of India*, Edinburgh and London.

Chandraiah, K. (1992), "The Awakening of Adi-Hindus of Hyderabad as Part of the National Movement for Freedom", *Souvenir*, Hyderabad.

Charsley, Simon, (2002), "Evaluating Dalit Leadership: P.R. Venkatswamy and the Hyderabad Example", *Economic and Political Weekly*, Vol. 37, No. 52.

Chauhan, Brij Raj, (1967), "Special Problems Regarding Education among the Scheduled Castes" in M.S. Gore (et. al. eds.), *Papers in the Sociology of Education in India*, New Delhi.

China Venkayya, Nakka, (1935), *Harijana Kirtanalu*, Eluru.

Chinna Rao, Yagati, (1992), *Literature and Ideology: A Study of Telugu Literature (1920-42)*, unpublished M. Phil Dissertation, Jawaharlal Nehru University.

Chinna Rao, Yagati, (1999a), "Dalit Education and the Question of 'Self-Identity' in Andhra: A Historical Perspective", Paper presented at South Asian Conference on Education, held at Department of Education, University of Delhi, (14-18 November).

Chinna Rao, Yagati, (1999b), "Education and Consciousness in Post-Colonial Societies: The Case of Andhra Dalits", Paper presented at

National Seminar on "Fifty Years of Independence: Economic Development of Dalits in India", held at Department of Economics, University of Hyderabad, (22-23 March).

Chinna Rao, Yagati, (1999c), *Dalit Movement in Andhra, 1900-1950*, Unpublished Doctoral Dissertation, Jawaharlal Nehru University.

Chinna Rao, Yagati, (1999d), "The World of Untouchables in Medieval Telugu Literature: A Study of Vemana", in R. Soma Reddy, M. Radhakrishna Sharma and A. Satyanarayana. (eds.), *Social Evils in Andhra Desa: 17th and 18th Centuries AD, (Proceedings of the Seminar)*, Hyderabad.

Chinna Rao, Yagati, (1999e), "Change in Nomenclature: A Historical Note", in Ambrose Pinto (ed), *Dalits: Assertion for Identity*, New Delhi.

Chinna Rao, Yagati, (2002), "Education and Identity Formation among Dalits in Colonial Andhra", in S. Bhattacharya (Ed), *Education and the Disprivileged: Nineteenth and Twentieth Century India*, New Delhi.

Chinna Rao, Yagati, (2003a), *Dalit Studies: A Bibliographical Handbook*, New Delhi.

Chinna Rao, Yagati, (2003b), *Dalits' Struggle for Identity: Andhra and Hyderabad*, 1900-1950, New Delhi.

Chinna Rao, Yagati, (2003c), "Rise and Growth of Dalit Movement in Andhra, 1906-1946", *Indian Social Science Review*, Vol. 5, No. 1.

Christian Missionary Society (1927), *Mass Movement Surveys, India*, (a series of Pamphlets), London.

Clarke, Sathianathan, (1998), *Dalits and Christianity: Subaltern Religion and Liberation Theology in India*, Delhi.

Clough, John E. (1914), *Social Christianity of the Orient: The Story of a Man, a Mission and a Movement*, New York.

Cohn, Bernard S. (1954), *The Chamars of Senapur: A Study of the Changing Status of a Depressed Caste*, Ph.D. Dissertation, Cornell University.

Cohn, Bernard S. (1994), "The Pasts of an Indian Village" in his *An Anthropologist Among the Historians and other Essays*, New Delhi.

Copley, Anthony, (1997), *Religions in Conflict: Ideology, Cultural Contact and Conversion n Late-Colonial India*, Delhi.

Craig, C.S. (1982), *The Archives of the Council for World Mission: An Outline Guide*, London, (revised edition).

Craig, John, (1908), *Fourty Years Among the Telugus: A History of the Mission of the Baptists of Ontario and Quebec, Canada to the Telugus, South India, 1867 – 1907*, Toronto.

Crooke, William, (1906), *The Tribes and Castes of North-Western Provinces and Oudh*, 4 vols., Calcutta, Office of the Superintendent of Government Printing.

Daniel Potts, E. (1967), *British Baptist Missions in India 1793–1837*, Cambridge.

Dasgupta, Sugata, (1973), *Voluntary organizations in Rural Development (A Global Model)*, New Delhi.

David, Kenneth, (1977), "Hierarchy and Equivalence in Jafna, North Srilanka: Normative Codes as a Mediator" in Kenneth David, (ed.), *The New Wind: Changing Identities in South Asia*, The Hague.

Deliege, Robert, (1992), "Replication and Consensus: Untouchability, Caste and Ideology in India" *Man*, Vol. 29, No.1.

Deliege, Robert, (1994), "Response", *Man* (N.S.), Vol.29, No.2.

Devitt, Richard B., (1976), *'For the Millions who surround us': Company Education Policy in Madras*, M.A. Thesis, University of Wisconsin.

Devitt, Richar B. (1977), "Progress Report: South Indian Educational Census Data-Quantitative History Project" (Mimeo), University of Wisconsin.

Dharma Rao, Tapi, (1992), *Devalayala Meeda Bootu Bommalenduku?*, Hyderabad, (first published in 1936).

Dharmapal, (1983), *The Beautiful Tree: Indigenous Indian Education in the Eighteenth Century*, New Delhi.

Diouf, Mamadou, (1999), "Historians and Histories: What for? African Historiography, Between the State and the Communities" Lecture at the *Young Historians' workshop on Social History* held at Dakar, Senegal (3 Oct.–5 Nov.).

_______(2000), "Des Historians et des Historires pourquoi faire? L' histoire Africaine entre l' Etat et les communautes" in the Canadian Journal of African studies, Vol. 34, No. 2.

Directory of Christian Missions and Churches in India, Burma and Ceylon, 1940-1941, Nagpur, 1940.

Downie, David, (1892), *The Lone Star: The History of the Telugu Mission of the American Baptist Missionary Union*, Philadelphia.

Dube, S.C. (1955), *An Indian Village*, London.

Dube, S.C. (1963), "Men and Women roles in India - A Sociological Review" in B.Ward, (ed.), *Women in New Asia*, Paris.

Dubois, Abbe J.A. (1813), *Letters on the State of Christianity in India*, London.

Dubois, Abbe J.A. (1953), *Hindu Manners, Customs and Ceremonies*, London, (3rd edition).

Duff, Alexander, (1988), *India and Indian Missions*, Delhi, (First Published in 1839).

Dumont, Louis, (1970), *Homo Hierarchus* (Trans. by Mmark Sainsbury), Chicago.

Duvvury, Nata, (1986), "Commercial Capital and Agrarian Relations: A Study of Guntur Tobacco Economy", *Economical Political Weekly* (July 26).

Duvvury, Nata, (1987), "Imperialism and the Social Framework of Commercialization of Agriculture in Dry Land South India: A Study of Tobacco in Guntur", *A.P. Economic Association Conference* Papers, vol. I.

Edwards. M. and Hulne D. (eds.), (1992), Making a Difference: NGOs and Development in Changing Words, London.

Eleyaperumal, L. (Chairman), (1969), Report of the Committee on Untouchability: Economic and Educational Development of the Scheduled Castes and Selected Documents, New Delhi.

Enthoven, Reginald Edward, (1920–22), *The Tribes and Castes of Bombay*, 3 Vols., Bombay.

Farquhar, J.N. (1967), *Modern Religious Movements in India*, Delhi, (First Published in 1914).

Findlay, G.G. and W.W. Holsworth, (1925), *History of Wesleyan Methodist Missionary Society*, 5 vols., London.

Fishman, A.V. (1941), *Culture Change and the Under-Privileged: A Study of Madigas in South-India under Christian Guidance*, Madras.

Forrester, Duncan B., (1974), "Indian Christians' Attitudes towards Caste in the 19th Century", *Indian Church History Review*, Vol. 8, No. 2.

Forrester, Duncan B. (1980), *Caste and Christianity: Attitudes and Policies on Caste of Anglo-Saxon Protestant Missions in India*, London.

Forrester, Duncan B. (1991), "The Depressed Classes and Conversion to Christianity, 1860-1960" in G.A. Oddie (ed.) *Religion in South Asia; Religions Conversion and Revival Movements in South Asia in Medieval and Modern Times*, New Delhi, (first published in 1977).

Freeman, James M. (1986), "Consciousness of Freedom among India's Untouchables" in Dilip K. Basu and Richard Sission, (eds.), *Social and Economic Development in India*, New Delhi.

Friedmann, John, (1992), *Empowerment: The Politics of Alternative Development*, Cambridge.

Frykenberg, Robert Eric, (1965), *Guntur District (1788-1848): A History of Local Influence and Central Authority of South India*, Oxford.

Frykenberg, Robert Eric (1986), "Modern Education in South India, 1784-1854: Its Roots and Its Role as a Vehicle of Integration Under Company Raj", *The American Historical Review*, Vol. 91, No. 1.

Ganapati Sastri, T. (1925), *The Arthasastra of Kautilya*, 3 vols., Trivandrum.

Gangadharam, Nedunuri, (1960), *Vemana Padyamulu*, Rajahmundry.

Gangawane, Kamalakar, (1994), "Social Awareness in Dalit Literature", in Bojja Tharakam, (ed), *The First All India Dalit Writers Conference*, Hyderabad.

Gatwood, Lynn E. (1985), *Devi and the Spouse Goddess: Women, Sexuality and Marriage in India*, New Delhi.

Gautam, M. B. (1953), 'The Scheduled Castes and Backward Peoples' Movement in Hyderabad', 30 November, (mimeo).

Gautam, M. B. (1976), 'The Untouchables Movement in Andhra Pradesh', *Souvenir*, A.P. State Harijan Conference, (10 – 12 April).

Gautam, M. B. (1977), "Dalita Jatulanu Samuddarincina Mahaniyulu-Bhagyareddi Varma", *Harijana Sanksema Samacaramu*, Vol I, No. 2.

Gautam, M. B, (1991), *Bhagyodayam: Maadari Bhagya Reddi Varma, Life Sketch and Mission*, Hyderabad.

Geertz, Clifford, (1966), "Religion as a Cultural System", in Michael Banton, (ed.), *Anthropological Approaches to the Study of Religion*, London.

Gledstone, F.F. (n. d.), *The Church Missionary Society, Telugu Mission: Being a Short Account of the Hundred Years, 1841-1941*, Mysore.

Gnaneswar, Ganumala (Ed.), (1983), *Boyi Bhimanna Sahiti Sastipurti Sancika*, Hyderabad.

Gooptu, Nandini, (1993), "Caste, Deprivation and Politics: The Untouchables in U.P. Towns in the early Twentieth Century" in Peter Robb (ed.), *Dalit Movements and the Meaning of Labour in India*, Delhi.

Gopi, N. (1980), *Praja Kavi Vemana*, Hyderabad.

Gordon, Andrew, (1888), *On Indian Mission*, Philadelphia.

Gough, Kathleen, (1956), "Brahmin Kinship in a Tamil Village", *American Anthropologist*, Vol. 58.

Government of India, (1898), "Progress of Education in India 1892-1893", *Third Quinquennial Review*, London.

Griffith, R.T. H. (1976), *Hymns of the Rigveda*, Delhi.

Grover, Charles E., (1871), *The Folk Songs of Southern India*, Madras.

Guha, Ranajit (ed), (1984), *Subaltern Studies: Writings on South Asian History and Society*, Vol I, Delhi.

Gupta, P.C. (1985), *Literature and Society: Selected Essays,* New Delhi.

Guru Prasada Rao, Nagalla, (1959), "Jashuva", *Bharathi* (April).

Guru, Gopal, (1997), *Dalit Cultural Movement and Dalit Politics in Maharashtra,* Mumbai.

Haq, Mohd. Rizwarnal, (1998), "Constitutional Provisions on Dalit Education and the Role of Voluntary Sector for its True Realization", Paper presented at a National Seminar on Dalits and the New Education System (January 5-7), held at Indian Social Institute, New Delhi.

Harrison, Selig S. (1956), "Caste and the Andhra Communists", *The American Political Science Review,* Vol. L, No. 2.

Harrison, Selig S. (1960), *India: The Most Dangerous Decades,* Princeton.

Havinghurst, Robert J. and Bernice L. Neugarten, (1964), *Society and Education*, Boston.

Hayter, O.C.G. (1930), "Conversion of Outcastes", *Asiatic Review,* no. 26.

Heimseth, Charles, (1964), *Indian Nationalism and Hindu Social Reform,* Princeton.

Heyzer, Neoleen, James V. Rickar, and Antonio B. Quizon, (ed.), (1995), *Government-NGO Relations in Asia: Prospects and Challenges for People Centred Development*, Kaula Lumpur.

Hornby, A.S. (1985), *Oxford Advanced Learners Dictionary of Current English,* Delhi, (8th impression).

Houska, William, (1981), *Religious Belief and practice in an Urban Scheduled Caste Community*, unpublished Doctoral Dissertation, Syracuse University.

Hughes, H.P. (1893), *Social Christianity*, London.

Huizinga, Henry, (1909), *Missionary Education in India,* Ongole.

Hunter, Robert, (1873), *History of the Missions of the Free Church of Scotland in India and Africa*, London.

Hutton, J.H. (1933), "Exterior Castes", in *Census of India,* 1931, Vol. I - India, Part I- Report, Delhi.

Hutton, J.H. (1963), *Caste in India,* London, (Fourth edition).

Hymavathi, (1978), *Paleru Nunchi Padmasri Varaku,* Hyderabad.

Ilaiah, Kancha, (1995), "Caste or Class or Caste-Class: A Study in Dalit Bahujan Consciousness and Struggles in Andhra Pradesh in 1980s", Research in Progress Papers, New Delhi, (mimeo).

Ilaiah, Kancha, (1996), "In Search of the Roots of Anti Caste Struggle: A

Dalitist Reading of the Buddhist Discourse" Research in Progress Papers, New Delhi, (mimeo).

Ingham, K. (1956), *Reformers in India 1793-1833: An Account of the Work of Protestant Missionaries on behalf of Social Reform*, Cambridge.

Inkeles, Alex, (1974), *Becoming Modern*, Cambridge.

Interviews with Sapati Samson, Dunna Seshayya, Karru Sriramulu, *Edureeta* Supplement, (August 1994), (Interviewed by Vu. Sambasiva Rao, Editor).

Irschick, Eugene F. (1969), *Political and Social Conflict in South India: The Non-Brahmin Movement and Tamil Separatism, 1916- 1929*, Berkeley and Los Angeles.

Issacs, Harold R. (1965), *India's Ex-Untouchables*, New York.

Jain, J C, (1947), *Life in Ancient India as Depicted in the Jaina Canons*, Bombay.

Jain, L.C. B.V. Krishnamurti, and P.M. Tripathi, (1985), *Grass without Roots: Rural Development under Government Auspices*, New Delhi.

Jashuva, Gurram, (1930), "Prabodamu", *Bharati*, Vol 7, No 4.

Jashuva, Gurram, (1991), *Gabbilam*, Vijayawada, (First published in 1945),.

Jha, Vivekananda, (1972), *Early History of Untouchables in India*, unpublished Doctoral Dissertation, Patna University.

Jha, Vivekananda, (1974), "From Tribe to Untouchable: The case of Nisadas", in R.S. Sharma and V. Jha (eds.), *Indian Society: Historical Probings*, New Delhi.

Jha, Vivekananda, (1975) "Stages in the History of Untouchables", in *The Indian Historical Review*, Vol.II,no.1.

Jha, Vivekananda, (1986-87), "*Chandalas* and the Origin of Untouchability", *The Indian Historical Review*, Vol. III, Nos.1-2.

Joshi, Barbara R. (ed.), (1986), *Untouchable; Voices of the Dalit Liberation Movement* New Delhi.

Joshi, P.C. (1946), *Among Kisan Patriots*, Bombay.

Juergensmeyer, Mark, (1982), *Religion as Social Visition: The Movement against Untouchability in 20th Century Punjab*, Berkeley.

Juergensmeyer, Mark, (2000), "Ad Dharm Movement", in Harish K. Puri and Paramjit S. Judge (eds.), *Social and Political Movements: Readings on Punjab*, Jaipur.

Kaleswara Rao, Ayyadevara, (1959), *Na Jivitha Kadha–Navyandramu*, Vijayawada.

Kananaikil, Jose, (1982), "Marginalization of the Scheduled Castes: A Sociological Interpretation", *Social Action*, Vol. 32.

Kapoor, Rakesh, (1996), "Voluntary Action: Survival politics and Transformation", *Social Action*, Vol. 46, No. 1.

Keen, Rosemary, (1968), *A Survey of the Archives of Selected Missionary Societies*, London.

Kesavanarayana, B. (1976), *Political and Social Factors in Andhra, 1900-50*, Vijayawada.

Khare, R.S. (1984) *The Untouchable as Himself: Ideology, Identity and Pragmatism among the Lucknow Chamars*, London.

Kooiman, D. (1989), *Conversion and Social Equality in India*, New Delhi.

Kotani, Hiroyuki, (1997), "Ati Sudra Castes in the Medieval Deccan" in H. Kotani (ed.) *Caste System, Untouchability and Depressed*, New Delhi.

Krishnamurthi, Bh., (1995), "Shifts of Authority in Written and Oral Texts: The Case of Telugu", in David Shulman (ed.), *Syllables of Sky: Studies in South Indian Civilization*, Delhi.

Kroebar, Alfred L. and Clyde Kluchohn, (1952), "Culture: A Critical Review of Concepts and Definitions", Papers of the Peabody Museum of American Archaeology and Ethnology, Harvard University, Vol. XLVII, No.1.

Kshirsagar, R.K. (1986), *Untouchability in India: Implementation of Law and Abolition*, New Delhi.

Kshirsagar, R.K., (1994), *Dalit Movement and Its Leaders (1857–1956)*, New Delhi.

Kumar, Dharma, (1968), *Land and Caste in South India: Agricultural Labour in the Madras Presidency during the Nineteenth Century*, Cambridge.

Kurmayya, Vemula, (1947), "Matru Desa Dasya Vimuktikai Andhra, Hari Janula Saktyanusara Krushi", *Andhra Patrika*, 15 August.

Kurup, K.K.N. (1996), "Inferior Caste Groups and the Development of Culture in South India in the 17th and 18th Centuries" in R. Soma Reddy, M. Radhakrishna Sharma and A. Satyanarayana, (eds.), *Caste Communities and Culture in Andhra Desa 17th and 18th Centuries A.D.: Proceedings of the Seminar*, Hyderabad.

Lalitha, N.V, (1975), *Voluntary work in India (A study of volunteers in Welfare Agencies)*, New Delhi.

Lamb, Frederic, (1913), *The Gospel and the Malas: The Story of the Hyderabad Westleyan Mission*, Mysore.

Lavanam, Hemalatha, (1986), *Ma Nanna Garu*, Vijayawada.

Laxmi Narasimham, Chilakamarti, (1957), *Sweeya Charitram*, Vizagapatnam.

Laxminarayana, Unnava, (1964), *Malapalli (Sangavijayamu)*, Machilipatnam, (first published in 1922).

Legge, James, (1971), *The Travels of Fa-Hein* .Delhi, (First published in 1886).

Lehmann, E., (1956), *It Began at Tranquebar*, Madras.

Lewis, Bernard, (1975), History: Remembered, Recovered, Invented, Princeton, New Jersey.

Lewis, J.P. (ed.), (1988), *Strengthening the Poor: What have we learned?*, New Brunswick, N.J.

Lovett, R. (1899), *The History of the London Missionary Society 1795–1895*, 2 vols. London.

Luke, P.Y., and John B. Carman, (1968), *Village Christians and Hindu Culture: Study of a Rural Church in Andhra Pradesh, South India*, London.

Lynch, Owen M. (1969), *The Politics of Untouchability: Social Mobility and Social Change in A City of India*, New York.

Macdonald, R.M. (1866), "Vemana", in *Madras Journal of Literature and Science*.

Madhava Rao, K. (Tr.) 1996), *Jashua's Gabbilam*, Hyderabad.

Madhaviah, A. (1905–1906), "The Matangi", *Madras Christian College Magazine*, Vol. 23, (New Series Vol. 5).

Mahalingam,T.V. (1969), *Administration and Social Life Under Vijaynagara*, Madras.

Mandelbaum, David G. (1970), "Cultural Variations and the Jati Order" in *Society in India, Vol.I: Continuity and Change*, Berkeley.

Mangamma, J. (1971), *The Rate Schools of Godavari*, Hyderabad.

Mangamma, J. (1992), *Andhra Desamlo Kraistava Mishanareela Seva*, Hyderabad.

Mani, Premkumar, (1975) *Munusmriti: Ek Pratikriya*, Lucknow.

Manor, J.G. (1971), "Testing the Barrier between Caste and Out-caste: The Andhra Evangelical Luthern Church in Guntur District", *Indian Church History Review*, Vol.5, No.1.

Marshman, J.C. (1859), *The Life and Times of Carey, Marshman and Ward*, 2 vols., London.

Massey, James, (1994), *Towards Dalit Hermenautics: Re-reading the Text, the History and the Literature*, Delhi.

Mathew, A. (1988), *Christian Missions, Education and Nationalism: From Dominance to Compromise, 1870-1930*, Delhi.

Mathew, A. (1988), *Pre- Independence Educational Policy of India*, New Delhi.

Mayhew, A.I., (1941), "The Christian Ethics India" in L.S.S. O'Mally (ed.), *Modern India and the West*, London.

Mencher, J.P. (1974), "The Caste System Upside Down, or the Not-so mysterious east", *Current Anthropology*, Vol. 15, No.4.

Menon, Saraswati, (1979), "Historical Development of Thanjavur Kisan Movement: Interplay of Class and Caste Factors", *Economic and Political Weekly*, Vol . XIV, Nos. 7 – 8.

Miller, Robert J. (1966), "Button, Button¼ Great Tradition, Little Tradition, Whose Tradition?", *Anthropological Quarterly*, Vol. 39.

Moffat, Michael, (1979), *An Untouchable Community in South India: Structure and Consensus*, New Jersey.

Moon, Vasanth W. (1986), "From Dependence to Protest: The Early growth of Education and consciousness among "Untouchables" of Western India' in Barbara R. Joshi (ed.) *Untouchable; Voices of the Dalit Liberation Movement* New Delhi.

Morris, Mary, (1989), *Voluntary work in Welfare state*, London.

Mosse, David, (1994), "Comment", *Man* (N.S.), Vol.29, No. 2.

Murali, Atluri, (1988), "Changing Perceptions and Radicialization of National Movement, 1920-34" *Social Scientist*, Vol.16, No. 8.

Narayana Moorty, J.S.R.L. and Elliot Roberts (Trs.), (1995), *Selected Versus of Vemana*, New Delhi.

Narayana Rao, K. V. (1973), *The Emergence of Andhra Pradesh*, Bombay.

Narayana Rao, Velcheru, (1978), *Telugulo Kavita Viplavala Swarupam*, Hyderabad.

Narayana Rao, Velcheru, (1992), "Kings, Gods and Poets: Ideologies of Patronage in Medieval Andhra", in Barbara Stroller Miller (ed.), *The Powers of Art: Patronage in Indian Culture*, Delhi.

Narayana Reddy, C, 1981, *Samikshanam*, Hyderabad.

Narla, V.R. (1969), *Vemana*, New Delhi.

Narla, V.R. (1971), *Vemana Through Western Eyes*, translated into Telugu by Maravuru Kodanda Rama Reddi, entitled *Vemana-Paschatyulu*, Nellore.

Narsimha Yogi, Mutyala, (1958), *Vemana Jnanamarga–3002–Padyamulu* Madras.

Natarajan, S., (1959), *A Century of Social Reform*, Bombay.

Nath, Trilok, (1987), *Politics of the Depressed Classes*, Delhi.

Nathan, Robert, (1908), *Progress of Education in India: 1897-98 to 1901-02*, Calcutta.

Neill, Stephen, (1954), *A History of Christianity in India*, 2 vols., Cambridge.

Nicholson, Sydney, (1926), "Social Organization of the Malas – An Outcaste Indian People", *Journal of the Royal Anthropological Institute of Great Britain and Ireland*, Vol. 56.

Nilakanta Sastri, K.A. (1976), *A History of South India: From Prehistoric Times to the Fall of Vijayanagara*, Madras, (First published in 1955).

Noble, John, (1867), *A Memoir of the Rev. Robert Turlington Noble*, London.

Oddie, G.A. (1975), "Christian Conversion in the Telugu Country, 1860-1900: A Case Study of One Protestant Movement in the Godavari-Krishna Delta", *Indian Economic and Social History Review*, Vol. 12, No. 1.

Oddie, G.A. (1979), *Social Protest in India: British Protestant Missionaries and Social Reforms, 1850 – 1900*, New Delhi.

Oddie, G.A., (1991), "Christian Conversion Among non-Brahmins in Andhra Pradesh: with Special Reference to the Dornakal Diocese, C. 1900-36", in G.A. Oddie (ed.)_*Religion in South Asia; Religions Conversion and Revival Movements in South Asia in Medieval and Modern Times*, New Delhi, (First published in 1977).

Oddie, G.A. (1996), "Missionaries as a Social Commentators: The Indian Case", Robert A. Bickers and Rosemary Seton (eds.), *Missionary Encounters*, Surrey.

Oglivie, J.N. (1915), *The Apostles of* India, London.

Omvedt, Gail, (1991), "The Anti-Caste Movement and the Discourse of Power", *Race & Class*, Vol 33, No 2.

Omvedt, Gail, (1993), "Who Are The Indigenous People of India" in M. Gopinath and Fr. Lazer (eds), *The Emergence of Indigenous Peoples: Collection of Papers Presented at the First All India Conference of Indigenous Peoples of India*, Bangalore.

Omvedt, Gail, (1994), *Dalits and the Democratic Revolution: Dr. Ambedkar and the Dalit Movement in Colonial India*, New Delhi.

Omvedt, Gail, (1995), *Dalit Visions: The Anti-Caste Movement and the Construction of an Indian Identity*, New Delhi.

Oommen, T.K., (1994), "Panchams to Dalits: The Context and Content of Identity", *Times of India*, 11 May.

Orans, Martin, (1965), *The Santal: A Tribe in Search of a great tradition*, Detroit.

Padfield, J.E. (1908), *The Hindus at House: being Sketches of Hindu Daily Life*, Madras.

Padma Rao, Katti, (1994), *Dalita Sahitya Vadam-Jashuva*, Ponnuru.

Pandey, Shashi Ranjan, (1991), *Community Action for Social Justice: Grosroots Organizations in India*, New Delhi.

Panikkar, K.N. (1975), "Presidential Address" (Modern Section) *Indian History Congress*, Aligarh.

Panikkar, K.N. (1990), "Culture and Consciousness in Modern India: A Historical perspective', *Social Scientist*, Vol.18, No.4.

Panikkar, K.N. (1991), "History, Politics and Culture" in K.N. Panikkar, (ed.), *Communalism in India: History, Politics and Culture*, New Delhi.

Panikkar, K.N. (1997), *Communal Threat Secular Challenge*, Madras.

Pantawane, Gangadhar, (1986), "Evolving a New Identity: The Development of Dalit Culture", in Barbara R. Joshi (ed.) *Untouchable! Voices of Dalit Liberation Movement*, New Delhi, (Indian edition).

Parsons, Talcott and Edward A. Shils, (1951), *Toward a General Theory of Action*, New York.

Partha Sarathi Ayya, P.T. (ed.), (1908), *Vemana Padyamulu*, Madras.

Pathank, Sushil M. (1964), *American Protestant Missionaries in India: A Study of their Activities and Influence 1813–1910*, unpublished Ph.D. Dissertation, the University of Hawaii.

Pearson, Hugh, (1839), *Memoirs of the Life and Correspondence of the Reverend Christian Frederich Swarts*, 2 vols., London, (3rd edition).

Pickett, J.W. (1933), *Christian Mass Conversion Movements in India: A Study with Recommendations*, New York.

Pickett, J.W. (1938), *Christ's Way to India's Heart*, London.

Pickett, J.W. (1938), *Christian Missions in Mid-India: A Study of Nine Areas, with Especial Reference to Mass Movements*, Jubbulpore.

Pradhan, A.C. (1986), *The Emergence of the Depressed Classes*, Bhubaneswar.

Prasada Rao, Mangalagiri (Comp.), (1993), *Souvenir of the Conference of Andhra Pradesh Relli Community Welfare Association*, (9-11 April), Kakinada.

Priyadarshini Vijaisri, K. (1997), *Patterns of Sacred Prostitution in Colonial Andhra*, Unpublished M Phil Dissertation, Jawaharlal Nehru University.

Priyadarshini Vijaisri, (2003), "Transcending the Devadasi: Reform and Patterns of Sacred Prostitution in Colonial Andhra", in Manas Ray (ed.), *Space Sexuality and Postcolonial Cultures: Papers from the Cultural Studies Workshop*, (Calcutta, 2003), [ENRECA Occasional Paper Series: 6].

Priyadarshini Vijaisri, (2004), *Recasting the Devadasi: Patterns of Sacred Prostitution in Colonial South India*, New Delhi.

Raja Gopal, Indu, (1985), *The Tyranny of Caste: The Non-Brahmin Movement and Political Development in South India*, Delhi.

Rajah, M.C. (1925), *The Oppressed Hindus*, Madras.

Rajaiah, (1961), *Choosen Vessels: Lives of Ten Indian Christian Pastors of the 18th and 19th Centuries*, Madras.

Ram Reddy, G. (1989), "The Politics of Accommodation: Caste, Class and Dominance in Andhra Pradesh", in Francine R. Frankel and M.S.A. Rao, (eds.), *Dominance and State Power in Modern India: Decline of a Social Order*, New Delhi.

Rama Murthy, Pamu, (1976), *Rashtra Harijana Nayakula Jeevitha Charitra*, Kakinada.

Ramakrishna, V. (1983), *Social Reform in Andhra*, New Delhi.

Ramanujachari, K. (1901), "The Conditions of Low Castes", in C.Y. Chintamani, *Indian Social Reform*, Madras.

Ramaswamy, Uma, (1974a), "Scheduled Castes in Andhra: Some Aspects of Social Change", *Economic and Political Weekly*, Vol. 9, No. 29.

Ramaswamy, Uma, (1974b), "Self Identity Among Scheduled Castes: A study of Andhra", *Economic and Political Weekly*, Vol.9, No.48.

Ramaswamy, Uma, (1984), "Preference and Progress: The Scheduled Castes", *Economic and Political Weekly*, Vol. 19, No. 30.

Ramulu Naik, D. (1992), *M.V. Bhagya Reddy Verma's Life and Mission*, unpublished M. Phil. Dissertation, Osmania University.

Ranga Rao, C.V. (1998), "Classification of Scheduled Castes: A Study in Public Policy Making", *Third Concept*, No. 142.

Ranga, N. G. (1949) *Revolutionary Peasant*, New Delhi.

Ranga, N. G. (n.d.) *Kisans and Communists*, Bombay.

Ranga, N.G. (1933), *Harijana Nayakudu*, Guntur.

Rangaswami, Jala, (1930a), *Antarani Varevaru?* Rajamahendravaramu.

Rangaswami, Jala, (1930b), *Malasuddhi*, Rajamahendravaram.

Ranier, G.J., (1950), *History: Its Purpose and Method*, London.

Ranke, Leopold von, (1874), Geschichte der romanischen und germanischen Voelker 1495-1535, Berlin.

Ratnaiah, K. (1991), *Social Change among Malas (An Ex-Untouchable Caste in South India*, New Delhi.

Ray, S. (1998), "Categorization of Scheduled Castes", *Andhra Pradesh*, (July).

Rice, Stanley, 1937, *Hindu Customs and Their Origin*, London.

Richter, J., (1908), *A History of Missions in India* (Tr. Sydney H. Moore), Edinburgh and London.

Risely, Herbert Hope, (1891), *The Tribes and Castes of Bengal*, 4vols., Calcutta.

Risely, Herbert Hope, (1909) *The Peoples of India*, Calcutta.

Rivera, Angel Quientero, (1976), Workers' Struggle in Puerto Rico: A Documentary Study, New York.

Rose, Horace Arther, (1911-19), *A Glossary of Tribes and Castes of the Punjab and North-Western Frontiers of Provinces*, 3 Vols., London.

Rouschenburschu-Clough, Emma, (1899), *While Sewing Sandals: Tales of Telugu Pariah Tribe*, London.

Roy Choudhary, S.C. (1982), *Socio-Cultural and Economic History of India*, New Delhi.

Russel, Robert Vane, (1916), *The Tribes and Castes of Central Provinces of India*, 4 Vols., London..

Sachau, E.C. (Tr.), (1914), *Alberunis India*, London.

Sagar, Sunderlal, (1973) *Hindu Sanskrititi Man Varna Vyavastha Aur Jati Bhed*, Lucknow.

Sambamurty, Vajrapu, (1992), *Valmiki Cheta Ramayanam Enduku Varayincharu?*, Hyderabad.

Sambasiva Rao, Gumma, (1991), "Jashuva Kavitvamto Jatiyata", *Telugu*, September.

Sambasiva Rao, Malyala, (1920–21), "Panchamula Pracheenata", *Andhra Patrika Ugadi Sancika*.

Sankaran, S.R. (1998), "The Mala-Madiga Controversy – An Appeal to the Scheduled Castes", *Sanghika Sankshema Samacharam*, (June-July).

Saraswathi, S, (1974), *Minorities in Madras State: Group Interests in Modern Politics*, Delhi.

Sargurudoss, M. (1961), *Educational Policy in the Madras Presidency*, Unpublished Ph.D. Thesis, University of Madras.

Sarini, (ed.), *Indigenous People in India*, (Sarini Occasional Papers no.1., 1997); *The Emergence of Indigenous peoples*, (Collection of papers presented at the first all India conference of Indigenous people of India, held at Bangalore 24-25 December 1993).

Sathianathan, S. (1896), *Sketches of India Christians: Collected from Different Sources*, London and Madras.

Sathinanadhan, S. (1894), *History of Education in Madras Presidency*, Madras.

Satyanarayana, A. (1979), *Kisan Movement in Madras Presidency: A Study of the Anti-Zamindari Agitation in Andhra, 1928-42,* M. Phil. Dissertation, Jawaharlal Nehru University.

Satyanarayana, A. (1986), "Rise and Growth of Left Movement in Andhra, 1934-39", *Social Scientist,* Vol. 19, No. 1.

Satyanarayana, A. (1990), *Andhra Peasants under British Rule: Agrarian Relations and the Rural Economy, 1900-40,* New Delhi.

Satyanarayana, A. (1993), "Land, Caste and Dominance in Telangana", Research-in Progress Papers, New Delhi, (mimeo).

Satyanarayana, A. (1994), "Caste and Class in Rural Andhra: A Historical Perspective", in K L Sharma (ed), *Caste and Class in India,* Delhi.

Satyanarayana, A. (1995), "Dalit Protest Literature in Telugu: A Historical Perspective", *Economic and Political Weekly,* Vol. 30, No. 5.

Satyanarayana, A. (1998a), "Dalit Identity and Consciousness in Colonial Andhra", *Vikalp,* Vol. 6, No. 2.

Satyanarayana, A., (1998b), *'Birds of Passages': South Indian Labour Communities, Burma, 1871 – 1964,* (mimeo).

Satyanarayana, A. (2002), "Growth of Education Among the Dalit-Bahujan Communities in Modern Andhra, 1893 – 1947", in S. Bhattacharya (ed), *Education and the Disprivileged: Nineteenth and Twentieth Century India,* New Delhi.

Satyanarayana, A. (2003a), "Ideology and Consciousness of Dalit-Bahujans in Colonial Andhra: Mid Nineteenth to Mid-Twentieth century", paper presented at a Seminar on "History of Socio-Economic and Political Thought in Modern India", (27-29 October), New Delhi.

Satyanarayana, A. (2003b), "Presidential Address", Modern Andhra Section, *A.P. History Congress,* Tirupati.

Satyanarayana, A. (2005), *Dalits and Upper Castes: Essays in Social History,* New Delhi.

Satyanarayana, Garimella, (1933), *Harijanula Patalu,* Mylapur.

Satyanarayana, Kambhampati, (1984-90), *Andhra Pradesh Lo Kammunist Vudyama Chritra,* 2 vols., Hyderabad.

Satyanarayana, S.V. (1993), *Dalita Sahitya Nepadhyam,* Hyderabad.

Saxena, R.N. (1967), "The Traditional System of Education in India" in M.S. Gore, I.P. Desai and Suma Chitnis (eds.) *Papers in the Sociology of Education India,* New Delhi.

Schwartz, Michael B. (1977), "Indian Untouchable Texts of Resistance: Symbolic domination and Historical Knowledge" in H.L. Seneviratne, (ed.), *Identity, Consciousness and Past: Forging of Caste and Community in India and Srilanka,* Delhi.

Searle-Chatterjee, Mary, (1981), "Reversible Sex Roles: The Special Case of Banaras Sweepers", *Women in Development*, 1.

Senart, Emile, (1930), *Caste in India: The Facts and the System*, London, (Originally Published in 1896 in French).

Sengupta, Kamalini, (1995), "Dalit is not a dirty word", *Times of India*, 9th January.

Sharp, H. (ed.), (1965), *Selections from Educational Records, Part-I 1781-1831*, New Delhi.

Sherring, M.A. (1882), *Hindu Tribes and Castes as Represented in Banaras*, 3 vols., London.

Sherring, M.A. (1884), *The History of Protestant Missions in India: From their Commencement in 1706 to 1881*, London.

Sherring, M.A. (1970), *The Tribes and Castes of Madras Presidency*, Delhi, Cosmos, (First Published in 1909).

Sheth, D.L. (1983), "Grass-Roots initiatives in India", *Economic and Political Weekly*, Vol. 19, No. 6.

Shivji, Issa G. (1976), *Class Struggle in Tanzania*, New York.

Shulman, David, (1985), *The King and the Clown in South Indian Myth and Poetry*, Princeton.

Shweder, Richard A. and Edmund J. Bourne, (1984), "Does the concept of the Person vary cross-culturally?" in Richard A. Shweder and Robert A. Levine (eds.), *Culture Theory: Essays on Mind, Self and Emotion*, Cambridge.

Singer, Milton, (1975), "The Great Tradition in a Metropolitan Centre: Madras" in Milton Singer, (ed.), *Traditional India: Structure and Change*, Jaipur.

Singh, T.R. (1967), "The Harijan Leather Workers—Some Aspects of Untouchability in Andhra Pradesh", *Voluntary* Action, vol. IX, No. 1.

Singh, T.R. (1969) *The Madigas: A Study of Social Structure and Changes*, Lucknow.

Sitapati, G.V. (1968), *History of Telugu Literature*, New Delhi.

Smelsor, Neil J. (1993), *Sociology*, New Delhi, (Fourth edition).

Smith, George, (1873), *The Conversions of India*, London.

Somasekhara Sharma, M. (1948), *History of the Reddi Kingdoms: (Circa 1325 A.D. to Circa 1448 A.D.)*, Waltair.

Souvenir (1976), (Sixth Andhra Pradesh Harijan Congressman's Convention), Kakinada, 6 June.

Stanley, Brian, (1992), *The History of the Baptist Missionary Society 1792–1992*, Edinburgh.

Stein, Burton, (1980), *Peasant State and Society in Medieval South India*, Oxford.

Stein, Burton, (1989), *Thomas Munro: The origins of the Colonial States and His vision of Empire*, Delhi.

Stock, Eugene, (1899), *History of the Church Mission Society: Its Environment, Its Men and Its Work*, 3 vols. London, 1899.

Subba Rao, Vanguri, (1951), *Vemana* Narsapuram, (reprint).

Subba Rao, Vanguri, (1957), *Sataka Kavula Charitramu*, Narasapuram.

Sudhakar, Yendluri, (1992), *Jashua Katha*, Rajahmundry.

Sundararaj, Manickam, (1977), *Social Setting of Christian Conversion in South India*, Wiesbaden.

Sundarayya, P. (1990), *Visalandra Lo Praja Rajyam*, Vijayawada, (First Published 1946).

Surgurdoss, M. (1961), *Education Policy in Madras Presidency: 1800-1900*, unpublished Doctoral Dissertation, Madras University.

Suryanarayana, K. (1956), *History of Minor Chalukya Families in Medieval Andhra Desa*, Delhi.

Suryanarayana, K.R., (1952), *Sir, R. Venkatararam*, Rajahmundry.

Suseela, M. (1913), "Andhra Desmuna Mishanula Bhavi Parinamamaulu", *Andhra Patrika Ugadi Sanchika*.

Talbot, Cynthia, (1992), "A Revised View of 'Traditional' India: Caste, Status and Social Mobility in Medieval Andhra", *South Asia*, Vol.15, No.1.

Tambiah, S.J. (1973), "From Varna to Caste through Mixed Unions" in Jack Goody (ed.), *Character of Kinship*, Cambridge.

Tarakam, (1976), *Telugunadu lo Samskritodyamam*, Hyderabad.

Tarakusu, J. (tr.), (1966), *A Record of the Buddhist Religion as Practiced in India and Malay Archipelago by I-Tsing*, Delhi, (Indian edition).

Thoburn, J.M. (1893), *India and Malaysia*, Cincinnati.

Thomas, M.M. (1969), *The Acknowledged Christ of the Indian Renaissance*, London.

Thurston, Edgar and K. Rangachari, (1909), *Castes and Tribes of Southern India*, 7 vols., Madras.

Trautman, Thomas R., *et.al.*, (1985), "The Study of South Indian Inscriptions" in Robert E. Frykenberg and Pouline Kolenda (eds.), *Studies of South India: An Anthology of Recent Research and Scholarship*, Madras.

Travelyan, C.E. (1838), *On the Education of the People of India*, Green & Longman.

Tylor, E.B. (1971), *Primitive Culture*, 2 vols., London.

Ullrich, Helen E. (1977), "Caste-Difference between Brahmin and non-Brahmin women in South Indian Village" in Alice Schlege (ed.) *Sexual Stratification*, New York.

Upadhyaya, Carol, (1988), "The farmer-Capitalists of coastal Andhra Pradesh" *Economic and Political Weekly*, Vol. 26, No.46.

Vagamare, Chandrakanth, (1994), *Devaraya Ingle Charatrani Kavita*, Athani.

Vaikuntham, Y. (1982), *Education and Social Change in South India, Andhra 1880-1920*, Madras.

Venkata Krishnamacharyulu, Nanduri, (1935), *Harijana Samasya*, Kakinada.

Venkata Rao, Dasari, (1926), "Adimandra Sabha", *Samadarshini*, 26 October.

Venkata Rao, Nidadavolu, (1954), *Dakshina Desiyandhra Vangmayamu*, Madras.

Venkata Reddi, Gurram and Pochana Rami Reddi, (1988), *Viplava Yogi-Viswakavi: Vemana Vedasastram*, Kurnool.

Venkata Sharma, Mangipudi, (1933), *Niruddha Bbharatamu*, (*Asprusysta Khandanamu*), Machilipatnam, (Third edition).

Venkata Siva Reddy, G. (2002), "Competition and Conflict among the Dalits: Madiga Dandora Movement in Andhra Pradesh", in Ghanshyam Shah (ed.), *Dalits and the State*, New Delhi.

Venkatarangaiah, M. (1965-69), *Freedom Movement in Andhra Pradesh*, 4 vols. Hyderabad.

Venkataswamy, P.R. (1955), *Our Struggle for Emancipation*, 2 vols., Hyderabad.

Venkateswara Rao, Akundi, (1939), "Andhra Desamu-Harijana Samasya," *Bharathi*_ Vol.16.

Veresalingam, K. (1954), *Sweeya Chritram*, Rajahmundry, (First published in 1911).

Vijaisri, Priyadarshini, (2005), "Contending Identities: Sacred prostitution and reform in colonial south India", *South Asia*, Vol. XXVIII, No. 3, (December).

Vijaisri, Priyadarshini, (2005), "The outcaste sacred prostitute in colonial India", *Women's History Magazine*, Issue No. 51.

Vincentnathan, Lynn, (1987), *Harijan subculture and self-esteem management in a south Indian community*, Doctoral Dissertation, University of Wisconsin.

Vincentnathan, Lynn, (1993), "Untouchable Concepts of Person and Society" *Contributions to Indian Sociology*, (N.S.) vol. 27, No.1.

Viswanatha Sharma, Vemuri, (1916), "Andhrula Vidya Vyapakamu" *Andhra Patrika Ugadi Sanchika*.

Viyaya Bharati, B. (1992), "Dalit Sahityam", in the *Souvenir*, Hyderabad.

Washbrook, David, (1996), "Land and Labour in Late Eighteenth Century South India: The Golden Age of Pariah" in Peter Robb, (ed.), *Dalit Movements and the Meanings of Labour in India*, Delhi, (First Published in 1993).

Waters, T. (tr.), (1904-05), *On Yuan-Chaung's Travels in India*, 2 Vols., London.

Weber, Max, (1964), *The Sociology of Religion*, Boston.

Webster, John C.B. (1992), *A History of the Dalit Christians in India*, San Francisco.

Whitehead, Henry, (1921), *Village Gods of South India*, Madras.

Wiebe, Paul D. (1988), *Christians in Andhra Pradesh: The Minnonites of Mahaboobnagar*, Madras.

Williams, John Bob, (1938), *Research Studies in the Economic and Social Environment of the Indian Church: A Study of the Economic Status and Self-Support of the Church of the Four Protestant Missions in the Andhra Area*, Guntur.

Yamazaki, Gen'ichi, (1997), "Social Discrimination in Ancient India and its Transition to the Medieval Period", in H. Kotani, (ed.), *Caste System, Untouchability and Depressed*, New Delhi.

Zelliot, Eleanor, (1988), "Untouchability", in Ainslie T. Embreee (ed.), *Encyclopaedia of Asian History*, New York.

Zelliot, Eleanor, (1996), From Untouchable to Dalit: Essays on the Ambedkar Movement, New Delhi.

Index